Successful Event Management

Also available from Continuum:

Principles of Hospitality Law, 2nd Edition: Boella and Pannett
Informative Writing, 2nd Edition: Goddard
The Tourism Development Handbook: Godfrey and Clarke
Passing Exams: Hamilton
Sales and Service for the Wine Professional: Julyan
The Fundamentals of Hospitality Marketing: Mawson
Using Computers in Hospitality, 2nd Edition: O'Connor
Becoming a Tour Guide: Reily Collins
Environmental Management in the Hospitality Industry: Webster
Dissertation Skills for Business and Management Students: White

Successful Event Management

A Practical Handbook

Anton Shone
with
Bryn Parry

continuum
LONDON • NEW YORK

Continuum

The Tower Building
11 York Road
London SE1 7NX

370 Lexington Avenue
New York
NY 10017–6503

www.continuumbooks.com

First published in 2001
Reprinted 2002

British Library Cataloguing-in-Publication Data
A Catalogue record for this book is available from the British Library.

ISBN   0–8264–5219–1

Typeset by Kenneth Burnley, Wirral, Cheshire
Printed and bound in Great Britain by Biddles Ltd, www.biddles.co.uk

Contents

Preface

My advice to the reader is to take this book all together: not just the text, but also the diagrams, case studies and the questions set in the case studies. This will help you learn more. For the beginner, or someone wanting 'a thirty-minute guide' to organizing events, your first step is to look at the forms listed on p. xiii, to give you some idea of what you are going to need, and then start with Chapters 5 and 6. The book is in two parts: Part I, Chapters 1–4, presents a picture of the events business; Part II, Chapters 5–12, is about how to organize events.

I have taken a deliberately European approach. This is for two reasons. First, many of the existing books in this subject area, events management, are either American or Australian, and tend to contain examples (especially the American texts) which may not have huge relevance to the European experience. Second, and perhaps more importantly, we, as Europeans, do not explore the extent and quality of our knowledge and mutual experience sufficiently. Partly this was due to language barriers, and, historically, to perceived cultural differences. However, in the age of the internet and in the new century, language is an increasing irrelevance, when the common language of the net is English, and culturally we are Europeans. More unites us than divides us, as most young people, having backpacked their way around the continent, watched MTV and drunk cappuccino in open-air cafés from Galway to Genoa, know very well. This being the case, the book contains material from all over Europe and all money is expressed in euros. For those who might have looked at their pounds, marks or francs with wistful patriotism, all things change.

I am extremely grateful for the contributions made to this book by many people and organizations, most especially my colleague and fellow author, Bryn Parry, for his excellent contributions to the structure, detail and organization of the book. I am also most grateful to James O'Neill, Chairman of the Inntel Conference Agency, and his staff at Marks Tey, near Colchester, for their kind help; to Albert Kemp, Chief Executive of Insurex Expo-Sure; to Hein te Riele, Director of the Deventer Tourist Service; and to Sally Looker, Tourism Officer of the Tendring District Council. I also wish to express my most grateful thanks to: Rudi Drost, Graham Lucas, Duncan Tyler, Crispin Farbrother, Mike Stapleton, Bays Boeijen, Ken and Christina Crossley, Eddie Shone, Jos Poth, Minesh Ghandi, Guiseppe Fontebasso, Andy Bell, Rachel Hollands, Steve Pateman, Joanne Webber, Steve Woodman, the Touristik Centrale Mainz, University College Cork, the Compass Group, Blue Arrow and all those who have contributed in some way, great or small.

This book is by no means definitive and I urge the reader to bear that in mind and to use it as a starting place. Any comments which readers may wish to make will be gladly received.

Finally, a note on conventions: for convenience, all costs are given in euros. Where the € symbol appears in sample tables and charts, the reader may possibly wish to substitute their local currency. In reference lists, full details of the referenced work are given, including page numbers, except where a book has been identified in the text as being of general interest only. Also, to differentiate between real locations and fictional examples, I have used the name 'Middleburg' to illustrate the latter. Those who live in the Dutch provincial capital of Middelburg, or any European town from Mittelburg to Middlesbrough, I hope you will excuse this small liberty, and not search too hard for the Arboretum or the Venetian Bridge.

ANTON SHONE
Derby, England

Table of Case Studies

For convenience, where costs are quoted these are given in euros. At the time of writing the exchange rate was one euro sixty-two cents to one pound sterling.

All case studies are real, as named. However, some more generalized examples are given to illustrate the text and to help the reader; in these cases the fictitious town of 'Middleburg' is used.

Forms for the New Event Organizer

If you have never organized an event before, you might like to refer to the example forms on these pages, which will help you get started:

PART I

The Events Business

CHAPTER 1

An Introduction to Events

Aims
- To consider a definition of, and framework for, special events.
- To provide a categorization and typology for special events, together with an overview of the historical context.
- To identify the key characteristics of events, in order to understand the business of events management as a service activity.

Introduction
Events have long played an important role in human society. The tedium of daily life in the past, with its constant toil and effort, was broken up by events of all kinds. In most societies, the slightest excuse could be found for a good celebration, though traditional celebrations often had strict ceremonies and rituals. In Europe, particularly before the Industrial Revolution, routine daily activities were regularly interspersed with festivals and carnivals. Personal events or local events to celebrate certain times of year, perhaps related to religious holy days, were also common. This role in society was, and is, of considerable importance. In the modern world some of the historic driving forces for events have changed. For example, religious reasons for having major festivals have, perhaps, become less important, but we still see carnivals, fairs and festivals in all sorts of places and at various times of year. Many of these events, although religious or traditional in origin, play a contemporary role by attracting tourists (and thus tourist income) to a particular place. Some major events, though, do still revolve around periods such as Christmas, Easter or Lent in the Christian calendar, and towns and cities throughout Europe hold major festivals based at these times. Even in those countries where religion is no longer as important as it once was, the celebration of originally religious and other folk festivals still takes place; so do older festivals related to the seasons, including the celebration of spring, with activities such as dancing round a Maypole,

decorating water wells and crowning a 'May Queen'. However, many historic, traditional or 'folk' ceremonies and rituals are, in practice, recent inventions or re-creations.

We can grasp, therefore, that special events were often historically crucial to the social fabric of day-to-day life. In modern times we are often so used to special events we do not necessarily see them in this context (e.g. Mother's Day). It is also sometimes difficult for the student of events to understand the full extent of these activities, their variety, their role and how they are run. Unlike in many industries, we cannot say, 'well, this industry is worth maybe thirty billion euros a year' or whatever. In fact it is almost impossible to quantify, in monetary terms, how much special events are worth 'as an industry'. Such a calculation would probably be problematic, because the range of events is staggering, from big internationally organized sports spectaculars such as the Olympics, to the family naming ceremony of the new baby next door. All we can reasonably say is, perhaps, that we could look at any one event, in isolation, and see what value it generated. Indeed, certain events have the purpose of creating wealth or economic value in some way, as well as entertaining and cementing society.

Definitions and Frameworks

For the student of events, we have to provide some context, or framework, to begin to understand the nature of the activity and the issues about management and organization surrounding it. This being the case, and for convenience, we need to attempt both a definition and a means of classification:

> Special events are that phenomenon arising from those non-routine occasions which have leisure, cultural, personal or organizational objectives set apart from the normal activity of daily life, whose purpose is to enlighten, celebrate, entertain or challenge the experience of a group of people.

Authors such as Goldblatt (1990, p. 2) have chosen to highlight the celebratory aspect of events: 'A special event recognises a unique moment in time with ceremony and ritual to satisfy specific needs.' Although this definition clearly works for events like weddings, parades, inaugurations and so on, it works less well for activities like engineering exhibitions, sports competitions, product launches, etc.

Getz (1997, p. 4), referring to the experience which participants have, states: 'To the customer . . . a special event is an opportunity for a leisure, social or cultural experience outside the normal range of choices or beyond everyday experience.' This definition, too, has its advantages, but seems to exclude organizational special events of various kinds. Nevertheless, it is a place to start and from it we can then begin to look at the vast range of events which take place. To do so, it helps to have some means of classification. Figure 1.1, for convenience, splits events into four broad categories (to be expanded on), based on the concept, in our definition of events, having leisure, cultural, personal or organizational objectives. It is crucial to bear in mind when considering this categorization that there are frequent overlaps. For example, the graduation of a student from university is both a personal event for the student and his or her family, and an organizational event for the university. A village carnival is both a cultural event, perhaps celebrating some aspect of local heritage or folklore, and a leisure event, possibly both for local people and for tourists. Therefore overlaps can be seen as inevitable, rather than exceptional, and any attempt to categorize an event, even by analysing its objectives, its organizers or its origins, will have to take account of this, even if we can say, yes, this event does fall into such and such a category.

Categories and Typologies

In this section we will begin to consider how this proposed categorization may need to be developed to take in the great variety of events. It is a useful starting point, and one we can adopt to help us look at the context and precedents for modern events and as a means of understanding their breadth and variety.

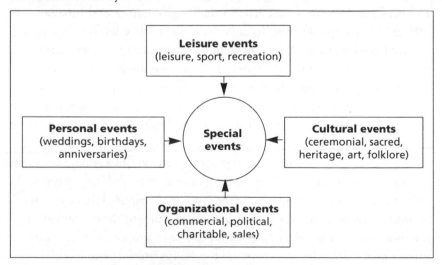

Figure 1.1   *A suggested categorization of special events.*

When we look at the various kinds of special event, whether these are leisure-based, personal, cultural or organizational, it is possible to identify a number of characteristics which are common to them, thus helping us to understand what special events are and how they work, as well as differentiating them from other activities.

Our definition of events could be given a shorthand version: 'Those non-routine occasions set apart from the normal activity of daily life of a group of people' does not necessarily give a feel for the specialized nature of the activity. We can say 'specialized' because of the uniqueness of events, but also because such events may often be celebratory or even ceremonial in some way. This is an aspect which other authors, such as Goldblatt, have highlighted. Clearly this approach can be applied to activities such as weddings, product launches or prize givings. On the other hand, it may be less suited to events such as exhibitions, sports days or annual conferences, although it can be argued that even an exhibition of paintings or a sales conference may have an element of ceremony about it – someone has to open it, but in so far as exhibitions, conferences and so on are non-routine, the definition is usable. For the purpose of illustrating the four categories, and to demonstrate historical progression, this chapter explores four case studies: for leisure events, the ancient Olympic Games; for personal events, a Roman wedding; for cultural events, the Coronation of Elizabeth I of England (which for those interested in the overlaps, could also be said to be political and therefore organizational); and for organizational events themselves, the Paris Exposition of 1889.

Special events vary tremendously in size and complexity, from the simple and small, such as the village fête, to the huge, complex and international, such as the Olympic Games. To understand the relative levels of complexity involved in various events, we can attempt to provide a typology. It is necessary to consider events as having both organizational complexity and uncertainty. Complexity is fairly easy to understand; uncertainty, as a concept, is a little more problematical. By uncertainty we mean initial doubt about such issues as the cost, the time schedule and the technical requirements. Thus, it can be understood that, at the beginning, the uncertainty about the cost, the timing and the technical needs of organizing the Olympic Games far exceeds the uncertainty of, say, a training conference or a small wedding reception. In order to quantify the complexity, in the typology in Figure 1.2, varying levels of organizational complexity have been used, ranging from individual to multinational. Using this typology it is possible to propose a classification of various events, in order to understand the comparative demands which such events might place on organizers or events managers.

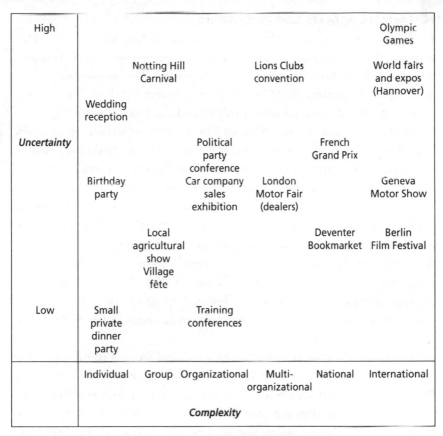

	Individual	Group	Organizational	Multi-organizational	National	International
High						Olympic Games
		Notting Hill Carnival		Lions Clubs convention		World fairs and expos (Hannover)
	Wedding reception					
Uncertainty			Political party conference		French Grand Prix	
	Birthday party		Car company sales exhibition	London Motor Fair (dealers)		Geneva Motor Show
		Local agricultural show Village fête			Deventer Bookmarket	Berlin Film Festival
Low	Small private dinner party		Training conferences			

Complexity

Figure 1.2   *A typology of events. Source: adapted from Slack (1998).*

Even where an event is relatively simple, the number of people attending may make it very complex indeed. There is the world of difference between a birthday party for six people and a birthday party for sixty, even though the format, structure and basic idea may be the same. The typology must be seen with this limitation in mind. Indeed, it is this concept of size which often means the difference between an amateur organizer, or a family member running an event, on the one hand, or having to employ an event manager, go to a hotel or find specialist advice, on the other. Size or number of attendees is something which easily catches people out. We can all organize a dinner party for eight or ten people, even a buffet for maybe twenty or thirty, but after that the sheer effort involved would overwhelm us: not enough space, not enough equipment, not enough people to help and so on. The events management business, whether it is about the annual dinner of the local town council or the European Figure Skating Championships, is often, in the contemporary world, about the need for trained staff, specialist companies and professional expertise.

Historical Contexts and Precedents

Events management can be thought of as an art, rather than a science. Historically, the organization of small local events was relatively uncomplicated and needed no extensive managerial expertise. The organization of a wedding, for example, could be done, most often, by the bride's mother with help from the two families involved and the vicar, priest, religious or other official representative. (Although in the past, especially up until the Victorian period, 'expert' advice often came in the form of a dancing master, employed to give the wedding festivities some formality of style; there were also quite specific local rituals to be observed, which acted as 'checklists' for the activities.) Some weddings are still done this way, and are within the ability of non-specialist people to organize and run: the bride and groom to deal with the ceremony; the bride's mother to order the cake and a buffet from a local baker, or with family and friends doing some or all of it; the reception held in one of the family houses or a church hall; flowers from gardens or obtained from a nearby flower shop and so on. All these tasks were, and can still be, coped with in an intimate and sociable way, without need of great cost or fuss.

While special events, by their nature, were (and are) not routine, pressure for formal organizational or technological skill was not so great for these local, family or small-scale activities in the past. This is not to say that large-scale events management is a particularly recent development, only that the modern world, with its many complexities, often requires specialists to do what, in gentler times, could be done by thoughtful amateurs, or ordinary people. We should not mistake the history, however. The scale and complexity of, say, the Greek or Roman gladiatorial games (which comprised vast numbers of activities, set piece contests and even theatrically mounted sea battles – the Romans were sufficiently advanced that they could flood their arenas) would certainly have had what today would be considered as professional events management organization to run them.

Looking back in history, we can see that events have always had a significant role to play in society, either to break up the dull, grinding routine of daily life (toiling in the fields, perhaps) or to emphasize some important activity or person (perhaps the arrival of a new abbot at the local monastery). We can trace all sorts of special events far back in time, even if those events are the result of some recent 'reinvention'. For as long as mankind has lived in family groups there will have been celebrations of weddings, births, religious rites and so on. In following up the categorization suggested above, of events being leisure, personal, cultural or organizational in origin, we can seek various historical examples or precedents.

Case Study 1

Leisure/sporting events: the Olympic Games

The modern Olympic Games are loosely based on the games of the ancient Greeks. Those games, first held in 776 BC at Olympia, in Peloponnesian Greece, had the purpose of celebrating the festival of Zeus, the most important Greek god. The games, organized by the temple priests and their helpers, carried on for hundreds of years at four-yearly intervals, even though Greece was normally at war (which was quite a usual thing in those times).

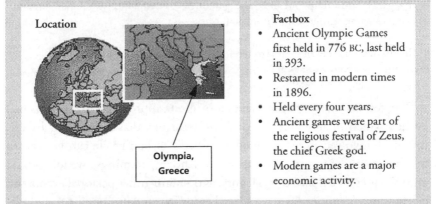

Location

Olympia, Greece

Factbox
- Ancient Olympic Games first held in 776 BC, last held in 393.
- Restarted in modern times in 1896.
- Held every four years.
- Ancient games were part of the religious festival of Zeus, the chief Greek god.
- Modern games are a major economic activity.

One of the most important aspects of the games was the truce which existed during the games to allow them to take place and to allow the participants, mostly the nobility and professional athletes, together with pilgrims (who were travelling to the temple of Zeus at Olympia), to get to the games safely.

The ancient games at first only had one component, the 'stade', a foot race, but later included not only the 'stade' (about 150 metres, hence the word 'stadium'), but also the pentathlon (the discus, the jump, the javelin, another race and wrestling), together with a chariot race, a horse race and the pankration – a very violent form of wrestling. All of these were performed naked, in the Greek style, although, as the games also celebrated military prowess, the final foot race was performed in full armour.

The games lasted for five days and included various religious ceremonies, the main religious aspect being the worship of Zeus, although the women had their own games, for the goddess Hera. (Married women were not permitted at the men's games, even to watch.) The games were organized by the religious authorities of Olympia and had professional trainers and referees for the events as well as judges (Swadding, 1999).

There were also social events, and rather like in the modern games, a parade of champions on the final day. The ancient games lasted, in all, for about 1,200 years and were closed down by the Roman Emperor Theodosius II in AD 393 (the temple at Olympia was destroyed later, about 426). The modern games began, again, at Athens in 1896, followed by Paris in 1900 and then, more or less every four years to the present day (Speake, 1994).

Based on this case:

Investigate the modern Olympic Games. Where were the most recent games held? How many people attended them? How many people participated? How were the games organized and what support services were involved? How many people did the games employ during the peak period? To what use were the games' buildings put after the games had finished? How much do the modern games differ from the ancient ones?

Related website for those interested in the Olympics: www.olympic.org

The second category of special events in our approach is that of personal events, which includes all the kinds of occasions that a family or friends might be involved in. Many modern aspects of family life can be seen to revolve around important occasions: birthdays, namings, weddings and anniversaries all fall into this category, as do many other personal events and celebrations (a dinner party is a special event in our definition). Of all these, weddings can be some of the most complicated to organize, involving friends and family, and a whole range of related service activities, from catering to entertainment, as well as the formal aspect of the marriage ceremony itself. (This is not to say that all weddings are a 'big performance'; some are small, friendly and relaxed, and just as good for it. Size is no measure of the success of an event.) Almost all cultures known to history have some form of partnership ceremony. The Romans can provide a historical precedent for personal events.

Case Study 2

Personal events: a Roman wedding

As with modern weddings, Roman weddings were organized by the families of the bride and groom (Dilke, 1975). A ring was often given as an engagement present, although no ring was involved in the ceremony itself. The bride wore a special bridal gown, generally with a flame coloured veil and garlands of flowers. The wedding would be arranged, with the respective families each dealing with various aspects. There was a legal contract to be signed by the two fathers on the day of the wedding. The joining of hands at the ceremony would be ensured, not by a priest, but by a married woman, known as a 'pronuba'.

Location

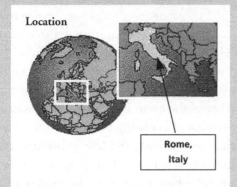

Rome,
Italy

Factbox
- The Roman Empire covered a huge area of Western Europe, from Britain to North Africa.
- Rome was pagan until the 300s AD, when it began to become Christian in religion.
- Roman weddings had many similarities to modern ceremonies, but also a number of differences.

At the ceremony prayers would be said to the family gods and especially to the goddess Juno, with a sacrifice offered to the god Jupiter. This might involve the killing of a donkey, as donkeys were thought to have considerable sexual prowess. Thus the sacrifice was thought to ensure a suitably exciting wedding night.

Following the ceremony the party would make their way to the bride's parents' house, where there would be a major feast in the Roman style, of some excess – a great deal of food and wine would be consumed. Once the feast was over, there would be a torchlight procession, from the bride's parents' house to the bridegroom's house. The procession would generally be led by the torch carriers, often children, and accompanied by flute players and the families, with friends, relatives and other locals joining in. There was a great deal of loud and happy singing during the procession and of the cheerful shouting of obscene poetry and jokes (known as 'Fescennine verses'). This was the Roman equivalent of writing obscene messages on the couple's car with foam, and often referred to how good the donkey was in bed.

On arrival at the bridegroom's house the bride would anoint the doorposts with oil as a sign of dedication to the gods and the bridegroom would carry the bride over the threshold. At this point we will leave them to it.

Based on this case:

From your own experience of going to a wedding, how did it differ from the Roman one? Who organized what? Suppose you have a wedding to organize with 100 guests: how long does it realistically take to get things done? Begin to look for possible similarities between the special events in these case studies: what are their common characteristics?

Related website for those interested in Roman history: www.roman-empire.net

Special events cover all kinds of human activity, not only sporting and family activities but also cultural and commercial or organizational activities. Culture, with its associated ceremony and traditions, has a role in all kinds of social activity, and for all kinds of people, organizations and institutions, but has been especially important for governments and leaders, such as royalty. In cultural events ceremony becomes very evident, often as a way of emphasizing the importance of the event itself or of the person at the centre of the ceremony, the intended effect being to secure support, or to allow as many people as possible to recognize the key individual. For example, the news media often shows heads of state (kings, queens, presidents) inspecting a 'guard of honour' when arriving at the airport of a country they are visiting: they listen to the national anthems and then go and walk past the guard of honour. The original purpose of this ceremony is not for the head of state to see the guards, but for the guards to see the head of state: for the guards to recognize someone they are to protect.

In the middle ages, special events and ceremonies had a major role to play in the life of the time, in ensuring that a dull daily existence was enlivened, and that people were entertained or at least impressed. There were no TV, video, movies or Internet for entertainment, as all these are less than 100 years old. It was, for example, accepted wisdom in England in the Tudor period (about 1500–1600) that 'In pompous ceremonies a secret of government doth much consist' (Plowden, 1982). Government, in this case the king or queen, was expected to make a good show, or put on a good sight for the people, and the people expected to see royalty in all its glory. This was intended to ensure, to a certain extent, respect and allegiance.

Case Study 3

Cultural events: the Coronation of Elizabeth I

At a time when the country had a huge foreign debt, and the treasury was empty, with a new queen not known for spending money, the Coronation of Elizabeth I had a huge amount spent on it, to put on a good show. This was felt to be important in order to generate loyalty and allegiance to the new queen and to ensure the stability of support for the monarchy and the government (which at that time were the same thing).

The ceremony ran for four days. It began with the queen travelling along the River Thames to take possession of the Tower of London, escorted by her guard (the 'gentlemen pensioners'), the royal court, the Lord Mayor of London and many others, including several groups of musicians, in a fleet of barges, boats and other water craft (Plowden, 1982). This river journey took

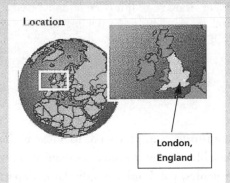

Location

London,
England

Factbox
- Coronation of Queen Elizabeth I of England took place over four days in January 1559.
- Run by the Lord Chamberlain.
- The event comprised:
  - a river procession on the Thames;
  - a foot procession through the city;
  - the coronation ceremony and a banquet.

most of the first official day of the event, after which the queen stayed at the Tower (then a royal palace as well as the most important fortress of the country), while other preparations were made.

Two days later a tremendous procession took place, on horses and on foot, from the Tower of London to the city of Westminster and the Whitehall Palace. This took the entire afternoon to travel through medieval London, so that as many people as possible could see the new queen. Unlike modern processions, the medieval one stopped frequently for the queen to look at displays and tableaux, to talk to all kinds of people from the great to the poor and to receive gifts and listen to loyal speeches. The coronation itself followed on Sunday 15 January 1559, in Westminster Abbey, the crowning place of English kings and queens for centuries. There then followed a great banquet which ended at one in the morning.

A task of this size would be a challenge to even a modern events manager: at Elizabeth's coronation it was the responsibility of the Lord Chamberlain and the Treasurer of the Household. The court of a medieval monarch was not only involved in the occasional coronation, but more or less existed in a constant state of pomp and ceremony, so much so that its organization reflected this. The Lord Chamberlain's department was responsible for entertainment of all kinds and had a special office called the 'Office of the Revels' which arranged anything from plays to pageants, and which consisted of a relatively large number of specialized staff, by the standards of the period (Plowden, 1982).

Based on this case:

Think of a recent ceremonial event you have seen, perhaps a royal or government event, a church event or some ceremony which takes place locally in your town or city, perhaps involving the mayor. What was this event about and what was special about it? Was there much ceremony – perhaps a procession, music, ceremonial dress or some kind of tradition being enacted? Does the ceremony still have a modern use? What is that use? If it is a traditional event, does it now have some other useful purpose, such as attracting tourists or emphasizing the long history which it relates to?

Related website for those interested in Queen Elizabeth I: www.luminarium.org/renlit/eliza

One of the things which these historic examples serve to show is that there have long been specialists available of various kinds to organize events (the temple priests for the Greek games, the Lord Chamberlain's department for Queen Elizabeth). Some events, such as the coronation of a king or queen, have been, and still are, highly complex. Very often, where great ceremony was needed for state events, the military could also be called on to organize them, and officers of the army were often seconded to do just that, as is still the case with much modern state ceremonial: parades, state visits, pageants and festivals.

Although the organization of historic ceremonial events might be seen as a matter of the injection of military organizational prowess, very often such prowess was no such thing. In fact great historical ceremonial disasters were quite commonplace. The modern events manager has no monopoly on things going 'pear shaped'. Many coronations and other great events were, in parts, famously shambolic. Even where these involved a non-military organization, such as the great royal fireworks held to celebrate the peace of Aix-la-Chapelle in 1749 for King George the Second, there was no guarantee of success, even though these were organized by George Frederick Handel, the famous composer, and set to his music. The fireworks were to be held in a specially built pavilion in Green Park, London. Handel was designated as 'Comptroller of the Fireworks'. This was such a major event that a full dress rehearsal was held, which went perfectly. However, on the night itself, Handel had an argument with Servandoni, the pavilion designer, at which swords were drawn, and during the middle of the performance, with 100 musicians playing and a crowd of over 12,000 people, half the pavilion burned down.

The modern world is no different: faster perhaps, more complex perhaps, but no less susceptible to things going wrong, falling down, being rained off, flooded out, with the guest speaker stuck in the traffic, the groom still drunk after the stag night, the buffet being dropped on the kitchen floor and the bride falling over the cake at the reception. In some ways, events management is a rather thankless task, one of those roles where everyone notices when something goes wrong, but few people notice the tremendous effort involved in getting even a simple event right. Indeed, some of the things which go wrong at an event may be beyond the organizer's ability to prevent: the weather, the traffic and so on.

Nevertheless, events can be considerable triumphs of organization and leave lasting legacies. The fourth in our categories of events is the organizational event. This may be anything from a political party conference to a motor show. There are any number of suitable examples. Some of the world trade fairs have left some interesting legacies. As trade and commerce developed following the Industrial Revolution, many countries sought to celebrate and display their industrial achievements. This led to a number of industrial and commercial exhibitions in many major cities. These exhibitions had often developed out of local trade fairs in towns and cities around medieval Europe. Fairs had been held for many centuries as a way to show off all kinds of products, goods and other wares. One of the first great international industrial fairs was the Great Exhibition in London in 1851 (there had been earlier ones, such as that in Paris of 1849), which was held in a specially built hall, the 'Crystal Palace', which held some 13,000 exhibitors from all over the world.

These fairs have taken place at irregular intervals in many major cities ever since. Recent fairs or 'Expos' having taken place in New York, Montreal, Seville and, in 2000, Hannover. In the Victorian period many cities held fairs, not only London, but also Amsterdam (in 1883 with the 'International Colonial Exposition' and several later fairs) and especially Paris, which held a series of fairs from 1855 to 1900 (and two since, in 1925 and 1937). One such event, which left a very obvious legacy, was the Paris Exposition of 1889.

Case Study 4

Organizational events: the Paris Exposition

The 1889 Paris Exposition was the idea of the French prime minister of the time, Jules Ferry. He wished to see an exhibition which would demonstrate France's industrial might, her commercial activity and her engineering skill. The result was the largest, most varied and successful world's fair ever held until that time.

The fair was opened on 6 May 1889, a wonderful spring day, by the French President, Sadi Carnot, who rode in procession from the Elysée Palace. The procession, led by a detachment of mounted cuirassiers, made its way along the Champs Elysées and the Avenue Montaigne among joyful crowds, and entered the exhibition area passing under the arches of the Eiffel Tower, arriving

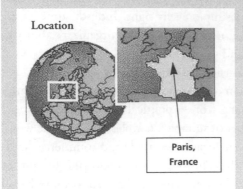

Location

Paris,
France

Factbox
- The Paris Exposition of 1889.
- Intended to display France's industrial power.
- Resulted in a major building programme in the Exposition area, including the construction of the Eiffel Tower.
- 32 million people visited the fair.

at the Central Dome at 2.00 p.m. A short ceremony took place at which the Exposition was formally presented to M. Carnot: 'This splendid result exceeds all hopes . . .' Indeed it did. The Exposition was huge. It covered the whole of the Champ de Mars and the Esplanade des Invalides, and stretched along the Quai d'Orsay and the Trocadero Gardens to the Eiffel Tower, some 228 acres (95 hectares), including a huge Ferris wheel, a precursor of the London Eye. There were almost 62,000 exhibitors from all over the world and by the time an exhausted President Carnot had left at 5.30 p.m., almost half a million people had streamed in through the 22 entrances to the exhibition, which then lasted 176 days. Some 32 million people visited the fair and among the exhibits was the world's first ever motor car, a Benz (Harris, 1975).

The lasting legacy of the exhibition is the Eiffel Tower. When the event was being planned, a member of the French cabinet, Edouard Lockroy, had suggested a thousand-foot tower to highlight its importance. The idea of a tower built of iron and steel was not new: one had been suggested by the Cornish engineer Richard Trevithick in 1833, and another by Clarke and Reeves, two American engineers, for the Philadelphia Exposition of 1876. But it was Gustave Eiffel who supervised the building of the Paris tower. The Tower was begun on 26 January 1887. It opened at ten minutes to twelve on 15 May 1889, to Eiffel's considerable relief, and has been the symbol of Paris ever since, though for the first twenty or thirty years it was rather disliked by some.

Based on this case:

Think of a recent engineering project you have seen launched, perhaps even the Millennium Dome. What was its purpose? How was it organized? In the long term, was there some benefit from having it, even if it was knocked down later? Does this apply to other kinds of events? How could a town or city benefit from holding an event? Could that event be used to help to renovate a run-down area? Who would pay for the event?

Related website for those interested in the Eiffel Tower: www.tour-eiffel.fr/indexuk

Characteristics of Events

In our definition of special events, we noted key characteristics of events as 'non-routine' and 'unique'. However, events have many other characteristics in common with all types of services, and in particular with hospitality and leisure services of many kinds. These characteristics can be grouped together as being: uniqueness, perishability, labour intensiveness, fixed time scales, intangibility, personal interaction, ambience and ritual or ceremony (see Figure 1.3).

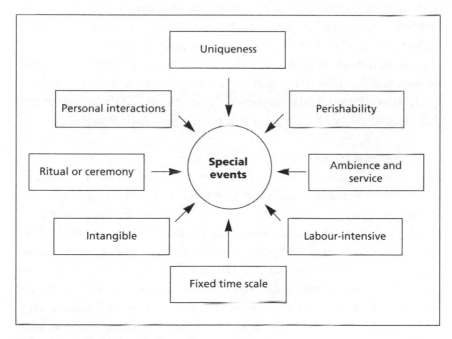

Figure 1.3   *Characteristics of special events as a service.*

Uniqueness

The key element of all special events is their uniqueness – every one will be different. This is not to say that the same kind of event cannot be repeated many times, but that the participants, the surroundings, the audience or any number of other variables will make the event unique. Even where we have looked at special events which are very frequent, such as weddings, all are different because of the different people involved, the choice of location, the invited guests, the timing and so on. The same is true of events which may have followed the same format for years and years. The ancient Olympic Games took place at four-year intervals for nearly 1,200 years, or put more simply, 300 sequential events. But each was unique, because each had different athletes, different organizers and a different audience. The format also changed slowly over time. At the beginning, it was a religious festival for the Greek god, Zeus, and only the 150 metre foot race, the 'stade', was run. At the end, there was no major religious aspect, but the athletics had become the main activity, with 12 or so different sports in the games.

The uniqueness of special events is therefore the key to them. We are not doing something which is routine, nor are we producing the same item of work repetitively. Nevertheless, it is important to recognize that certain types of event do recur; they may recur in the same kind of format (such as weddings – each wedding is different but the format or structure is similar), or they may recur on the basis of time interval (such as an annual conference – again the format or structure is the same, but the participants and the subjects will be different). Uniqueness alone, however, does not make a special event. Events have a number of characteristics and the uniqueness of them is closely related to the aspects of perishability and intangibility.

Perishability of events

Almost by definition, if we regard events as 'unique', then the event is tremendously perishable, and cannot be repeated in exactly the same way. Two wedding anniversaries at the same location, with the same number of people, will not be the same. Even where a reasonable level of standardization is possible, such as with activities like training seminars, each will be different and will be very time dependent. The perishability issue also relates to the use of facilities for events. Let us suppose we have a banqueting room. It may be used to its peak capacity only on Saturdays, for weddings, so for the rest of the week its revenue generating potential may not be exploited. If the room is empty for even one day of the week, the revenue generating potential of that day is lost for good – it is perishable. Yes, you can use the room on a different day, but the day on which it is empty cannot be replayed and used for an event.

One of the key issues in the events manager's role is therefore the extent to which facilities and services can be used effectively, given the uniqueness or irregularity (perhaps it is better to say infrequency) of use. In consequence events can be expensive to provide. Many things will have to be produced on a one-off basis and cannot be used again; for example, a large banner saying 'Happy Wedding Anniversary Anna and Frederick' would be a unique item and thus (relatively) expensive to provide. On the other hand, a banner saying 'Happy Anniversary' may have a number of potential uses and can be stored.

The issue of perishability also means that events venue managers may have to use a variety of techniques, such as differential pricing, to try to encourage activities in quiet periods when a facility or service on offer might not sell. So, perhaps, a mobile disco can be obtained at a discount for an event on, say, a Tuesday, rather than at a peak period of the week or year, perhaps a Friday or Saturday night or New Year's Eve. This too illustrates the perishability issue; if the disco is not booked on one night of the week it will have lost the revenue for that night for ever.

Intangibility

When you go out to buy a chocolate bar or a pair of socks, you are buying something tangible – you can see it and touch it. With special events, however, the activity is more or less intangible. If you go to a wedding, you will experience the activities, join in, enjoy it and remember it, but there are only a few tangible things which you might have got from it – perhaps a piece of wedding cake and some photographs, or a video you took of the happy couple and the rest of the guests. This intangibility is entirely normal for service activities – when people stay in hotel bedrooms they often take home the complimentary soaps and shampoos from the bathroom, or matchbooks from the bar. These are efforts to make the experience of the event more tangible – something to show that the experience happened and something to show friends and family. It is important for event organizers to bear this in mind, as even the smallest tangible item will help to support people's idea of how good an event has been. A programme, a guest list, postcards, small wrapped and named chocolates, even slightly more ambitious give-aways, such as badged glasses or colour brochures, help in the process of making the intangible more tangible.

Ritual and ceremony

This is, for authors such as Goldblatt, the key issue about special events, or, simply, the major thing which makes them special. In our historical case studies it was very evident that ritual and ceremony often played an important part. In practice, many modern ceremonial activities are 'fossilized' or reinvented versions of old traditions. The old tradition might originally have had some key role in the ceremony, now lost, but the ritual of doing it (like the inspection of honour guards) still continues. Often, the ritual ceremony is there because it does, in fact, emphasize the continuity of the tradition, even though the reason for the tradition has gone. In Ripon, in England, at dusk, a horn is blown to signify the setting of the night watch. In olden days this had real purpose (now it is just a small event for tourists). The town was in open countryside and could be invaded or attacked by brigands or barbarians, and the sounding of the horn was to set the guard on the town walls and to ensure that the night watchmen, known as 'wakemen', came on duty. Even this was not thought enough, and Ripon being a cathedral city, God was appealed to: 'If God keep not ye citie, ye wakemen waketh in vain.' Or put into modern English: if God didn't look after the town, the watchmen were wasting their time. Thus, for hundreds of years, this short ceremony has taken place in Ripon and continues every nightfall even now. The watch is still called to the walls, though the walls are long gone and the last watchmen long dead.

Modern special events may not, by any means, rely on old tradition and old ceremony. If you think of a contemporary ceremony, such as the Hollywood Oscars, which are essentially prizes given for good film-making and good acting, the whole ceremony was specially made up. This is true of all kinds of events. In fact, it is often the case that a town or city wishing to attract tourists might do so by creating a brand new special event, containing a brand new ceremony, something for the visitors to watch. This can be done for all kinds of special events, and the creation of new ceremonies and 'new' traditions is very common, although it can be argued that for a special event to have a 'traditional' element in it, that traditional element should have some basis (however tenuous) in historical reality.

Ambience and service
Of all the characteristics of events, ambience is one of the most important to the outcome. An event with the right ambience can be a huge success. An event with the wrong ambience can be a huge failure. At a personal event, such as a birthday party, the ambience may be simply created by the people who are there, without the need for anything else – good company among friends can make an excellent event.

Some events, however, may need a little help to go well. At a birthday party, there might be the need for decorations, music and games, as well as food and drink. But it is very important to realize that the presence of these things does not guarantee that things will go well: one can have a wonderful environment, expensive themed decor, large amounts of excellent food and drink and the event could still be a flop. One of the roles of an events manager is to try to ensure the event succeeds by careful attention to detail and by trying to encourage the desired outcome. Nevertheless, people cannot be compelled to enjoy themselves. If they've had a bad day, or feel grumpy, your wonderfully well organized event might turn them round, or it might not.

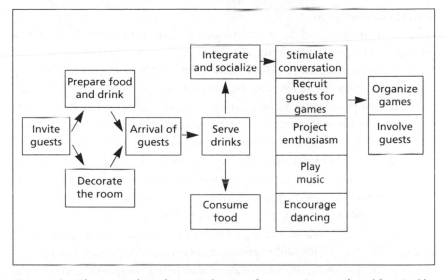

Figure 1.4   *Elements in the ambience and service of an event. Source: adapted from Berkley (1996).*

High levels of personal contact and interaction

In manufacturing situations, customers have no contact with the staff producing the goods, only with, perhaps, the sales team. In service situations, customers have frequent contact with staff, and often this contact determines the quality or otherwise of the experience. People attending special events are frequently themselves part of the process; that is to say, for example, the crowd at a sports tournament is not only watching the event, it is also helping to create the atmosphere, it is interacting with itself, with participants and staff and is part of the whole experience. Much the same is true of the guests at a Christmas party: it is the guests themselves interacting with each other, with the hosts and perhaps with entertainers who create the atmosphere and contribute to how enjoyable the event is. A room decorated for a party may look nice, but will not come to life until it is full of guests. Therefore, in considering how to make an event successful, event managers must be fully aware that this is largely dependent on the actions and reactions of people attending. It is perfectly possible to have the same event twice in a row, such as a pageant or procession, and have one event a complete success and one event a complete failure due to audience reactions, interactions or backgrounds. An awareness of the attendees is vital on the part of event planners.

Labour intensiveness

The more complex and the more unique an event is, the more likely it is to be more labour-intensive, in terms of both organization and operation. The organizational issue relates to the need for relatively complicated planning to enable the service delivery to be efficient, or, put more simply, for the event to be a good one (this being the reason why some events may be out-sourced to event management companies, caterers or other types of event suppliers). The uniqueness of this type of service implies a high level of communication between the organizer and the event manager. Such a high level of communication and planning will take time and effort, even where the event may be repeating a well known formula, or operating within a common framework, such as a conference. The operational element may also require high levels of staffing in order to deliver the event properly. A banquet for 300 people will require not only food service staff, but bar and drinks staff, kitchen staff, management and perhaps support staff, such as cloakroom attendants, cleaners and staff to set up and break down the room. Staffing needs are also likely to peak at certain times. In the case of the banquet, peak staffing will take place at service time, but a long sequence of preparation has also to be taken into account.

No two events are likely to require the same number of staff, except in so far as events which have an element of routine, such as banquets and con-ferences, will require a known number of staff. Managers can forecast staffing needs for these types of events from experience, depending on the number of guests, the types of service, the experience and quality of the staff, the time required to complete the service and even the layout of the building. Staffing ratios are dealt with below in more detail. The labour intensiveness of special events is rather less predictable, as it depends entirely on the type of event, in addition to all the above conditions. An event such as an athletic competition will require a completely different staffing structure to support it (including competitors, judges, timekeepers, etc.) from a company annual outing to a theme park. An event manager will have to forecast staffing needs directly from the requirements of running the event, based on what the organizer specifies as the event's objectives and needs as well as on the experience of department heads.

Fixed time scale

Events, rather like building projects, run to a fixed time scale, unlike routine activities which carry on indefinitely. The time scale can be very short, such as for the opening ceremony for a new road, or can be very long, as with the Paris Exposition noted above – the planning phase taking about three years. Even these are not extremes. Many special events are actually composed of a sequence of short bursts of activity, with pauses or breaks in between. Constant ceremony, lasting many hours, might become dull and tiring. The example of the coronation of Elizabeth I shows that while the event lasted for four days, this was composed of several shorter activities of varying lengths, depending on what was going on and why. For those planning special events, this issue of timing must be kept in mind. For an event to be successful and striking, it will need to hold people's attention and interest them; it is better that it is broken up into sections than that it takes place all at once, without a respite. This is not to say that the fixed time scale cannot be varied. Some events, such as a birthday party, may carry on longer than intended because 'it just happened'; other events may even be extended in a planned way for some special reason, e.g. to recoup the costs.

Summary

Special events have always had a major role to play in human society. In many respects, modern events are not that much different from those of ancient times, especially in helping to enliven routine and daily life. In understanding this, we can also see that society has developed and changed. Increasing public knowledge, and technology, often means higher expectations of modern events managers. Whatever role events play in the social context, the management of events should be seen as a service activity. This context helps us to understand how events work, what their major elements are and how we can classify them.

Reference List

Berkley, B. J. (1996) 'Designing services with function analysis', *Hospitality Research Journal*, **20** (1), 73–100.

Dilke, O. A. W. (1975) *The Ancient Romans*. Newton Abbot: David and Charles, pp. 82–3.

Getz, D. (1997) *Event Management and Event Tourism*. New York: Cognizant, p. 2.

Goldblatt, J. J. (1990) *Special Events: The Art and Science of Celebration*. New York: Van Nostrand Reinhold, p. 4.

Harris, J. (1975) *The Tallest Tower*. Washington, DC: Regnery Gateway, pp. 3–13, 108–18.

Markland, R. E., Vickery, S. and Davis, R. (1995) *Operations Management: Concepts in Manufacturing and Services*. Saint Paul, MN: West, pp. 43–51.

Plowden, A. (1982) *Elizabethan England*. London: Readers Digest, pp. 10–15.

Slack, N. (1998) *Operations Management*, 2nd edn. London: Pitman, p. 591.

Speake, G. (1994) *The Penguin Dictionary of Classical History*. London: Penguin, pp. 448–9.

Staines, J. and Buckley, J. (1998) *Classical Music*. London: Rough Guides, pp. 174–81.

Swadding, J. (1999) *The Ancient Olympic Games*. London: British Museum, pp. 53–93.

Tomlinson, A. and Whannel, G. (1984) *Five Ring Circus: Money, Power and Politics at the Olympic Games*. London: Pluto, pp. 16–29.

CHAPTER 2

The Market Demand for Events

Aims
- To examine the scope and scale of the events business.
- To consider the determinants of demand for events.
- To illustrate the structure of demand for events.

Introduction
It is very common for individuals and organizations to like to quantify things. We like to be able to say that a particular industry or its market is a particular size. There are several reasons why statistical measurement of events activity might be considered useful. First, data are required from which we can evaluate the significance of events to a particular location, whether that is a town, city or some other geographical region. In this respect data help to quantify the role that events play in the economy and in society. Second, data are essential to the planning of facilities and services. This has been particularly shown in the construction of special sporting facilities, for example, but also for the development of tourism and other community facilities. Third, data are particularly needed by organizations (stakeholders) in the events business, government departments and individual event organizers for the marketing and promotion of events, the prediction of demand and statistical comparisons.

There is a view that an expansion of events activity has been and is taking place. This is reflected in the increasingly rapid development of specialist events management companies and related service providers. There may be a number of reasons for this. In Europe, increased wealth (and associated benefits of disposable and discretionary income) and many years of peace in the industrialized countries have strengthened the inclination to travel, to experience new ideas and to enjoy recreational activities; this, coupled with an active awareness of traditions, has seen an increase (in some cases a rein-vention) of many kinds of events, especially in the cultural field (such as opera at Glyndebourne and film at Deauville). As much as this is true culturally, it is also true of the commercial, sporting and personal fields, for much the same reasons. As demand has grown, so have the mechanisms to supply services to satisfy it; hence the reason why major international organizations and companies take an interest in event activities. (Cause and effect can be argued here: is the increase in the number of organizations providing events services entirely due to the effects of demand, or has the potential demand been suppressed because of lack of available services?) Nevertheless, many of these general demand factors are not apparent to the organizers of individual events, who are probably more interested in the individual motives of participants and visitors to ensure their event is a success. In so far as events are often 'unique activities', even where an activity recurs, perhaps on an annual or more frequent basis, there are some unusual features of demand which have to be considered.

Whereas demand for a routinely manufactured product is known and largely predictable, demand for events is less easy to predict. This is partly an issue of participants' motives to attend an event, but also because demand might be suppressed by factors not immediately obvious to organizers (such as lack of disposable income for the target market group at a particular time of year). This leads to some unpredictability. The demand expansion for Eurostar services through the Channel Tunnel has significantly exceeded the expected demand, because it tapped latent (hidden) demand: there were always going to be people who wanted to travel between Britain and mainland Europe with ease, in speed and in moderate comfort, without having to bother with a ferry crossing. This latent demand turned out to be very large indeed. Similar demand aspects may be at work in the events business – who knows how successful an event might be if demand is hidden or latent.

Size and Scope of the Events Market

The events market is so diverse and so fragmented that it is problematic to say what the business is worth as a whole. In fact, to attempt to quantify it might be a fruitless exercise of the first order. Although such a quantification might be seen as a challenge for some academics and researchers, the nature of the events business and the limitations of data collection have to be appreciated. Imagine trying to accumulate attendance data for carnivals in every European town and city.

The student of events management would therefore be best advised to steer clear of this problem; even the serious researcher should not regard an assessment of the total value of the market as a particularly viable exercise given the lack of suitable frameworks (although as better quantitative information becomes available this position may change). So how can we seek to address the issue of the scope and scale of the events business? This can be done to some extent by breaking the business down into small components. We can then say that a certain part of the business is worth a given amount of money, has a certain number of participants or has a particular impact. We could take a geographical region and ask, 'can we quantify this type of event in this area?' In some cases this is possible. For example, the total wedding business in a region such as the UK is thought to be worth some €2.6 billion. This is based on the known number of weddings (which are recorded officially) and an estimate of the average cost of having a wedding. A similar kind of exercise could probably be done on a European scale, thus giving us a notional figure for the European wedding market. For a few categories of events, estimates have been made on a European scale. These estimates range from those which have been done in reasonable depth, such as the economic impact studies of the European grands prix (see Case Study 5), by Lilley and DeFranco (1999), to the study by Nils Klevjer Aas (1998) of European film festivals, which is an example of the approach taken to assessing a type of event, in a European context, where information is limited and incomplete, but the best that can be made in the circumstances.

In building up a picture of event activity we are, in effect, 'building a wall'. At present all we have for this wall are a few bricks, from widely different sources, and not much by way of foundations. As the events industry is not typically seen as a homogenous whole, there has been no drive to seek common statistical information, either by the industry or by other users of statistical data, such as governments and academics. In the range of events activity, the nature of personal events, voluntary events and similar activities means that almost no data are collected for many kinds of events, except by occasional sampling, or perhaps by the event organizers for their own use or for a few household surveys. Even where events are organizational or commercial in nature, the extent of data collection is very limited indeed, and often particular only to that event. There is no common format even for the collection of attendance data, nor in the foreseeable future is there likely to be (although some countries, such as Germany, do require a certain type of attendance and other data to be collected for tourist-related festival activities). This means that data collection relies predominantly on a few sources and most often on casual estimates. The accuracy of much event reporting tends to be limited, for a whole range of reasons, not least that accurate data are often collected only for admission to paid events, and even then the likelihood of publication is small. Many events organizations record data mainly for their own internal use, if they record it at all.

Case Study 5

The size and scope of events: the European grands prix

The study of European grands prix by Lilley and DeFranco, possibly a model of good practice, looked at the economic impact of the eleven annual grands prix held in the European Union (this included the Monaco Grand Prix, as its economic impact was felt almost wholly within the EU). Although this was a study of a fairly uniform type of event, it offers a framework for analysing other events.

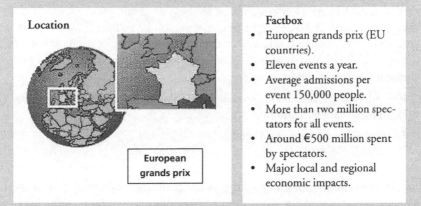

Location

European grands prix

Factbox
• European grands prix (EU countries).
• Eleven events a year.
• Average admissions per event 150,000 people.
• More than two million spectators for all events.
• Around €500 million spent by spectators.
• Major local and regional economic impacts.

The methodology used by Lilley and DeFranco could also be adopted for other major event categories, since the purposes of the study were to:

• measure the size of the total attendance at each event;
• measure the size of the non-local attendance;
• determine how much money was spent by non-local attendance in the local area.

Data were collected directly from the race tracks' own attendance information, used in conjunction with a number of interrelated surveys dealing with where the attendance came from, and what was spent on tickets. In addition, phone interviews of sample sections of the local hotel, restaurant, retail and other services industries were undertaken to assess the impact of race visitors on them. This large-scale data collection effort was then analysed to produce the survey results, in terms of both the eleven individual races and the total impact.

This approach clearly highlights the potential for major studies to enlighten us about the nature of events. However, it is intensive, costly and time consuming (the study took three years to complete). In normal circumstances our knowledge of the events business is limited by the meagre data available and methodological limitations (professional studies being rare). In general terms there is a need for a level of uniformity and comparability in the collation of basic statistics of events, and a need for a start to be made on a framework. This is, initially, a task for academics and industry professional bodies (of which there are few). Consequently, it may be some time before even the most sketchy outline of the full scale and scope of the events business is built up.

Based on this case:

Identify an event or festival in your region: investigate what information the organizers collect about the participants, visitors, income and size of the event. Is this information kept internally or is it disseminated publicly, and if so how? What key elements of information might help us to build up a picture of the events business and how might this information be collected? What are the current problems and limitations of data collection? For any given activity or group of activities what sources of information might be available, and how might we classify such sources?

Related website for those interested in this study: www.fia.com/etudes/f1_impact/sommaire.html

Source: Lilley and DeFrance (1999).

On the other hand, and looking at the problem positively, we can focus on individual events. A practitioner, researcher or student could make a fairly accurate analysis of the size and scope of an event, given time, effort and the cooperation of the organizers. More importantly, in terms of the market demand, once this focus on an event has been made, the market for the event can be analysed too – we can say what kind of people are likely to attend, or have attended in the past, we can say something of their likely media habits, of their motives for going to the event and what benefits they get from attending or participating. These issues do help our understanding. Richards (1992) makes good use of this approach in discussing how events and festivals can be planned and marketed and how market information should be recorded. He identifies five basic areas for continuous monitoring:

- visitor numbers;
- visitor spend;
- visitor activity and participation;
- advertising effectiveness;
- visitor satisfaction.

On this basis, any assessment of the scope and scale of the events business could achieve its ends by looking at the component parts of the business. At an industry level, a note of caution is necessary: we have financial assessments of only a few parts of the total market. The vast majority of component parts of the events business have no available estimates of demand, income, expenditure or impact. Indeed, many types of events may never have realistic estimates, especially smaller voluntary events. If we, in our categorization of special events, have included personal events as a key category, there is no way in which the amount of money which is spent on private informal gatherings, such as birthday parties, is ever going to receive much more than reasonable estimates; nor, for the sake of privacy, should it. The need for usable statistical data is a key one, however. This being so, event organizers and events management companies do need to record more comprehensively the key indicators, and publish them in the public domain, in order to raise the profile of the industry, assist the planning of facilities and services and help to focus marketing and promotional efforts.

For an indication of the possibilities of estimating the market for the events business, consider the adaptation of the earlier typology of events in Figure 2.1 (p. 32). From this, you may wish to insert your own event, or another event known to you, to see how the typology can be applied.

The typology, rather like the first periodic table in chemistry, is incomplete, but a framework into which we can insert and apply other examples. The vast range of events not listed far exceeds the small number of events which are given, as examples of their class, in the typology. However, there is nothing to prevent an assessment of one event being made in terms of its worth, or in terms of its market. There are even a number of classes of events which could have their worth, market size and market components realistically estimated. This approach, of taking one element (and recognizing it as part of a much greater whole), may be a more useful means of gaining an impression of the scope of the events business.

Case Study 6

Estimating events market size and scope: the UK wedding market

The wedding market is one of a large number of discrete sectors of the events business. It is also one of the few for which there is some assessment of size and extent. Many component parts of the events business cannot be quantified because of their *ad hoc* nature (for example, charity events, school sports days, private dinner parties), and even where there might be the potential to collate data about a particular sector of the market it might be difficult to disaggregate the size and extent of the business from other activities.

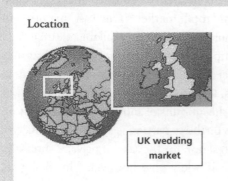

Location

UK wedding market

Factbox
- UK wedding market.
- 325,000 events a year.
- Average €8,000 per event.
- Estimated €2.6 billion market.
- Largest components are the catering, the reception venue and the honeymoon.

Mintel (1997), attempting to quantify the size and extent of the UK wedding market, observes that there is considerable regional, cultural and socio-economic variation in what a wedding costs. Therefore, even though the national average cost of getting married is thought to be of the order of 8,000 euros, this can vary from 5,000 to 20,000 euros, depending on the location and extent of the celebrations, and comprises a long list of items:

- engagement and wedding rings;
- engagement party, stag night, hen night, evening wedding party, music, band;
- wedding dress, shoes, accessories and bridesmaids' outfits, groom's outfit, going away outfit;
- bride's bouquet, other flowers, posies and corsages;
- cars or carriages;
- registry or church fees;
- invitations and other stationery;
- photographs, video;
- reception venue or marquee;
- catering and drinks, wedding cake;
- first night hotel, honeymoon;
- various other expenses.

In terms of market demand, the UK wedding market has been gradually declining, with a fall in total number of events from about 400,000 a year in 1981 to 327,000 in 1997, although the average cost of an event has been rising. This decline in overall demand suggests a change in the social determinants for getting married, in so far as marriage is becoming less popular, and not only are UK couples getting married later in life, but many are happy not to be married at all. This reflects a change in the family and social structures of the UK, and in the underlying social determinant for being married. In comparison to many other types of event, the determinants for getting married are primarily social, although there are a range of secondary motives such as the ability to have family and friends at a major life event, and the ability, in the case of some types of wedding, to display wealth or status.

Based on this case:

If you have attended a wedding recently, what type of event was it, formal or informal? How many people attended and what was their background – were they family, friends, acquaintances, neighbours, work colleagues? Who was involved and why? Was there anything unusual about the event, such as special costumes or a historic venue? Is the market for weddings in your location changing? If so, why? Are these changes due to social factors and if so what are they? How are data collected for this type of event, and how do researchers and analysts use the information to produce reports and estimates of size and scope?

Related website for those interested in consumer research reports: http://sinatra2.mintel.com

Source: Mintel (1997).

Determinants and Motivations

The events business cannot be seen in marketing terms as a homogenous whole. The wide range of events, the fragmentation of the business and the wide range of differences in determinants and motivations make an assessment of the total market driving forces for events rather a challenge. Until a more complete framework for the categorization of events exists it is only possible to look at individual sectors or individual events to assess market demand and demand determinants. Historically, the demand for events can be seen to have been determined largely by social factors. These social factors included the need for the integration of society, interaction between individuals and communities, mutual support, bonding and the reinforcement of social norms and structures. In addition there were issues of status, the need for public celebration and the development of religious, civic, trade and community rituals and ceremonies.

In the modern world these determinants also exist, and events continue to be driven by social and psychographic factors. Human society, while it may have developed technologically, still has the need for integration, interaction and community. In addition to these key social needs, events are also driven by economic, organizational, political, status, philanthropic and charitable needs. The development of events management companies and a larger and more cohesive service infrastructure for events is itself indicative of change in the forces which underpin demand for events activities. In examining the determinants for events we can conclude that the creation of

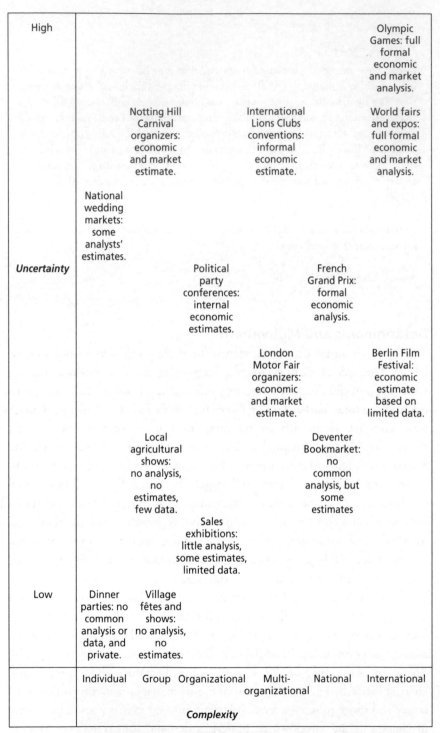

Figure 2.1   *Some approaches to assessing the scope of the market and economic impact of events. Source: adapted from Slack et al. (1998).*

events is also driven by economic factors, an increasing standard of living, changing demographics and the increasing education of the population. Within the European Union the high level of industrial development and general wealth ensures relatively high levels of disposable income, which is increasingly spent on hospitality, tourism and recreational activities such as visiting or participating in events. Much the same is true of the commercial sphere of activity (contrary to some views of the effect of technology on commercial enterprises) – the demand for commercial events, such as conferences, exhibitions, product launches and so on continues to increase.

In attempting to analyse the key drivers of demand for the events business we can perhaps conclude that for any given event there is a range of motives or determinants and these motives could be said to be both primary and secondary (Figure 2.2). For example, the primary motive for putting on a dinner party may be to entertain one's friends, but there may be secondary motives, such as to increase one's status by showing off a new house where the dinner party is to be held.

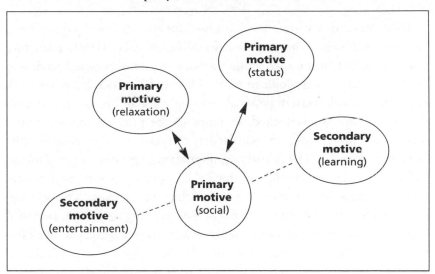

Figure 2.2   *A combination of motives for participating in an event such as an opera gala. Source: adapted from Teare* et al. *(1994).*

The primary motive for holding an athletics competition may be to provide an opportunity for local athletes to measure their abilities against others; the secondary motives may be to provide a social integrating mechanism for people with the same interests, and, perhaps, to raise money to support an athletics club. We can see from these examples (and Figure 2.3) that there is unlikely to be one single motive for most types of event.

Examples of Social Motives	Examples of Organizational Motives
Social interaction with others	The need to make sales
Creation of community spirit	The need to have an organizational presence
Status or recognition of achievements	
Philanthropy or charitable contributions	Status or recognition
	Sponsorship or community support
Examples of Physiological Motives	**Examples of Personal Motives**
Relaxation or recreation with others	Seeking new experiences
Sexual enjoyment with others	Learning and education
Exercise or physical challenge	Creativity and exploration
To eat, drink or be entertained	Fulfilment of ambitions

Figure 2.3   *Possible motives for attending events (these may be primary or secondary). Source: adapted from McDonnell et al. (1999).*

There is a tendency to see the motivation for attending and participating in special events in terms of personal motivation. Getz (1991) takes this general approach in considering the satisfying of various personal needs as a mechanism for getting people to events. Motives for participation in events might be physical, social or personal, but might also be organizational, and this should not be overlooked. In terms of the primary and secondary motives described above, the satisfaction of needs can vary considerably from event to event. The primary need for attending a dinner party might well be the maintenance of friendships; the secondary motive might be to explore the possibility of starting a relationship with the host. The primary need for attending a motor show might have nothing to do with personal needs, but everything to do with the fact that the organization you work for has sent you for organizational reasons. In this respect, the classical and often over-quoted theories of motivation, such as those by Maslow, do not provide us with a real picture of why people go to events. Equally, a marketing approach which seeks only to satisfy one single need might not be enough to get people to the event without there being some additional benefit or package of benefits.

Participation in events may be a result of a wide range of potential motives, not just social ones: personal expectations, tourism, support for other participants in the activity or the propensity to attend events as a form of relaxation or entertainment may be reasons. In the case of those events for which an admission charge is made, the ability and willingness to pay the price is an issue, and secondary cost implications may also impact on personal events. In the case of the dinner party, whether one's friends attend is not simply a matter of the wish to interact with each other, it is also a matter of their ability to do so, in terms of transport to get there, travel costs, distance, time and effort or whether some other personal priority (like the need to look after the kids) exists at the same time as the proposed date for the party.

This does not mean to say that knowing the motives for attendance will necessarily help organizers in trying to find out how many people will actually attend an event. We might find that there is no useful market information whatsoever for an event we are planning, no studies, no collated data. This should not stop us searching for clues. What might be the total market size? What proportion of that total market is in our catchment area? Are there any clues from previous or similar events? Suppose our proposed event is industrial heritage. For whom might this kind of industrial heritage be of interest? How big is the market for it and what might the catchment be? Without research data on market size, we might look initially for other evidence, say the circulation numbers of popular magazines about it (these can be obtained from magazine marketing circulation information, which will usually be printed somewhere in the magazine itself), though this approach is still little more than guesswork.

The same might be true of small events. Our 'first ever' village fête might only have a total potential market of the village population, say a village of 500 people, and not all of these will be there. So, in short, attendance estimates are just that – estimates. However, the process can, and should, be helped along by a little market research: take a sample of the target market and ask them if they are going to attend, but beware – there is a difference between interest and action!

Case Study 7

Motives for attending events: the Berlin Film Festival

The Fiftieth Berlin Film Festival took place between 9 and 20 February 2000 in a number of venues and cinemas throughout Berlin, many of which, including the Berlinale Palast, the CinemaxX and the Sony complex, were newly opened, as part of the large-scale redevelopment of the city which had been taking place during the 1990s, especially around the Potsdamer Platz, where much of the Festival activity goes on. The Festival is a major international cultural event for Berlin and attracts not only the movie-going public but also large numbers of celebrities and journalists.

Location

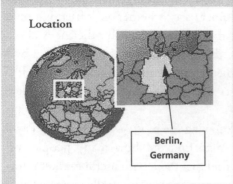

Berlin,
Germany

Factbox
Berlin Film Festival.
- Sells 35,000 tickets for a 12-day event.
- Screens 240 films.
- Attracts major film stars.
- Attended by 12,000 journalists and film-makers.
- Helps to promote Berlin as an international city.

The Festival is a means of launching new films, made not only in Europe but also abroad, including the USA. The event is competitive in so far as a jury awards a range of prizes for film-making activities: these are known as the 'Golden Bears'. (The bear is the symbol and mascot of Berlin.) During the twelve days of the year 2000 festival, some 240 films were shown. These were not only feature films, but also documentaries and shorts. They included some well known international films and many lesser known ones. Some films attracted major audiences not only for the film itself but also to see some of the stars who attend the festival, particularly where the launch of a new film is taking place. The major films and the presence of their stars can bring frantic scenes, with the attendance of international celebrities attracting the panting attention of fans and journalists.

The Festival not only deals with the mainstream of film-making: there are fringe activities including the 'Panorama' section which gives advance previews of the next season's films, the Kinderfilmfest (children's film festival), the International Forum of Young Cinema and, separately, the European Film Market, for producers, distributors and other film professionals. Such a major event also attracted political interest, including a visit by the German Chancellor Gerhardt Schroeder, who mingled with the stars at the awards ceremony.

Based on this case:

What kind of people would visit the film festival? If these visitors were classified into various categories of, say, film goers, film-maker, the local public, film stars, film stars' fans, politicians, etc., what would be their respective motives for going to the festival, in terms of both their primary motives and their secondary motives? Identify a film festival in your region. How many people go to it ? What might be the total market size and what do you think is the relationship between the total market size and the actual attendance?

For those interested in the Berlin Film Festival: www.filmfestivals.com

Source: Downey and Schutze (2000).

The range of motives can also impact on the attendance for those types of events, such as large-scale festivals, where more than one activity is taking place. In this respect it is highly likely that more than one market segment will be present with more than one motive for being there, an issue which Hall (1992) addressed in his generic product/market model, adapted in Figure 2.4.

THE EVENT 'UMBRELLA'

Example: **The North Sea Jazz Festival, The Hague**

Event emphasis
The core event   **The fringe event**

Example: Music festival   Free ancillary activities

Specialization within the market for the event
Core events activities   **Fringe events activities**

Example: Bands Solos   Bands Kids
            Big concerts Masterclass   Open air Sales

Individual components or specialized activities at the event

Example: 70 bands, 50 soloists, etc.   30 bands, 1 clown, 48 sales stalls, etc.

Individual target market groups attending an element of the event

        ❶ ❷ ❸ ❹ ❺ ❻   ❷ ❹ ❺ ❼

Example: Various age/interest   Different groups attend fringe
            (market) groups

Figure 2.4   *Event component mix. Source: adapted from Hall (1992).*

In the case of the model, it has been supposed that the event is composed of a number of activities, some of which are core activities and some of which might have 'grown up around it'. This is often true of many kinds of events: conferences, for example, may have associated exhibitions. Carnivals may be composed of a large number of different activities linked by the carnival theme. Although an event may be a single activity (such as an anniversary dinner) with one homogenous group of people attending (one market segment), certain types of events comprise a range of parts, and these parts are attended by different groups or segments, with possibly different motives for being there.

Case Study 8

The North Sea Jazz Festival: The Hague

There are a very large number of cultural and arts festivals held every year throughout Europe, ranging from folk festivals to poetry festivals, from highland dancing to classical music. Jazz is a major music medium, and there are perhaps some 300 major and minor jazz festivals and events throughout Europe each year. These are held in all kinds of places, from major cities to small villages, and attract both jazz fans and the general public. There are well known jazz festivals in Glasgow, in Scotland, Cork, in Ireland, San Sebastian, in Spain, Aanekoski, in Finland, to name only a few. One of the major European jazz festivals, however, is that held in the Hague in the Netherlands: the North Sea Jazz Festival.

Location

The Hague,
The Netherlands

Factbox
- North Sea Jazz Festival.
- Total participants and visitors: 150,000.
- Number of musicians: 1,200.
- Three-day festival in July.
- No formal economic analysis found.
- Predominant market: jazz fans aged 35–55.

The festival attracts, directly, some 70,000 people. The three-day event is held in July at several venues in the Hague, including the Congress Centre. The programme of jazz bands, groups and musicians is one of the major cultural events in the European calendar, and includes not only the main festival programme itself but also activities for kids, supporting sales activities and exhibitions and an additional free programme for the public in the city centre, called 'Jazz Heats the Hague' (www.northseajazz.nl). This part of the festival is held in the evenings from 7.00 p.m. until midnight, in the form of summer open air concerts in the city. This open air programme attracts a further 75,000 people, and adds much to the general atmosphere of celebration and relaxation. It also serves to bring jazz to a wider audience than jazz fans.

In total, the festival, in its twenty-fifth year in 2000, reached almost 150,000 people, not only from the Netherlands but also from all over the world. The programme, over its three days of events, concerts and open air entertainment, is provided by almost 1,200 musicians. The market for the event comprises people from all age groups, with the key age group of jazz fans being 35–55, and includes families, tourists and people living in the Hague itself, from office workers to government ministers. Many of the visitors stay in the city's hotels and guest houses, for which this is a peak period.

Based on this case:

What might be the primary and secondary motives for a jazz fan attending this event? What might be the primary and secondary motives for a family attending one of the summer evening open air concerts? What are the marketing benefits, to the main festival at the Congress Centre, of having three days of free evening open air concerts in the city, for the public? Do these extra events, for example, help to create demand for the main event? What kinds of businesses in and around the Hague would benefit from the festival?

Related website for those interested in the North Sea Jazz Festival: www.north-seajazz.nl

The Structure of Demand

In general, for the events organizer, an interest in the potential sources of demand is key to providing a successful event, because without this knowledge it will be impossible to provide what the target market expects (Swarbrooke, 1995). Indeed, the target market for the event, even if properly promoted, might or might not materialize. This is because, for a number of events, we are doing something new. Therefore the estimate of the potential market is just that – an estimate. On the other hand, there are events where the market is known and is fixed, personal events being one example. Equally, there are events which, while retaining their uniqueness, recur at intervals, such as annually or bi-annually, and in this case the market is relatively well known from previous experience. If 5,000 people came to a town's firework fiesta last year, and have done so for the past five years, then, assuming all other factors remain more or less the same, there can be a reasonable degree of certainty that 5,000 people will come this year. Here, though, is a limitation to the marketing theory that people will come and buy your product or attend your special event provided you have done everything right – it might rain on your firework fiesta. To take up a point made in Chapter 1, events are perishable. A one-day event might well suffer from an unexpected external factor: the weather (as with the British Grand Prix at Silverstone in 2000, when rain made access by car to the car parks, which had become muddy fields, impossible, Silverstone having no public transport facilities worth mentioning, the event attendance was very nearly ruined), the traffic, a clash with another event; all factors beyond the control of the organizers.

In consequence there may be all kinds of reasons why an event might not attract the numbers its organizers expect. People might not be attracted to the event at all. On the other hand, the assessment of the market for an event could be based simply on known 'current' demand. This current demand may only be part of the event's potential. In terms of new events we may perhaps be tapping demand which has been latent or suppressed in some way. There are, in the sense of demand potentials, four kinds of demand:

- Current demand: that demand which our event satisfies at the moment.
- Future demand: that demand which our event could satisfy over a normal growth period.
- Latent demand: that demand which is sleeping until you provide an event for it.
- Frustrated demand: that demand which exists for our event but which cannot get to it owing to being suppressed by price, time, availability, lack of disposable income or other reasons.

Suppose a town has a range of cultural and sporting events in its calendar. These events take place every year and will often attract different target market groups: those who attend the regional soccer tournament might not be the same people as those who attend the annual early music festival. The market for events is therefore diverse and changing. Some events will also be more popular than others, some events will be new that year, some events might not, for a range of reasons (from costs to popularity, or shortage of volunteer expertise), run again next year. So the issue about running an event is not simply about the current market, it is also about whether the expertise, inclination, funding and support exist for an event to be planned and run. In the case of the North Sea Jazz Festival, the event began in 1975 with a small number of visitors, a few venues and fewer than 300 musicians. The level of demand was relatively small, but in each successive year the event has grown, and the level of demand to visit and participate in the event (150,000 visitors and 1,200 musicians) could not have been foreseen 25 years ago. At that time, demand for a jazz festival in this location was latent. Rather like the building of Eurotunnel between Britain and France, the effect was to create a new market, and then expand on it. Equally, it is perfectly possible that there might be further potential – unexploited demand for the jazz festival – which is not being tapped for a variety of reasons. This is true of many types of event.

Summary

In examining the scope and determinants of demand for events, we have concluded that owing to the unusual and fragmentary nature of the events 'industry' (which includes anything from private dinner parties to the Olympic Games), an overall assessment of the market size of the business is a difficult process. It is preferable to look at individual events, or groups of the same kinds of events, to assess their scope, impacts and extent; and although it is possible to make some estimates for certain sectors of the events business, this is not sufficient to provide a picture of the whole. People attend special events for a whole range of reasons: these may be social, organizational, physical or personal. Indeed, the motives for attendance are often a combination of several reasons or stimuli.

Reference List

Aas, N. K. (1998) *Flickering Shadow: the European Film Festival Phenomenon*. Strasbourg: European Audiovisual Observatory (http://www.obs.coe.int/oea/docs/00001262.htm). (26 June 2000)

Downey, M. and Schutze, S. (2000) *The Future Is Now*. Paris: Filmfestivals (http://www.filmfestivals.com). (25 June 2000)

Getz, D. (1991) *Festivals, Special Events and Tourism*. New York: Van Nostrand Reinhold, pp. 1–21.

Hall, C. M. (1992) *Hallmark Tourist Events: Impacts, Management and Planning*. London: Belhaven, pp. 137–48.

Lickorish, L. J. and Jenkins, C. L. (1997) *An Introduction to Tourism*. Oxford: Butterworth Heinemann, pp. 134–68.

Lilley, W. and DeFranco, G. (1999) *The Economic Impacts of European Grands Prix*. Brussels: EU Sports Workshop (http://www.fia.com/etudes/fl_impact/sommaire.html). (25 June 2000)

McDonnell, I., Allen, J. and O'Toole, W. (1999) *Festival and Special Event Management*. Brisbane: Jacaranda Wiley, p. 115.

Mintel (1997) *Leisure Intelligence Report: Wedding Venues*. London: Mintel Marketing Intelligence, pp. 8–11.

Richards, B. (1992) *How to Market Tourist Attractions. Festivals and Special Events*. Harlow: Longman, pp. 26–32.

Slack, N., Chambers, S., Harrison, A. and Harland, C. (1998) *Operations Management*, 2nd edn. London: Pitman, p. 591.

Swarbrooke, J. (1995) *The Development and Management of Visitor Attractions*. Oxford: Butterworth Heinemann, pp. 58–84.

Teare, R., Mazanee, J. A., Crawford-Welch, S. and Calver, S. (1994) *Marketing in Hospitality and Tourism*. London: Cassell, pp. 44–63.

CHAPTER 3

The Events Business: Supply and Suppliers

Aims
- To consider the fragmentary nature of the events business.
- To provide an overview of events services.
- To examine the role of public sector, private sector and voluntary bodies.

Introduction

The reader will have observed that we have, so far, tended not to refer to the events business as 'an industry'. This is mainly because of the fragmented nature of the activities which go to make up the huge breadth and range of the events business. There is comparatively little explicit structure to the business, unlike in many industries which perceive themselves as a cohesive whole: for example, banking or retail. There is no one single major supply element to events, although there are some representative bodies, and some understanding that events are a major economic activity, however difficult to quantify.

In contrast to many industries, the special events business is not completely driven by the need to make money. Indeed, the business has a very large element of personal, voluntary, charitable and philanthropic activity. The broad range of special events allows all kinds of organizations and individuals to participate in an enjoyable way for the mutual benefit of all concerned. The social benefits of this approach are very considerable, not only in terms of social integration and the contribution which people can make to their community, but also in terms of friendships and good neighbourliness.

This is not to say that a large commercial sector does not exist: that sector has developed rapidly during the past fifteen years or so, and will continue to do so. The market for events has expanded to the point where the need for a professional infrastructure is evident (especially for a European Association of Event Managers). The increasing number of events management companies and professional events organizers is an indication of this demand. This is not to say that events management suddenly appeared out of nowhere – these businesses have long existed as part of the tourism and hospitality industries – simply that events management, as a standalone role, is now commonplace.

The Structure of Events Services: Public Sector

As the events business has developed, the levels of specialization and technical requirements have increased, owing to greater expectations on the part of organizers and participants. This has led to a rapid development in event-related services and support organizations. While it is still the case that a small personal event, such as an anniversary, may be a comparatively simple affair, with little need of organizational or technical support, larger activities, VIP events, launches and corporate hospitality activities often require a great deal of support from conception onwards (Hall, 1992). This support may be via commercial organizations or public sector bodies.

The extent of these support services may be rather startling to the uninitiated, but think of all the activities which are involved in a carnival, and the potential for complexity in the support of the larger events business may become more evident. In fact, many of the support activities which we think of as being 'the events business' are really only the commercial organization element.

A developing public sector infrastructure exists (see Figure 3.1), which takes in:

- European Union and national government departments responsible for tourism (or sport, depending on the type of event): for example, the Tourism Division of the UK Department of Culture, Media and Sport, the Secretaria de Estado de commercio, turismo y de la pyme (the Spanish Government Department of Commerce, Tourism and Small Business) and similar government departments throughout Europe.
- National (and regional) tourist organizations (NTOs) responsible for developing and marketing tourism activities: for example, the British Tourist Authority (BTA), the Netherlands Board of Tourism (NBT) and similar national authorities, who collate information on tourist-related events, promote and support some of them.
- National trade associations and industry professional bodies: for example, the UK Association of Events Managers, the European Federation of Conference Towns.
- Regional or local tourist offices and visitor and convention bureaux: for

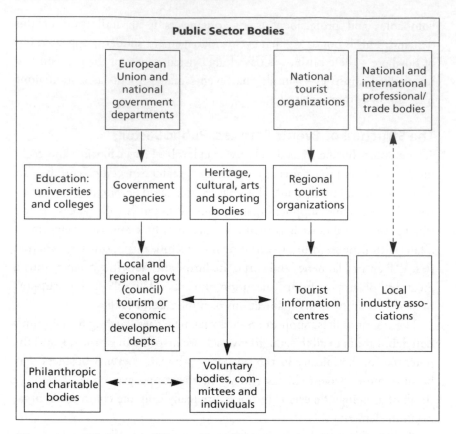

Figure 3.1   *Infrastructure of the events business. Source: adapted from Tribe (1995).*

example, the Birmingham Visitor and Convention Bureau, the Scottish Tourist Board, the Dutch VVV (Vereniging voor Vreemdelingenver-keer), tourist information offices in towns and cities.
• Educational Institutions, including colleges and universities teaching events management.

In many cases, such as with professional bodies, and with events education, these are at a fairly early stage of development, largely because of the current nature of the events business. However, as the business matures, it is likely that public sector organizations will begin to play a greater role (especially where there is a public agenda for social inclusion or tourism development activities), and clearly at the moment, some of these types of organizations are better developed in some countries than others.

Case Study 9

Example of public sector organizations:
European Federation of Conference Towns

There are a large number of public sector organizations involved in events management and the related activities of tourism and leisure. These range from national government departments covering tourism to small voluntary committees set up to provide a particular event. The European Federation of Conference Towns (EFCT) is a trade body whose primary objective is to provide a focal point for the European conference industry. It particularly promotes those towns and cities that are members, and are significantly involved in the provision of major, large-scale, conference and events venues.

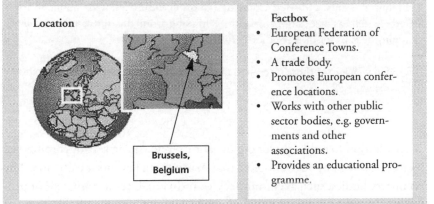

Location

Brussels,
Belgium

Factbox
- European Federation of Conference Towns.
- A trade body.
- Promotes European conference locations.
- Works with other public sector bodies, e.g. governments and other associations.
- Provides an educational programme.

The Federation has been in existence for almost 40 years and is based in Brussels. It has sought to promote its member towns and cities as venues, and in this respect provides worldwide publicity as part of the promotional effort. However, as it has been in existence for a comparatively long period of time, in an industry which has been rather underrepresented by professional bodies, associations and similar organizations, the remit of the EFCT has gradually expanded to take in a wider role, particularly in giving the industry a voice in government and the ability to lobby on behalf of the business tourism sector in general, at European level.

The EFCT is also involved in education, and provides short courses at operations level for those interested or involved in conference and events activities. Many of these courses are run as part of a summer school programme which is held each year in a different member city. This programme is backed up by workshops, meetings and seminars, as well as a two-day annual forum for more senior members of staff. However, this is not an educational programme in the recognized sense for professional status. The EFCT is a trade promotional body and a lobbying group, rather than a professional body with educational aspirations.

The EFCT's objective is to promote its member's facilities, such as congress halls, purpose built conference and exhibition centres and other larger-scale (i.e. over 300 people) venues (member towns and cities must fulfil certain criteria in terms of capacity of venues and accommodation to join). It provides publicity for these facilities, exchanges information and gives advice to members (as such it acts as a distribution channel). The EFCT is run by a secretariat and an executive committee made up of seven members from its 30-member board of directors, which normally meets twice a year.

Based on this case:

Identify a number of public sector bodies involved in events management. What do they do, and why? What government departments might have an interest in events, and why? Compared to other industries, what public sector bodies, such as associations, might be missing from this industry, and how might the gaps for those bodies be filled?

Related website for those interested in the European Federation of Conference Towns: www.efct.com

In addition to public sector organizations (and the private or commercial sector), it must not be overlooked that many special events are organized by voluntary bodies, such as committees, or individuals (either amateur or professional events organizers). Voluntary bodies can organize a whole event based on voluntary help, or a mixture of voluntary help, support from local authorities and other organizations, or with partial use of commercial organizations in some roles. Essentially, personal events such as dinner parties follow this 'voluntary' framework: you do it yourself or receive help from friends and family to do it; perhaps you buy in food from a caterer. The other type of organization is the voluntary organization supported by the public sector, as noted above – a town carnival might be organized by a voluntary committee, but it also might be helped by the local council's events or tourism department (or a combination of these). Special events organizations should not, then, be seen as simply the business of profit-making companies or individuals – these are only part of the whole.

The Structure of Events Services: Private Sector
The events business is not solely concerned with the provision of activities, entertainment, refreshment and equipment: it encompasses a wide range of interlinked activities. Although the most basic type of event may require only those things, the larger and more elaborate events become, the greater

the need for increased technical and logistical support of one kind or another. With an increasing complexity of needs and demands, the standard of organization required for large-scale events is very high and a whole series of specialist activities have grown up to service these needs. Although many of the organizations in production, distribution, venue and ancillary services might be thought of as 'commercial' (i.e. profit-making), this is not entirely the case, as Figure 3.2 shows.

Production	Distribution
Event management companies	Individual events and venues
Event catering companies	Event and conference agencies
Party planners	Trade media
Production companies	Hotel booking agencies
Exhibition and theatrical contractors and designers	Incentive travel agencies
Technical services	Visitor and convention bureaux
Professional events organizers	Exhibition organizers
Multimedia support companies	National and local tourism bodies
Voluntary bodies, committees and individuals	
Education and training	
Venue Services	**Ancillary Services**
Event room/hall/grounds hire	Accommodation providers
Catering and kitchen facilities	Photographers and video makers
Accommodation	Transport and guiding services, ground handlers
Food and drink supplies	Translation services
Business support services	Music and entertainment providers
Medical and crèche services	Travel companies
Information and customer services	Costume hire services
Technical support	Marquee hire services
Waste disposal and grounds clearance	Printers
Toilets, washrooms and public facilities	Floral contractors
Parking	Database support services
Security	Professional and trade bodies
	National and local government services

Figure 3.2   *Events organizations (private sector and others).*

These organizations, typically, either package services and provide the whole thing or provide one element of the service needed by event organizers or organizing committees, which may wish to do the rest themselves. The types of organizations which are capable of providing complete packages for events are normally:

- event management companies;
- production companies;

- event catering companies;
- party planners and professional events organizers;
- exhibition and theatrical contractors;
- technical service and multimedia companies.

A wide range of companies provide other services which can be hired in, contracted or purchased (depending on the service). These cover directly related services such as the provision of hospitality, or indirect services which not only provide something for the events business, but also perform a function for the local community. These include transport and guiding services, whose role is to get participants and audiences from the point of arrival to, and sometimes around, a venue. Then there are various other services, such as retailing, medical support, administration, secretarial and travel (Kotas and Jayawardena, 1994). It can be seen from this approach that a matrix of distribution activities already exists in the events business. There are a range of distribution channels, like those of most industries. For example, when buying a holiday, the purchaser may go to a travel agent, who might provide a whole package holiday (in the same way that an event management company can provide a whole event package). Alternatively, the purchaser might put together a holiday from various component parts, such as a flight and a hotel, having chosen the destinations using information from a tourist office (equally, clients wanting an event could do it themselves by assembling the various parts – a venue, a caterer, an entertainer and so on). So the distribution channels are the mechanism by which venues, markets and events activities are put together. The choice of channel depends on the experiences and expectations of the buyer, and the influences, such as through marketing, which the various companies or other sellers can exert.

The use of these various organizations is a matter not only of budget, but also of the experience (or lack of it) on the part of buyers, of the standard to be achieved at a given event, of the time available to make arrangements and of the requirements of the organization making the booking and completing the planning process. Needs and, therefore, the approach, vary.

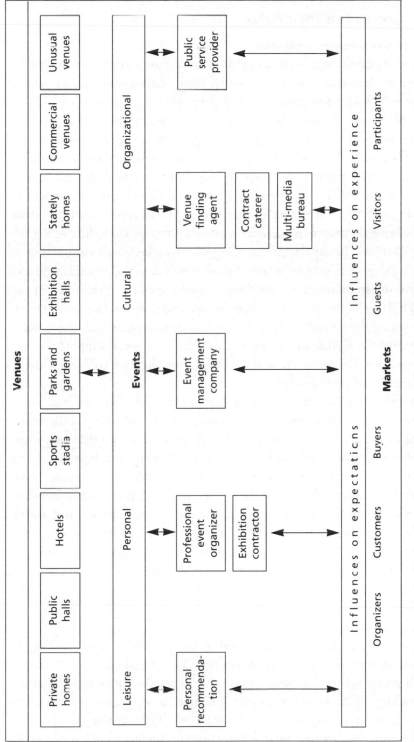

Figure 3.3   *Matrix of sample distribution channels and activities. Source: adapted from McIntosh et al. (1995).*

Companies and Their Roles

Event management companies

Event management companies (EMCs) are a quite recent innovation (but there are historical precedents) which have often grown out of related service or hospitality providers, and have specialized in provision of the complete event. Events, as we have noted, may range from product launches and dinner dances to themed gala evenings or charity sports competitions. EMCs tend to be involved where the organizers have a requirement for major or VIP events and corporate hospitality, or where, for example, a product launch demands specialist design and innovation. The benefit of having an EMC is the range of expertise, ideas and experience it can draw on. Taking the case of the need for a gala evening, such as a themed dinner, the EMC will be capable of providing the expertise for almost any theme the organizer may wish to choose. This will include the planning, menu and theme design, in terms of identifying a suitable menu to go with the theme and full catering support in food production and service at the event. Development of the theme would include specialist sets, props and, if necessary, costumes for participants or guests, and all the range of support requirements, from the provision of special effects and lighting to music (live or recorded) and entertainment.

The creation of special events of this type is highly complex, and above all requires extremely careful planning and costing. The choice of the theme itself should also be a matter of careful discussion between the event management company and the buyer or client. A great deal depends on the objectives, the venue, the nature of the facilities (such as kitchens and even washing up areas), the size of the venue, its design features and elements such as the availability of licensing, parking, loading, power and access. However, all these things are within the expertise of an EMC to arrange and sort out, so that clients do not have to do the hard work of organizing an event themselves, but simply employ the EMC, give it a brief and let it get on with it.

Production companies

Organizers are often confronted with unique problems when seeking to create an event of a professional standard. This is particularly the case for high profile events. The ability to develop such events may be beyond the knowledge of the average organizer delegated to do the job within a committee or other organization. Nevertheless, high profile events, VIP ceremonies, roadshows, major competitions or product launches all require specialist technical facilities and knowledge. Increasingly, events of this kind are put into the hands of production companies. These companies are able to package together the wide range of technical support which high profile activities often require. This technical support might range from set design to the training of presenters.

A production company will probably be able to undertake most, or all, of the following activities: project management, in the case of large-scale projects where the whole event is delegated by the organizer to the production company as a contractor (especially those events which might also involve building or construction, either of the permanent or temporary kind); design, including set and backdrop design, staging, lighting and all the range of audio-visual support needed for high quality presentations; venue management, where an organization may, for example, wish to take over a unique venue, such as a castle or stately home, to use for its event, and which therefore requires expertise to be brought in that the venue itself might not normally possess (outsourcing); participant or audience handling, which ranges from the simplest issues of ticketing and security to the full provision of VIP seat booking or allocation of accommodation or pavilion space; technical support, ranging from simple provision or hiring in of equipment to the full preparation of computer graphics, slide or video production and related facilities; training of presenters and speakers, often including not only the basic training but also scriptwriting and video production. Naturally, the packaging of the whole production process does not come cheaply, but production companies have a level of expertise which most organizers simply do not possess, so that while it might be possible for an organizer to put together a highly complex up-market event, the organizer would have to be both well trained and extremely experienced to do so. Given that few organizations, especially volunteer ones, possess experienced organizers, it is often necessary to bring in production companies for events of a high profile nature.

Case Study 10

Example of private sector organizations: the Inntel Agency

There are a large number of private sector organizations (companies, etc.) involved in commercial activities in the events management business. Some of these companies have a single line of activity, some are multi-activity. Inntel is a well established company providing various linked services in conferencing and event management, based in Colchester in the south-east of England. Established in 1984, it now employs some 64 staff who cover a number of key departments.

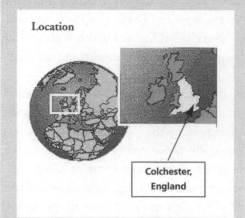

Location

Factbox
* Inntel, Colchester, Essex, England.
* Specialist conference, hotel and events agency.
* Sixty-four staff in four key operating departments.
* Family-run business established in 1984.
* Turnover in excess of €32 million.
* One of the UK's largest agencies of its type.

Colchester, England

Inntel began life as a hotel booking agency, dealing with hotel reservations for companies and other organizations within the UK. It has gradually expanded to take in conference activities, especially conference venue finding, and finally events management activities. It therefore maintains a multi-role portfolio of business and has a national profile as an agency in this field of business. Inntel is organized into four primary operating departments.

Conference placement

This is the main element of Inntel's conference business. Clients who are looking for a suitable venue for their event can do so themselves, which can be time-consuming, or they can place their enquiry with an agency such as Inntel, which will lessen their effort and possibly benefit them by obtaining more competitive rates at venues. The agency will take details of the prospective requirements of the client and will then identify a number of suitable venues to enable the client to choose. This process may involve further assistance by the agency for the client, such as the provision of brochures or the organization of site visits. The agency will then receive a commission from the chosen venue. The benefit to the hotel of agency business is that of adding a distribution channel, particularly one targeted at corporate or group business. The benefits to the client are ease of finding suitable venues, especially those which the agency would regard as reliable.

Hotel reservations

Much the same process is involved for hotel reservations as for conference placement (Horner, 1995). Enquiries come in to the agency from individuals or organizations (which may or may not be conference related) and the agency identifies suitable accommodation, and an element of skill is needed in matching the client with a choice of suitable venues. Owing to the large amount of business that Inntel handles, it is capable of obtaining discounted rates from accommodation providers such as the major hotel companies, which act as an incentive for clients to use the agency. In a similar way to the conference placement activity, agencies receive commission from the hotel where the booking has been made.

Event management

Increasingly, as organizations have begun to concentrate on their core activities, they no longer have the staff to do their own event organizing and have therefore needed an event organizer or agency. The task of putting together often complex conference and event activities is taken on by the agency, which has the necessary expertise and time to achieve a better result. Sometimes this can be via a professional event organizer, or often the agency can provide the total package: venue finding and event organization. This role is undertaken by Inntel through its Event Management Division, which not only covers the prior arrangements and general at-conference organization, but also deals with the in-event activities (such as registration) and post-event activities (such as feedback and reporting).

Contract management

This is probably the least understood role of agencies. We have noted that many organizations simply do not have the staff, or inclination, to become involved in venue finding or event organization (it could be inferred that this simply means small organizations, but often it is quite the opposite). A number of extremely large public companies and national organizations prefer to contract out their conference activities to an agency. This enables organizations to concentrate on their own main activity, but also to draw on the agency's expertise whenever conferences or events are required. Where this is the case, a contract is developed between the organization and the agency. Once set up, the agency will become a 'nominated supplier' for that organization. It is incorrect to believe that this implies that all events for the contracted organization go through the agency directly. Very few of these contract arrangements mean the agency becomes 'mandatory' supplier (most are non-mandatory) and the agency may have to make its presence felt physically in various divisions of a company to get the business. This is often done by site visits, familiarization presentations or, for example, setting up the agency's stand in the foyer of the contracting organization's office or offices. Basically, to get the business, the agency has to go to the company and sell itself to individuals in the company who buy conferences and events.

Based on this case:

What are the advantages and disadvantages of an events organizer using an agency? As an event organizer, what choices do you have to organize your event – who else could you go to besides either doing it yourself or getting an agency to do it? Do agencies make their turnover just in commission from venues, or do they do so in fees and other revenues from their professional activities?

Related website for those interested in Inntel: www.inntel.co.uk

Source: Author, with grateful thanks to James O'Neill of Inntel.

Event catering companies

Probably the most major input to the events business is the need for catering. This covers all aspects of refreshment for participants, audiences, crew and staff. Catering can be provided in three main ways: it is undertaken in-house (i.e. by an organizer or venue), by contractors permanently employed at the venue or on an *ad hoc* basis at the venue. A venue might not be able to provide specialist catering for an event: for example, for a church fair, the church hall might have a kitchen but no caterer to run it. A larger venue may be needed nearby or a marquee may have to be erected. For these situations the catering arrangements will have to be determined well in advance.

Catering operators range in size and in the types of service they provide. EMCs were mentioned above as sometimes having developed from catering operators. The larger contract catering companies also run the in-house services of a number of venues and *ad hoc* provision for conferences, exhibitions and other events including, corporate hospitality. Independent caterers also have a share of the *ad hoc* conference business. Moreover, in the price restricted part of the market, such as for charitable events, there are small independent caterers, who provide basic, but sound, catering in the form of buffets. This type of catering for small events may be unserviced; that is to say, the food/drink is delivered with disposable plates, etc., and the organizer simply lays it out for participants or guests to eat. Bakeries often provide this kind of unserviced buffet, simply delivered and paid for on the spot and perfectly adequate for the job. A similar service is also sometimes provided by supermarket companies.

Many major hospitality or catering companies have divisions dealing with events catering, sometimes, perhaps wrongly, known as 'outside catering'. Events catering companies range in size from small family businesses, which look after things such as local weddings or village fêtes, to major international caterers who hold contracts for significant large-scale events such as international airshows and sports tournaments, major 'society' weddings, VIP dinners, corporate hospitality and so on. Think, for a moment, of the complexity and size of the catering provision for the Wimbledon Lawn Tennis Tournament, the Paris Airshow or the Olympics, and it can be seen that this is a very large business indeed.

An organizer may choose any one of the above 'packaging' organizations depending on the requirements of each particular event. What are its objectives? Who are the participants? How large will the event be? In some cases it might even be conceivable that all three types of company are needed together, but this is not very common.

Party planners and professional events organizers

Although major companies, like those above, are increasingly common in the events business, so too are a wide range of smaller organizations and individuals willing to provide events-related services. The most common of these are probably party planners and professional events organizers; the first tend to offer a range of services particularly for the personal events market, the second for the corporate market. This includes the organization of parties, celebrations, weddings, anniversaries and many other types of similar events. While many people are happy to organize their own events on this small and more intimate scale, not all have the time or wish to expend the effort on doing so, and are happier to pay a professional to come along and deal with all the nitty-gritty detail of planning, organizing, operating and managing an event so that everything goes smoothly. Professional party planners or event organizers are obviously more used to doing this than is the average person, who might only have to put on a biggish event occasionally and might have to rely, otherwise, on friends and family to help.

Case Study 11

Events management as a career

Events management has only comparatively recently been seen as a potential career. Many of the people involved in events management have developed their jobs through related activities, such as corporate hospitality and entertainment, travel agency and tour operation, theatre and media. There are a large number of quite small event management operators, individuals and partners. However, a number of major companies have taken an increasing interest in events management, especially those historically involved in the activity, or through acquisition of similar companies. Outdoor catering companies are one example: there has always been a major market for outdoor catering at (for example) sporting events and competitions; these companies have then expanded into the events market as it has matured.

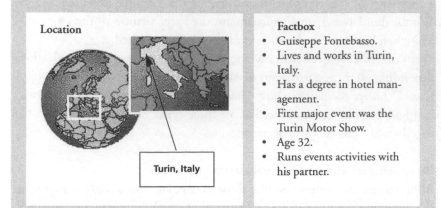

Guiseppe Fontebasso's career in events management developed from his parents' restaurant business in Turin, where he grew up. Having a restaurant background, he took a degree in hotel management in Switzerland, and helped to cover his fees by working in vacations in the family business and also in related banqueting and corporate hospitality activities. On graduating, his first major events experience was at the Turin Motor Show, a major annual event for motor manufacturers and dealers.

Guiseppe also spent a year in the UK with a contract catering company, Ring and Brymer. During this year he participated in a number of large-scale events, such as the Farnborough Air Show, Wimbledon Tennis Championship and various golf events at St Andrews, Turnberry and Wentworth, through which he was able to develop his management and interpersonal skills, and increase his knowledge of event planning and production techniques. The year also included a range of private functions and smaller events providing parties and corporate hospitality all over the UK. Following this experience and using his existing qualifications and knowledge of the hospitality industry, Guiseppe then returned to Italy to set up his own small events management company with his partner.

Based on this case:

Using the national and trade press, identify a range of possible jobs which might lead to a career in events management. Which are the main companies in your area involved in this activity? What qualifications, skills and experience might you need? What might the advantages and disadvantages be of a career in events?

Related website for those interested in events management as a career: www.world-of-events.co.uk

Exhibition and theatrical contractors

Exhibition (and some theatrical) contractors are a surprisingly mature part of the industry and have existed for many years. Their function is to provide exhibition (or backdrop) services of one kind or another ranging from design and management for large exhibition-type events to the provision of relatively simple one-off stands. Some venues in the field are able to provide in-house services but may rely on exhibition contractors to create and supply complete shell schemes for exhibitions. Given that some parts of the events market (manufacturing companies, for example) have a long history of organizing combined launch and exhibition events, a number of exhibition contractors also have expertise in events production. However, some specialize and act as suppliers of systems either for hire or for purchase. Typically, contractors will provide the shells in a venue and individual exhibitors will fill the shell with their own material, displays and staff for the duration of the exhibition or show. The contractor will then come in and break down the shells and clear the area.

Technical services and multimedia support

In addition to catering, technical services may also be bought in. Not all venues have the technical support or equipment to cope with the full range of services sometimes demanded by organizers. Indeed, the small hotel, marquee or village hall used by parts of the market may have no facilities at all beyond the space and the furniture. Equipment and technical support can be hired in from a range of companies, some of whom simply provide equipment, some of whom provide equipment, training and technical support. Basic presentation equipment can be hired in, ranging from overhead projectors to slide projectors and video players.

The higher levels of technology can also be hired in to provide complete presentations on anything from multimedia to video walls. Print shops are capable of copying both black and white and colour material for guest packs, tickets, handouts and support material such as badges or place cards. Video production companies are also common and are used for videoing the proceedings themselves, those companies often having their own recording, sound editing and production facilities. The range of technical facilities provided by the companies in this field is extremely wide and reflects the importance that organizers, particularly of high profile and VIP events, attach to the need for technical facilities, whether those facilities are a simple overhead projector, computer video or liquid crystal display (LCD) projection, prompting systems (autocues) or any other of a wide range of systems to support a stage presentation, ceremony or commentary.

Voluntary Bodies, Committees and Individuals

Event management is one of those activities in which there is a large and active voluntary input. Many events, ranging from charity functions to village sports days, from birthday parties to local traditions, are undertaken by volunteers. This might be the family or friends for a birthday or wedding; it might be a volunteer group for a sports day or a fête. It might be a small committee set up for the purpose of running the event – anything from an annual rose growing competition to the re-creation of a historic battle in full costume.

This type of organization is often significantly overlooked in studies of events activity; there is a (perhaps natural) tendency to look at larger-scale professional events as the model for events management. To take such a restricted view would be wrong, and would ignore the long social history of events, festivals and traditional folklore activities. A typical voluntary committee might be made up of six or so people interested in putting on a particular event. This group might be already elected to perform some task, in, say, running a voluntary society, as a hobby or recreational interest, or might be formed specially to do the job. The effectiveness of voluntary bodies is often very high, due to the commitment, work and effort which the volunteers are willing to put into the activity, and also due to the lengths they might go to in order to obtain resources, help, facilities and services for their event.

It is also the case that larger or more important events might be planned and managed through cooperation between volunteers and professionals. An event might be volunteer managed, through an executive committee, but employ a professional events organizer to plan and run it. On the other hand, a professionally managed event might not only employ volunteers as staff, but also coordinate the activities of a range of voluntary bodies to produce it (such as at a carnival, where the organizers might be the city council tourism department, coordinating the efforts of everyone from the city band to the local majorettes).

Summary

The increasing complexity of events management has seen the development of companies with specialist roles in management, production and hospitality; some of these companies, such as exhibition contractors, have been around for many years; some, such as production companies and events management companies, are relatively recent. The public sector infrastructure of the events business is also becoming more evident, with an expansion of interest from tourist authorities and government, and an increasing number of trade and professional bodies. The breadth of the events business is such that there is also a very considerable voluntary sector, organizing anything from small personal events to local shows and sporting competitions. The size of this voluntary sector is difficult to judge, but it is as much a key component of special events activities as are the developing private and public sector structures.

Reference List

Davidson, R. (1994) *Business Travel.* London: Pitman, pp. 32–8.

Goldblatt, J. J. (1990) *Special Events.* New York: Van Nostrand Reinhold, pp. 17–28.

Hall, C. M. (1992) *Hallmark Tourist Events.* London: Belhaven, pp. 100–17.

Horner, P. (1995) *Travel Agency Practice.* Harlow: Longman, pp. 223–4, 242–8.

Kotas, R. and Jayawardena, C. (1994) *Profitable Food and Beverage Management.* London: Hodder and Stoughton, pp. 192–235.

McIntosh, R. W., Goeldner, C. R. and Ritchie, J. R. B. (1995) *Tourism: Principles, Practices and Philosophies*, 7th edn. New York: Wiley, p. 133.

Richards, B. (1992) *How to Market Tourist Attractions. Festivals and Special Events.* Harlow: Longman, pp. 101–10.

Tribe, J. (1995) *The Economics of Leisure and Tourism.* Oxford: Butterworth Heinemann, pp. 21–32.

CHAPTER 4

Social, Economic, Political and Developmental Implications

Aims
- To consider the impacts of special events in the community.
- To examine the social, economic, political and deveopmental implications of running events.

Introduction
It would be very easy for us to see special events purely in a social context; in the past, many events were largely personal and private affairs; the implications of having a special event in a community were largely social. An event such as a village wedding was both a cause for celebration and a means by which the whole village could interact together. Indeed, events of this type often involved the whole community in some way, in addition to the immediate families of the couple to be married. There were often local rituals to be undertaken; these rituals varied from place to place and were part of the social fabric and history of the area. Such rituals, often now long forgotten, served to reinforce community ties and make local events different in many small ways from those of their neighbours. Local village events, for example, were sometimes much rowdier and more spontaneous than today (e.g. Mayday), but many of these local traditions faded away during the Victorian period as the nature of society changed, to be replaced by a rather more constrained way of doing things. The reason for this loss was the rather fossilized nature of Victorian society and a tendency in our modern society to regard spontaneity as odd or out of place, having forgotten many of the traditions and differences which characterized our communities until the 1840s.

However, the social context is only one element of events – there are often other implications. We can look back and understand that events such as the Roman gladiatorial games and public festivals such as Saturnalia had both religious and political implications. In the modern world similar parallels can be drawn from festivals such as the Welsh National Eisteddfods, which have many of these aspects: social and community impacts, political and economic impacts.

Contemporary events are, perhaps, most often seen in terms of community impacts, and often events managers go to some lengths to involve the local community. These impacts are not the only outcome of many modern events, because, as the size and complexity of events has increased (especially size and complexity of organizational and sporting events), so the potential impacts on the economic and political life of the area, or community, whether that is a town, city or region, have often increased. For example, tourist towns and resorts have long understood the benefits of running special events in the tourist season, perhaps to bring more people to the town (and thus encourage further spending in local shops and businesses) or to extend the season in some way. The Blackpool illuminations, that great triumph of light and colour, with its miles of lights, displays, tableaux and illuminated trams, was intended to extend the tourist season for the resort. In this it has very much succeeded and the event attracts a huge number of people from all over the North of England and Scotland every year, giving the resort's economy a very significant boost.

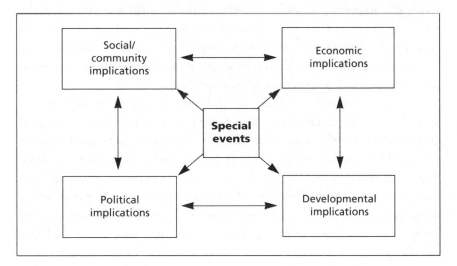

Figure 4.1   *The implications of special events.*

Some types of events, especially sporting events, play a political role, in addition to the social and economic roles. The Olympics are a key example of this. There is considerable international competition to stage the games, on the one hand because of the economic implications of doing so, but on the other because there are also positive political impacts, such as improving the international image of a country. Some types of special event are used as a means of gaining other political benefits, such as kudos or public exposure. For this reason politicians often attach themselves to activities such as the Hollywood Oscars or the Brit Awards, as they gain from the reflected glory of the stars attending such events.

Social and Community Implications of Events

Human society is complex and interactive, and all human societies, whether they are modern and technological or old and traditional, celebrate. The means of celebration are very diverse. Sometimes special events are spontaneous – your friends at work find out it's your birthday and, almost straight away, you find they've got you a card, found a cake (even if it's just a muffin with a candle in it) and opened a bottle of wine (which, being alcohol, was banned from the premises by the tedious management, but hidden by the wise staff). These events serve to strengthen social bonds as well as spread joy around. Many events are less spontaneous and more carefully planned, but even events whose progress is frequently planned down to the last detail, (such as weddings), have intense social implications (Goldblatt, 1990). They serve to impact on participants' emotional and intellectual senses, in terms of enjoyment, social interaction, stimulation of the mind and the senses – ranging from the consumption of food and drink, through enjoying the atmosphere (or not enjoying the atmosphere – not everyone enjoys every event), participating in activities such as games or dancing to doing unusual or (sometimes outrageous) things.

There are a number of more general social implications of having a special event. In community terms, many events, particularly personal events and events run by the community itself, have the benefits of improving social ties, and are an opportunity for the community to demonstrate that it can pull together for the greater good. These can be anything from local arts festivals to the Eurovision Song Contest. Even a tree planting day or street party can provide such opportunities. The role of events in encouraging social interaction and the celebration of happy occasions is probably more important in a society which, owing to modern media, modern work methods and the relative decline of the 'traditional' family structure, feels a greater need to maintain social contact. Without the social contact which events often give, the feeling of social isolation in a society where even work can be conducted in a solitary way, from a computer in the spare room, can be very great. Human beings are social animals (an issue typically overlooked in the hype which goes with some new 'technological innovations'), and the growth of the events business may in part be due to the need to increase opportunities for social interaction in the community, at a time when less interaction is possible in the work or home environment than at any time in the past. In such a case, organizations (particularly those which rely on technology) may have to give more serious thought to how to help their employees to interact and develop the social skills and interests which are the key to the maintenance of a cohesive inter-social structure.

Social impacts could also be seen in a wider context, perhaps as one potential mechanism for strengthening weak community structures in a particular location. The Notting Hill Carnival in London was one of the major driving forces behind improvements in relations between local communities with different ethnic backgrounds, and ultimately helped to drive forward many community social and political initiatives. But care must be taken not to see special events as some kind of panacea for local social or economic problems. There are no panaceas, only a range of tools which might, if handled correctly, and if well received on the part of local people, work positively for the benefit of all. You cannot impose a special event and say: 'There you are, enjoy that.'

Case Study 12

Social impacts of community events: the Notting Hill Carnival, London

The Notting Hill Carnival began in 1966. The Notting Hill area of London had become the home to a large number of people from the Caribbean, particularly from Trinidad, who wished to celebrate their own culture and background. From its beginnings as a relatively small and colourful festival of West Indian (and in general Black African) culture, it has gradually expanded to reputedly become one of the largest outdoor street festivals in Europe (Owusu and Ross, 1988). The event is one long open air party, featuring live music and bands, not only West Indian, but from cultures all over the world, mainly based around Portobello Green.

Location

Notting Hill, England

Factbox
- Notting Hill Carnival, London.
- Annual celebration with parades and music.
- Attracts a million people.
- Consists of several themes, including the Mas (the Masquerade), steel bands and soca (the music combination of soul and calypso).

The Carnival takes place on the last Sunday and Monday in August, and attracts large numbers of participants, sightseers and tourists. There is a tremendously colourful street procession (the Mas) with music and dancing, traditional calypsos and soul music mixes, with some (extremely loud) house, reggae and rap rhythms. There are floats and fancy dress, Caribbean and many other types of food are sold from front gardens to the passing public and the carnival attracts huge numbers of people to what is essentially a free street party. Prizes are awarded for various parts of the Carnival, such as the best steel band or soca (in the 2000 Carnival, there were some 25 soca music systems in the procession).

The Carnival has developed from a relatively small community-based event to a major part of London's summer calendar. It has, during its existence, been the focus of community will, community cohesion, community celebration and, occasionally community issues and community anger. The Carnival, now much respected, has had its ups and downs. Large numbers of people interacting together are largely peaceful, but occasionally there were violent incidents, sometimes not helped in the past by occasional incompetent policing. Today, the Carnival attracts more than a million people each day, many of whom are tourists coming to experience the spectacle. This does put some strain on the local infrastructure, such as public transport, toilets and emergency services, but the local authorities have become more practised in the event, and public services are better geared up to it than was the case when the Carnival first began.

The Carnival helped to raise the profile of the West Indian and Black African community in London, over the years, and has brought not only the benefits of community involvement but substantial economic benefits to what had been a relatively run-down area, one which has now become increasingly gentrified and popular, due in part at least to the success of the Carnival in attracting economic benefits and political attention.

Based on this case:

Examine a community-based event in your local area. What benefits does that event bring in social terms: what does the community get out of it? Why is the event worth the effort? How is the event organized? Is it voluntary or has it a professional organizer? Does the event bring economic benefits, or is it enough just to celebrate and have an enjoyable time? What special plans might be needed for the infrastructure to deal with large numbers of people?

Related website for those interested in the Notting Hill Carnival: www.nottinghillcarnival.net.uk
Also: www.london.gov.uk/mayor/carnival/index.htm

Events can be seen in terms of both performing a social role and, for certain types of events, acting as a stimulus for other social activities, such as tourism. For a town or city wishing to become a tourist destination, elements such as attractions, accommodation, transport and infrastructure or facilities must be present. Looking back at the historical development of some major destinations, it can be seen that all four elements are present, although the destination may not have had anything in the beginning apart from a natural attraction (such as a beach or a countryside view). This has been the case for resort towns such as Brighton in England, Howth in Ireland or Scheveningen in the Netherlands. In addition to the attractions of the seaside or countryside, some towns have relied for their tourist development on the architectural attraction of a great building, such as a castle or stately home, or on an event such as a market, fair or religious festival. Some destinations developed simply because royalty or the upper classes visited them.

Brighton, England:	Sea bathing; Prince Regent's Pavilion for his mistress	Natural/man-made attraction
Salzburg, Austria:	Historic medieval city	Man-made attraction
Scheveningen, Holland:	Sea bathing. Proximity to The Hague	Natural attraction
Interlaken, Switzerland:	Lake views and scenery	Natural attraction
Galway, Ireland:	Galway Arts Festival, Galway Races	Event attraction
Gleneagles, Scotland:	Golf and golf tournaments	Event attraction

Figure 4.2   *Development of tourist destinations: some examples.*

A destination was often intended to build on existing elements, such as: a pleasant location, warm climate or tourist attraction in or near the town (Shaw and Williams, 1997); the availability of local accommodation and places of refreshment (restaurants and cafes); good transport networks (by road or rail also helped). In many tourist resorts there was no major physical attraction, such as a national museum or theme park, but the tourist season could be driven entirely by special events, anything from a seaside airshow to a jazz festival or a carnival.

Looking at the social implications of events, we can see that the main impacts are for events to create better social interaction, help to develop community cohesion, increase cultural and social understanding, and

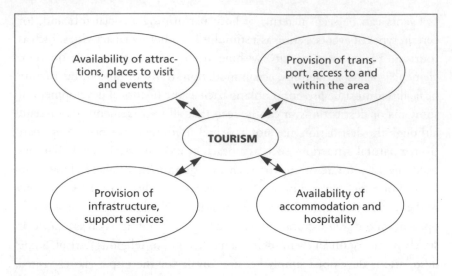

Figure 4.3   *Elements of tourism.*

improve the community's identity and confidence in itself. These are very important gains for many communities. We must, though, give a note of caution, particularly for large-scale, mega events. As with some of the issues of sustainable tourism, depositing a major international event on a small undeveloped community could do some damage to that community, perhaps resulting even in the destruction of its identity – particularly if the activity is badly handled, done without thought for the outcomes or without regard to the carrying capacity of the location (i.e. how many people the location can cope with). Nevertheless, the vast majority of events have tremendously positive outcomes, they serve to celebrate and to entertain, they serve to strengthen and improve social bonds and they increase community involvement and confidence. It is in this light that most events can be seen.

Economic Implications of Events

The impacts on a local community of a major event, be it a sporting event or a large cultural event such as a festival, could be looked at in terms of cost–benefit analysis or through economic multiplier analysis (Braun and Rungeling, 1992; Tribe, 1995). An event itself may not, for example, provide huge direct employment, but the indirect effects on local businesses, local services and local infrastructure and environment could be extremely significant. These indirect effects may include the support of activities such as retailing (visitors buying anything from magazines to clothing), catering (visitors using restaurants, coffee shops and pubs) and less obvious support in terms of services such as transport, taxis, printers, technical equipment, local musicians and entertainers, marquee contractors, photographers and many other types of supplies and suppliers. Some towns, cities and resorts have seen special events as their economic salvation when other forms of tourism, such as business tourism or heritage tourism, might not be appropriate to their area. It is also thought that events which have many participants, as opposed to many spectators, have a greater economic impact on a destination. Thus it might be quite reasonable to say that a fairly low key event, such as a three-day international conference of dentists, might have more economic impact than, say, a premier league soccer match because, even though the soccer has a higher profile, the spectators are more transient. A number of event-stimulated developments have been undertaken on this economic basis, such as the construction of Symphony Hall in Birmingham or the Exhibition and Congress Centre in Maastricht.

Case Study 13

Economic impacts of international events: the French Grand Prix, Nevers

The French Grand Prix held at the Circuit de Nevers Magny-Cours is a major international sporting event with significant economic impacts for the central France region. It is one of the most popular international events of the year, attracting some 185,000 people (1997 figures), putting it in the top rank of French events. For comparison, the UK Grand Prix at Silverstone attracted some 170,000 people.

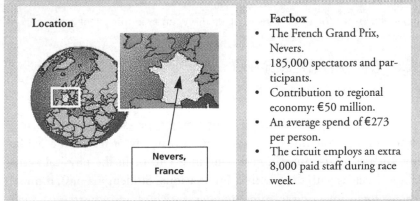

Location

Nevers, France

Factbox
- The French Grand Prix, Nevers.
- 185,000 spectators and participants.
- Contribution to regional economy: €50 million.
- An average spend of €273 per person.
- The circuit employs an extra 8,000 paid staff during race week.

The study (carried out by Lilley and DeFranco, 1999), which looked at European grands prix, concluded that the event at Nevers resulted in very significant impacts indeed. The visitors to the event came not only from France, but also from other parts of the EU and further afield. This resulted in some very high average spending patterns, as many visitors not only attended the race days but also stayed overnight in local hotels, or at nearby campsites, spent money in local bars and restaurants, used local transport services including taxis and coaches, and spent money in shops and retail outlets in the surrounding area as well as at the facilities at the Circuit de Nevers Magny-Cours itself. In 1997 the contribution to the local economy amounted to some €50 million. This can be broken down into several elements: money spent at the circuit, at food and drink outlets, at retail outlets, at hotels and other accommodation, on local transport and related services.

On average, each visitor to the grand prix spent about €273. The data are identified from a range of sources, including ticket sales. The businesses which benefited from the 185,000 visitors included: restaurants and pubs, accommodation providers, newsagents, petrol stations, chemists, photo shops, gift shops, booking and travel agents. Although it is less the case at Nevers (because of its location), some European grands prix also provide major business for local nightclubs and discos, and local specialist retailers (e.g. clothes and designer shops), as well as food shops and supermarkets.

Based on this case:

Can you identify the direct economic benefits and the indirect benefits? What are they, and why are they important? Can the local economy be sustained without them? Can any local economy survive without special events? What are the alternatives? Why are some locations better suited to events as an economic activity than others? Does an event of this type displace income from other activities (e.g. might local hotels be full anyway, and might this existing business be displaced – if so, will it return?).

Related website for those interested in the economic impact of the event: www.fia.com/etudes/f1_impact/sommaire.html

Source: Lilley and DeFranco (1999).

This is not to say that the running of a major special event is the correct solution to the economic problems of any town, city or resort. If a public body, such as a city council, invests in an event, or in the physical event facilities (such as with the Sheffield International Student Games), it must, perhaps, forgo investing in something else, such as an industrial or retail development. There is an opportunity cost, and even a danger that, as in the case of the Sheffield Games, the event might itself run at a loss. In consideration of the possibilities for the economic regeneration of an area, the running of a major event is only one option, not a panacea, and may be a significant cost or burden on the sponsoring organization (say a city council). For this reason, special events are often used as part of some wider initiative, so that an element of synergy can be gained from the event in conjunction, say, with building a new arena. Equally, it might be recognized that the objectives of a particular event are to provide short-term gain, not long-term gain. This objective alone might be worthy enough.

In the context of a community, the running of a major event is often perceived as having a positive social and economic impact, in much the same way as the construction of a factory or tourist attraction would. This economic impact is not terribly well documented, but some studies, especially of sporting events, such as games and grands prix, give us various clues as to the benefits of events. In the case of some events, their operation and running is seen as a matter of civic business; that is to say, the event may be organized or even sponsored by the city or town council and based, partly at least, on the economic and social benefits which it brings to the community, in terms of increased numbers of visitors or an increased visitor spend. Given the size and extent of some events, the economic and social benefits may be very great (Law, 1993).

Political Implications of Events

It might be thought that the political implications of events in the past were relatively modest. However, this is clearly not so. For example, the political nature of the Roman gladiatorial games is well understood: the ability of the Roman Emperor or members of the Roman upper classes to put on a major spectacle contributed much to their status. Similarly, in medieval times much political status was attached to royal events, such as jousts and tournaments. Therefore, certain types of events do have political impact, even if that impact is only to provide a mechanism to indicate some form of political status. The opening of the town's festival or a civic reception, to celebrate some new feat of a town's progress are opportunities for the mayor and council to be seen in public, officiating at the ceremony with due purpose and dignity. The political implications are simply that the town's dignitaries are expected to be seen doing what the town's people elect and pay them to do. In this respect many modern events fulfil the same purpose, and politicians gain the benefit of being associated with useful civic activities and positive special events.

The gentle pride with which civic dignitaries were regarded is often neglected today, but towns and cities often organized events or constructed things which demonstrated their commitment to the good of the general population and to technical or civic progress. This might be anything from the construction of a new hospital to the maintenance of some curious quirk of local tradition (such as 'cheese rolling' as performed in Brockworth in England). Old photographs of ceremonies and celebrations often focus on this aspect of civic pride, something which, in our modern age, can be overlooked in an effort to seem 'modern', but which was, in the past, crucial to the ritual and traditional nature of events, and which added to the political status of those dignitaries involved.

Today, it is major events which tend to attract the attention of politicians (and media). Hall (1992) comments on the very political nature of events such as the Olympics and events designed to influence public opinion about a particular politician or ideology.

Case Study 14

Political implications of events: the return of the Stone of Scone, Edinburgh

It is not to be supposed that just because an event can be staged, it will be a success. This is not so. Such an outcome is amply illustrated by the 'ceremony' which accompanied the return of the Stone of Scone from London to Edinburgh in 1996. The stone, also known as the 'Stone of Destiny', is reputed to be the stone upon which the ancient Scottish kings were crowned. It was removed from Scotland in 1296, by the expansionist and acquisitive King Edward I of England, at about the same time as he removed the Crown of King Arthur from the Welsh. The stone was kept for 700 years under the coronation chair in Westminster Abbey.

Location

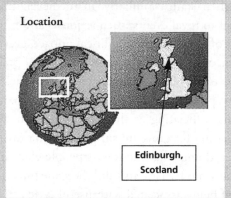

Edinburgh, Scotland

Factbox
- The return of the Stone of Scone.
- Ancient rock that Scottish kings were crowned on.
- Removed from Scotland in 1296.
- Returned to Scotland in 1996.
- Handled badly as a political exercise.
- Lack of attention to local political feeling.

In 1996 the deeply unpopular Conservative government in London sought to make political capital by returning the stone to Edinburgh. In this way, it was reasoned (wrongly) that the Conservatives might gain some votes in the elections due to take place thereafter from this 'gesture of magnanimity'. It has been argued they would have been better to put it in a box and send it quietly to Edinburgh on the first train out of London King's Cross railway station. However, it was felt that there would be a political benefit in returning it with some ceremony. Therefore the stone was sent to Edinburgh with a military escort in what 'came across as an unsuccessful publicity stunt' (Godfrey-Faussett, 1999) in which much of the London-based media, including the BBC, were involved.

The Stone was sent north carried on (of all things) a khaki green military Land-drover. It was escorted to the border at Coldstream (the site of its removal 700 years before), and handed over to the Scots on the Scottish side of the border bridge, where it was received by pipers and the Royal Scottish Archers (Elizabeth, Queen of Scots' ceremonial bodyguard).

This contrived effort was met with considerable public indifference. It was seen as a political 'lollipop'. Although the Scots were happy to have the stone back, and it now lies in Edinburgh Castle with the Honours of Scotland (the Scottish crown jewels), the manner of its return did not achieve the political gains the Conservatives wished, and resulted in much embarrassment for them.

Based on this case:

Why might a politically inspired special event not work? Could this event have been planned in a more sensitive way towards the Scots, and if so, how? Would this have meant the elimination of the obvious political stimulus for the event? What kind of event might have gained some positive outcome – could an event with no political overtones actually gain a positive result for the politicians involved?

Related websites for those interested in the Stone of Scone: www3.cnn.com/WORLD/9611/15/stone.of.scone/, also www.scone-palace.co.uk

High profile public events are attractive as mechanisms for producing social and economic benefits of the type noted earlier, and these events can focus and stimulate political will to promote and run them. Many events can be extremely positive in creating useful outcomes for the nation, region or area concerned. Nevertheless, political interest in an event may not be related to the good of the community or the local population: there may be a hidden political agenda behind the event (as in the case of the Stone of Scone). Indeed, there are also examples of dictators and unscrupulous politicians using events to distract attention from some political problem, or as a mechanism to improve their image (the Berlin Olympic Games of 1936, in which the Nazi Party attempted to get political kudos out of the event, is a classic example of this). Therefore it is important to understand that some types of events may well have a political element, and for the student and practitioner of event management to be able to recognize when that political element may or may not be positive.

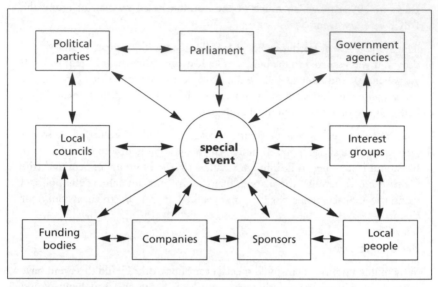

Figure 4.4   *Political stakeholders for events.*

Following this note of caution, it should be remembered that the most common political outcomes of events are positive and useful. A major event held in a town or city could not only help to provide social and economic benefits such as community cohesion, jobs, income to local people, but might significantly alter the image of the place in the long term. This can be a useful outcome, especially for those locations which might have endured a long period of economic decline or social drift. For them a major special event could not only rekindle community involvement and civic pride, but also transform visitors' perceptions of the place, from negative to positive. The series of garden festivals held in various towns and cities during the 1980s and 1990s performed just this task. A similar role is performed by the creation of a city as a 'European City of Culture', as in the case of Glasgow, whose image was transformed by this method.

The Developmental Implications of Events

By their nature, the vast majority of special events are fleeting things, with little or no developmental impact. It is only necessary to consider the large number of, say, weddings which take place to recognize the limitations of most kinds of event in terms of developmental and environmental impact –

there is no impact, apart from having to sweep up the confetti. This is true of most events. Even some larger-scale events, such as horse racing, might have little long-term impact except to provide some manure for one's roses. It is therefore important not to get carried away on the bandwagon of environmental impacts, sustainability and disturbance. To do so would demonstrate a poor understanding of the nature of most events as being modest, passing, affairs.

A few events, however, have some developmental impact, usually because this is a specific aim of their creation. Developmental events may be used as one tool in a toolbox of potential mechanisms for redevelopment, image building and regeneration, as a means to produce some positive outcome. This outcome might be to support tourism or to improve the environment of a given location. There could be other ways of achieving this. It might be easier and more cost-effective to construct a new business park, a new hospital or a new conference centre, rather than to invest time and money in a developmental event in order to get some longer-term outcome from it. Indeed, the developmental impact of events will mainly relate to some physical construction or re-use needed to put the event on, rather than to the running of the event itself. It depends entirely on the purpose of the event. Within these caveats, some events have been well known for their impacts, most notably the series of garden festivals sponsored by the UK government during the 1980s and 1990s. These were intended as a mechanism to regenerate run-down areas, and have been a modest success in achieving this aim, but not as great a success as might have been possible, as, in some cases, the post-event planning mechanism was a shambles, and the job was left partly unfinished.

Case Study 15

Developmental impacts of events: the Welsh Garden Festival, Ebbw Vale

During the late 1980s, the UK government was wrestling with the problem of land reclamation in a number of run-down industrial areas, where the former industrial base had collapsed because of economic and industrial change. Such change had left large areas with derelict land, for which there was no immediate hope of re-use without substantial work and investment. These areas, typically, also had severe image problems and included parts of the North of England and Scotland (Liverpool, Stoke-on-Trent, Glasgow and Gateshead near Newcastle), as well as Ebbw Vale in south-east Wales (the last in the sequence of festivals).

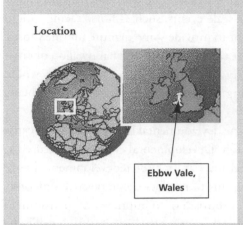

Location

Ebbw Vale,
Wales

Factbox
- Garden Festival, Wales, at Ebbw Vale, 1992.
- Purpose: redevelopment of a derelict steelworks.
- Two years to prepare, open for six months.
- The long-term outcome was the provision of a large business park providing employment and a better local environment for residents and visitors.

The mechanism chosen for the regeneration was to be the 'garden festival'. These festivals had three primary aims: first, to reclaim the land from its derelict and unusable state; second, to improve the image of the area, by making the chosen location over to gardens and parkland; third, to encourage inward investment in new businesses, to create employment and a better local economy. A large number of areas were submitted for consideration, most of which, like Liverpool, were in very urban locations. The Ebbw Vale location was somewhat different, in that it was a very derelict and damaged former industrial site (steelworks and coal mines) in what was otherwise a relatively rural location, near the Brecon Beacon mountains, at the head of a valley near Merthyr Tydfil. The organization of the Festival Company comprised local councillors, members of the Welsh Development Agency and the Wales Tourist Board (Meudell *et al.* 1993), who can also be considered as the political stakeholders (see Figure 4.4).

The festival ran for six months between May and October of 1992, after some two years of preparation work in planning and in reclaiming the site, planting it as gardens, parkland and countryside. Over a million people visited the festival site, which required some 800 staff at its peak, and which was intended to provide an excellent family day out. The key issue from the developmental point of view was, however, the legacy of the festival in terms of its original aims.

Clearly, the objective of land reclamation had been achieved. The area of the festival had been transformed from its almost unusable state to a condition where it was pleasant and suitable for further re-use once the festival had finished. Second, it helped the image of Ebbw Vale considerably. People visited the festival grounds who would never have otherwise been to such a run-down area. These visitors would have included not only families but also politicians, civic officials and business people. The change of image has helped to stimulate the third and final aim of economic regeneration and to achieve inward investment (i.e. to attract new businesses and thus provide jobs). The festival grounds have become a 36 acre business park as part of the Blaenau Gwent development area, with some of the reclaimed land remaining in use for the Victoria Festival Park (Ebbw Vale) – a country park with nature trails, a lake, gardens and woodlands, and a number of the features which were originally in the garden festival itself, including sculptures and a tropical plant house. The park has its own visitor centre and restaurant, and remains popular with tourists and visitors to the area. The outcome has been both economic regeneration and (on a smaller scale in terms of the Festival Park) the provision of an improved local environment capable of attracting visitors and visitor spend.

Based on this case:

How and why does the developmental impact of the Welsh Garden Festival differ from the vast majority of special events? Are hallmark special events of this type the only mechanism for stimulating tourism? Are such events necessary, or are there other methods of improving the environment in run-down or derelict areas? In order for special events to have this kind of positive impact on the environment, what legacy is needed in terms of infrastructure, transport and communications?

The Festival Park does not have a website.

Source: Adapted from Meudell *et al.* (1993).

The developmental and environmental impact of events do vary. The garden festivals were intended to have both an image building and an environmental impact; other events have had image building and reconstruction impacts. The Festival of Britain in 1951 left a legacy of the Royal Festival Hall and the Hayward Gallery on London's South Bank. The Sheffield Student Games in 1991 resulted in the development of a range of sporting facilities, including the Ponds Forge Pool, the Don Valley Athletic Stadium and the Sheffield Arena. The redevelopment of Sheffield was also supported by investment in a tram system and in the private sector construction of the Meadowhall Shopping Centre, plus more recent associated work in terms of a multiplex cinema and other businesses along the route of the tramway between Meadowhall and the Arena. The curiosity of the Sheffield development was that the Student Games made a loss in direct financial terms (and left a €64 million debt), but their longer-term impact in helping to turn round Sheffield's once grim image and in helping to stimulate other developments has been tremendous. Yet this scale of development is unusual – most special events have no such impacts, and do not need to, as it is not part of their objectives to do so.

Summary

The extent to which special events impact on our lives may be rather surprising to the uninitiated. Daily life is improved in many ways. If this were not so, events would have had little or no impact on the cohesion of human society. In fact events have a major impact and have been a feature of society from its earliest beginnings. Events serve to strengthen social bonds, to bring enjoyment and celebration to individuals, families, communities and society as a whole. There are also economic and political benefits, including the provision of direct and indirect employment, the enhancement of facilities and the improvement of local services, which are often stimulated by events. While some large-scale or developmental events may give us pause for thought about the wider impacts, especially culturally or politically, the vast majority of events serve to improve and enhance our society, at a time of significant social change.

Events can also be seen in the context of promoting and sustaining tourism. Not all tourist destinations have great physical attractions. Consequently, some destinations rely on a continuing programme of events, during the tourist season, to sustain them. This ensures the provision of short-term events related jobs and, crucially, helps to secure permanent jobs, which a small town might not otherwise be able to retain without the continuing stream of event visitors and tourists. In this respect, the involvement of locals, for example, in running their own small sales stands at fairs and shows, in catering and in employment in key activities, helps to keep tourist spending in the local economy (much more directly than it would if tourists simply spent their money at national chain retailers in the town). The focus on community involvement in events is therefore important, and methods of engaging the community need to be carefully considered, especially by event tourism providers.

Reference List

Braun, B . M. and Rungeling, B. (1992) 'The relative economic impact of convention and tourist visitors on a regional economy', *International Journal of Hospitality Management*, 11, pp. 65–71.

Godfrey-Faussett, C. (1999) *Edinburgh.* London: Cadogan, p. 83.

Goldblatt, J. J. (1990) *Special Events.* New York: Van Nostrand Reinhold, pp. 1–3.

Hall, C. M. (1992) *Hallmark Tourist Events.* London: Belhaven, pp. 84–99.

Law, C. M. (1993) *Urban Tourism.* London: Mansell, p. 39.

Lilley, W. and DeFranco, G. (1999) *The Economic Impacts of European Grands Prix.*

Brussels: EU Sports Workshop (www.fia.com/etudes/f1_impact/sommaire.html). (28 August 2000)

Meudell, K., Mullins, L. and Scott, H. (1993) 'Developing culture in short life organisations', *International Journal of Contemporary Hospitality Management*, 5 (4),15–19.

Owusu, K. and Ross, J. (1988) *Behind the Masquerade: the Story of the Notting Hill Carnival*. London: Media Arts Group, pp. 86–90.

Shaw, G. and Williams, A. (1997) *The Rise and Fall of British Coastal Resorts*. London: Mansell, pp. 65–9.

Tribe, J. (1995) *The Economics of Leisure and Tourism*. Oxford: Butterworth Heinemann, pp. 186–7.

PART II

Managing Events

PART II

Managing Events

CHAPTER 5

Making a Start

Aims
- To introduce some of the critical planning issues for events.
- To consider the process for screening event ideas.
- To discuss the potential objectives of running events.

Introduction
This chapter is the first in the sequence of chapters which deal with how to run an event. We have tried to present this as following a series of steps. In practice though, as the event begins to come together, many parts of the process will overlap, so if you are using this book for the first time, you might want to follow the order of the chapters, or you might simply want to dip in and look at the elements you need. For most events, time, money, people and effort could be in short supply and the end result needs to be the best possible blend of resources available.

It is necessary at the beginning, to recognize that existing organizational structures (such as a company management hierarchy or a standing committee), which serve an organization so well ordinarily, might not be suitable for the non-routine activity of organizing and running a special event (Badmin *et al.*, 1988). At a professional level, and for those organizations regularly involved in the production of events, there is a need to use those techniques which will ensure an effective, enjoyable and safe outcome, and this may require a more organized and structured approach than the cheerful informality of a family party.

Getting started involves finding people to do the job (it might be yourself and some friends, or a committee of some kind), and sorting out or screening the idea. The idea might be ready made. You might have been set a task: 'Your job is to organize this year's flower show.' Or the task might not yet be known, except that it has to solve some problem or other: 'We need to raise some money to paint the village hall.' So the first few steps in getting started are deciding who will do the job, what the idea is and whether it is feasible.

Getting Organized

The initial stage of getting an event started depends on what kind of activity is going on, or, put more precisely, what the objectives are (and whether there are primary and secondary objectives). The event can be a personal event, a leisure event, a cultural event or an organizational event. It may be organized by volunteers or by professionals. Some events are organized by one dedicated individual with a little support and encouragement; some events are organized by committees or groups of enthusiastic people. Getting started partly depends on what we know about the event and who will be doing it. In some cases we know what the event will be but not who will do it; in others we might have people who can organize it, but we don't know what sort of event can be offered. So, for convenience, and because we have to start somewhere, let's start with who is going to do it.

We might already know. If you are reading this book, it might be you. You may not be doing it alone, but might have other people to help, you might be part of an organizing committee looking for ideas or your job might be to organize the organizers. Mostly, a group of people will be involved. Sometimes the group may already exist – the committee which runs a club of some kind, perhaps a sports, social or hobby club, will also run the event. This has the benefits of not needing to form a committee from scratch, and of the existing committee members knowing each other and their respective strengths and weaknesses. For a special event, the committee might want to add one or two extra members or advisors from people who have done similar events before, or might form a smaller sub-committee to deal with the event, rather than the 'parent' committee doing it. A useful size for a committee is thought to be about six key people, but group size does vary, although the larger the group the more difficult it may be to get an integrated approach (Kakabadse *et al.*, 1988). Even with a small group there may be problems of cohesion, or difficulties getting people to work together, so careful leadership might be essential to the group's progress.

Equally, it may be necessary to build a new organizing committee. Forming this group may not be easy, because of the range of expertise which might be needed (and not necessarily available). Hall (1992) and Richards (1992) make a number of important points about finding suitable candidates. Our initial instinct may be that we can get our friends to be on the committee, but they might not have the right kind of skills needed, or have the time or inclination. The search for people will need to consider:

- How much time will organizing the event need from the committee? Can they spare this time to do the job properly?
- Have they any background of doing it before? Have they done anything similar? Have they a reputation for good work in an activity we might need, e.g. keeping accounts?
- Do they have good working relationships with other people? Will they pull their weight and do they get on well with others?
- If a member has some particular weakness in organization, has another member of the committee got that as a strength, so that the committee has a balance of expertise?

Most of all, the composition of the committee needs to be such that it is able to deal with the key jobs, whether these are organizing, marketing, finance, finding resources, recording or just plain being enthusiastic and keeping things going. In essence, the organization structure, whether it is a committee, a working party, an advisory group or a coordinating team, will need to be able to achieve the requirements of the job, but it must be noted that, especially for volunteer groups, the pool of expertise may be limited and this can act as a constraint on how fast things can be done, how well they might be done and how good the outcome will be.

Chair/president

Operations officers

Finance officer

Marketing officer

Health, safety and legalities officer

In addition, various other people might be invited to attend some of the meetings, depending on the type of event and the agenda of the meeting:

Representatives from the venue, licence holders, sponsors, police, first aid, fire service, local council, local associations related to, or attending, the event, bank manager, chamber of commerce, insurance advisers, professional specialists etc

---

Figure 5.1   *Example of an events management committee*

The organization of events also varies somewhat depending on how an event has grown. What was originally a one-off volunteer organized event may have grown to the point where it is annual and organized by profession-als. As events grow and their organization possibly changes, there may also be changes in the culture of the organizing body (for example, from informal to formal, or from amateur to professional) and sometimes this kind of change may lead to conflict about how the event is to be run. This also implies that there is a continuum of organizational types, perhaps dependent (though not entirely so) on the growth stage of the event (see Figure 5.2)

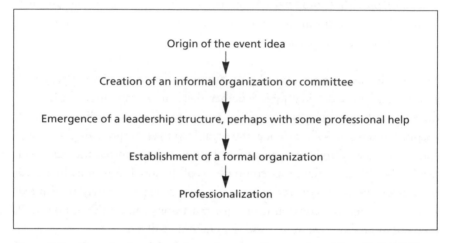

Figure 5.2   *Organizational development in events. Source: adapted from Hall (1972).*

As a starting point, we will assume an early stage of development of the event, and that there is a largely volunteer committee doing the work. (As Hall (1992) notes, some events organizations do not get beyond the volun-teer approach, nor may they need to.) However, once the organizing committee members have met and got to know each other a little, perhaps informally as well as formally, the first issue is what the event is going to be. As noted above, we might already know, but perhaps we don't know, and have no ideas – so what happens next?

Case Study 16

The Salzburg Festival – informal organization

After several years work, the first festival director, Max Reinhardt, with several friends and colleagues, succeeded in establishing the Salzburg Festival, in the Cathedral Square, Salzburg, Austria, during 1920. Although a lack of finances prompted a break in 1924, the festival grew into an international event, expanding into several venues and, beyond music, into drama. Quickly moving on to the international stage, the festival began radio broadcasts within five years (radio being relatively new at that time). The festival has continued to the present day, despite various political difficulties in the eighty years of its existence. Today, a public square in Salzburg is named after Max Reinhardt.

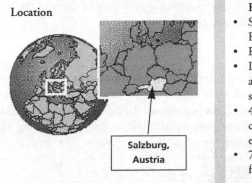

Location

Salzburg, Austria

Factbox
- Salzburg International Festival, Austria.
- Established in 1920.
- In 1998, 210,000 visitors attended 185 events and spent €21.8million.
- 4,876 journalists, from 30 countries, attended the event.
- 75 per cent of visitors are from outside Austria.

Despite the festival's early success, and its ability to attract foreign visitors, various political actions affected it in its early years, while it was still run, informally, by Max Reinhardt. In 1933, the German Nazi regime imposed a 1,000 mark visa charge on visits to Austria, cutting the number of German visitors from over 15,000 to just over 800. In 1938, Austria was annexed by Germany, and the Nazis took over, but not all Austrians supported this. The film *The Sound of Music*, not only contains the famous scene of the Austrian Captain Von Trapp tearing the Nazi flag down from outside his home, but also deals with the escape of his family from pursuit (including scenes from the Salzburg Festival itself, some of which were filmed in the Mirabell Castle and other parts of the city). Germany and Austria made war on much of Europe and were defeated. In 1945, the festival radio broadcast is credited as being the first common act in Austria by the occupying powers (Britain, America, France and Russia).

In 1950 the Salzburg Festival Foundation was set up, which put the event on to a formal and professional basis with a board of directors, and in 1952 the festival became a founding member of the European Festivals Association. The festival benefits from the efforts of a broad base of supporters, ranging from high profile managers to experienced arts patrons, operating, since 1961, under the umbrella of 'The Association of Friends of the Salzburg Festival'. In 1983, performances were relayed live for the first time to visitors in the Cathedral Square. During the 1990s, organizers began long-term cooperation with sponsors such as Nestlé, ABB and Allianz, and a reorganization of the festival's board and activities – introducing such innovations as subscription tickets for youngsters and 'Curtain Up' access to rehearsals – took place.

The expanding 'Festival District' now encompasses permanent venues (e.g. the Festival Halls), historic properties (e.g. Felsenreitschule or Summer Riding School) and uses, both open air (e.g. Cathedral Square), and temporarily covered spaces (e.g. the courtyard of the Residence). This evolution demonstrates both the financial scope of large festivals and the civic pride which they can build upon. The festival, during its long existence, has contributed significantly to the revitalization of Salzburg as a cultural centre (together with the city's association with Mozart), and to the imaginative use of many of the city's fine historic buildings for public activities.

Based on this case:

What benefits has the festival brought to Salzburg and for whom? What problems might be associated with the success of a festival and how might these problems be addressed? What impacts might political changes have on festival activity and can festivals have political effects (see also Notting Hill Carnival)? How has the organization of the festival changed over the years?

For those interested in the Salzburg Festival:
www.salzburgfestival.at/home.htm
and the European Festivals Association: www.euro-festival.net

Event Feasibility: Finding and Testing an Idea

The feasibility of an event might not have been considered because it seemed 'such a good idea'. But, without doubt, most events planning would benefit from a brainstorming stage, where various ideas are thrown in and tossed around to 'see which is the best'. Unfortunately, this 'seeing which is the best' often involves little more than the organizing committee having a couple of beers and going 'Yeah, we've got it, it's going to be fantastic.' To a detached observer, this conclusion will probably result in the response 'Is it?'

In practice, there is a need for a systematic approach, as with much of events management. A systematic approach helps us in situations of limited expertise, where the time period during which events are to be held may be quite short, and we may have to rely on volunteer labour and community support. In the case of feasibility, major events might well get into intensive methods of assessment, such as cost–benefit analysis or investment appraisal. For the more common type of event, perhaps of the kind being put on by a town or village or by a voluntary organization, a relatively straightforward series of tests could be applied, in the form of 'screening'. From this first phase, more detailed planning can follow.

There are three screens (or filters) that we can put suggestions for an event through. These are the marketing screen, the operations screen and the financial screen. All are intended to sort out less viable ideas and help to identify the idea(s) which will work the best when tested against the objectives (or criteria) set. It is important to recognize, though, that owing to the varied nature of special events, there may not be one 'perfect fit'. The end of the screening process may still result in several acceptable ideas, or none. The organizers will finally have to make a choice about what to accept. In addition to these processes, once an event has been agreed upon, the first of many planning activities must begin. This first planning activity is about the 'lead time' for the event or, put more simply, whether there is enough time to get it booked and organized (in much the same way as key dates apply to organizing conferences or exhibitions; Seekings, 1996). In most cases the answer will be yes, it can be done in the time scale, but careful planning and forethought about the critical timing issues will focus attention on whether the event really is achievable in the time available. Many events go badly because of lack of time to organize them properly – many project management texts argue that a poor level of planning during the early stages creates problems that will surface later.

We should bear in mind that all special events require a feasibility process, although some events happen simply because they have to. Typically, it is unlikely that personal events require a feasibility test – you don't obviously feasibility test a dinner party, but you do think about what is needed to get it right. With personal events the 'feasibility' does not take on a formal process, it is much more likely to be an informal, even unconscious, decision about what will happen. There may be constraints, such as the availability of money to pay for it and where to hold it, but these may simply affect the size or magnificence of the event rather than whether it goes ahead or not. In this case the event is predetermined and the real issue is how to make it happen.

On the other hand, many events do not develop by such a simple process, especially given the vast range of special events which take place. Suppose the scouts need to raise money for a new roof for the scout hall. There may be many possible events which could be put on to raise the money but there has to be some way by which a selection is made. Perhaps a list of ideas is put together of what the scouts could do:

- a car wash day;
- a theatrical play;
- a sponsored swim;
- a sale of pledges (a pledge being a gift contributed, then auctioned);
- a table-top or 'jumble' sale.

The criteria for what to do might include: what type of event has been successful in the past; what can be organized given the resources of the scout pack; what might earn the most money. These are relatively simple considerations, but they still represent a very basic kind of feasibility.

For larger-scale, public and organizational events in particular, there may well be an issue of how to choose from a range of possible activities for, say, fund-raising, or for a product launch, and how to screen the choices down to the one most likely to be effective. Camacho (in Richards, 1992) noted: 'However good an idea may seem to be, if it cannot win sufficient support, and if it is unlikely to attract the public of a locality . . . the best thing to do is to drop it.'

The Screening Process

The process of screening is very important. Not only has the event got to be possible to do, but it must also attract sufficient support to be successful. Let us consider this process in more detail. The first stage of the screening is to come up with the initial concept or set of ideas which might be tested (see Figure 5.3).

In some cases, a better range of ideas might be obtained by skipping through this general process and simply brainstorming a long list of

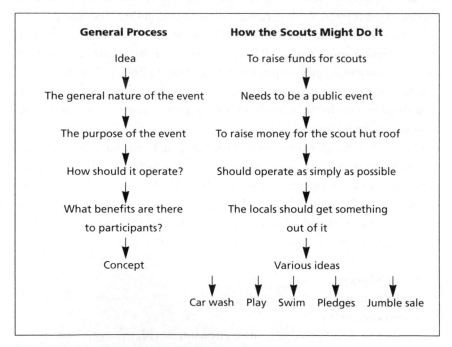

Figure 5.3 *Screening.*

(possibly) raucous, heroic, obvious, typical or ludicrous events and then dealing with the list in a serious way through a series of criteria to evaluate what really is feasible (see Figure 5.4). There are several possible ways of doing this, by using evaluation criteria (such as cost–benefit analysis; Tribe, 1995) or concept screening.

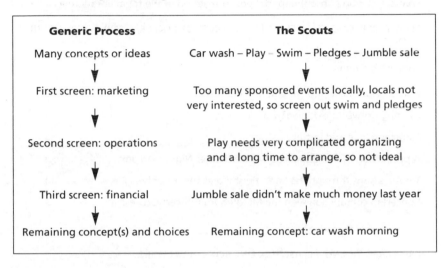

Figure 5.4   *Concept screening.*

The marketing screen

When a number of ideas or concepts for a possible event have been identified, there has to be a process whereby the organizers or clients can sort out what concepts will be most suited to the target market. This implies a good knowledge of the target market – the type of people, their demographic or social profile, age group, familiar activities, past experience of events, size of the target group and so on. This can be approached in two ways. Either the results of the initial brainstorming or listing session can be checked roughly against the opinions of the organizing committee (who, after all, will have to be committed to an idea in order to make sure it has a chance of success) or some pilot research can be done to see what the potential market makes of the list of potential events. This may be essential, as there is the possibility that the organizing committee may not be representative of the target market (in terms of age group, life experiences, gender, etc.). Detailed research about the event finally chosen could be carried out in the planning phase, but an initial pilot questionnaire might explore first reactions to the range of ideas (Goldblatt, 1997).

SURVEY OF MIDDLEBURG RESIDENTS AND VISITORS

The Middleburg Garden Club is proposing to raise money to revitalize the Arboretum and Venetian Bridge. We would like to put on a suitable fund-raising event in the Arboretum walled garden in July and would be most grateful if you would return this questionnaire, either in the post to the secretary (address on reverse), or pop it into the special post box set up in the town library foyer.

PLEASE PICK TWO CHOICES – 1 FOR YOUR FIRST CHOICE, 2 FOR YOUR SECOND CHOICE.

Suggested Events:

Garden Club show of prize-winning blooms ❏

Evening fireworks extravaganza ❏

Summer dance and buffet ❏

A production of Shakespeare's 'A Midsummer Night's Dream' ❏

Treasure hunt through the park, finishing at the 'Knobbers Rest' bar ❏

Concert in conjunction with the Middleburg Concert Orchestra ❏

Have you another idea? _____

PREFERRED TIMING: PLEASE TICK ONE BOX ON EACH LINE:

Monday ❏ Tuesday ❏ Wednesday ❏ Thursday ❏ Friday ❏ Saturday ❏ Sunday Morning ❏ Afternoon ❏ Evening ❏

Many thanks for your kind help. We look forward to welcoming you at the event, which will be advertised soon.

Name:_____

Address:_____

Figure 5.5   *Example pilot questionnaire for proposed events.*

The essential factor which the marketing screen is intended to deal with is whether the various ideas or concepts will work in the target market. In addition, it will be necessary to consider whether the ideas are sufficiently different from (or even similar to) successful competing events. Often, special event organizers are very poor at pulling in information about other events which may be taking place at the same time and targeted at the same market as their own concept. This may result in clashes of dates or two different organizing groups putting on almost the same type of event. 'Environmental search' (or 'environmental scanning', as given by Costa and Teare, 1996) is a way of avoiding this. Identification of competing events can be difficult, but should at least involve compiling a list of dates when similar events take place in the area, such as from tourist information, from local 'What's On' publications, magazines or trade press, together with a knowledge of activities in the calendar, or by checking the local newspapers for the same period in the previous year, and by getting people in the organizing committee to ask their friends and other contacts if anyone is aware of similar events. This should produce a list of what else is going on, which will serve a number of purposes:

- it will identify dates to avoid;
- it will give a feel for what goes on and what the local market likes;
- it may give additional ideas or identify gaps in the market not being filled.

In this way it will be possible to create a shortlist of events which will satisfy the overall objectives of the clients (if this is a commercial or paid event) or organizing committee, but will also suit the available target market and run at an appropriate time, not competing with other activities. This done, there is the final question of whether the list of 'possibles' fits in with the organizational type and market. There is not much point putting on a 'Tarts and Vicars' theme for the Sisters of the Immaculate Conception annual fund-raising tea. The marketing screen is intended to identify what will work in a given market, what else might be going on by way of competition, what an organization would see as appropriate and, most of all, what demand there should be from the target market. Having done this, the organizer can move on to the operations screen.

The operations screen
So far, from a list of ideas or concepts screened against the marketing criteria for an event, there will probably still be a large number left that might work. However, the event manager needs to consider what is achievable. All events have various resource needs, based on how adventurous or ambitious the ideas are, what expertise and staffing are available, what locations or venues can be found, what capacity at the required dates, what time scale and what technology or other equipment are needed. Due consideration also needs to be given to legalities. Do you need licences? (see Figure 10,6).Will insurance be needed? Are permits required, etc.? This is the role of the operations screen.

Events often fall into two operational styles – volunteer or professional (though some have parts of both). For example, many events, especially in the personal, sporting and cultural categories, are run by volunteers. A volunteer committee may well consist of people who have had no experience of events before or who have only their own experience and innate good sense to go on. On the other hand, there are those events (particularly organizational, but also some sporting, cultural and personal) which are professionally run, or for which a professional advisor, consultant or events management company has been employed. The level of expertise available is, then, an issue of the operations screen – what events can be done within the style of organization preferred. As there are some excellent amateur organizations and some lousy professional ones, there is nothing to say that volunteer organizations are necessarily worse off than professional ones in terms of putting on events. They may have less experience and (perhaps) lesser knowledge of what can be achieved, but it should not be assumed that professional organizations or companies know everything or will produce a perfect result. Any number of things may go wrong, including the professionals not paying sufficient attention to the brief or to key issues. On the other hand, volunteer organizations might be more enthusiastic, more resourceful with limited means and have a better local knowledge than a professional events company.

Case Study 17

Volunteer organizers and event screening: University College Cork

Volunteer organizations are extremely common in events management. Clubs, societies, associations and charitable bodies often rely on volunteers to run the organization. Often volunteers have little or no training, but they do have enthusiasm and dedication to what they are doing. Many people get some experience of committee activity and voluntary organizations at college or university, where clubs and societies dedicated to a whole range of sporting, leisure, recreation and special interest activities are common. The Hockey Club of University College Cork is one such example. Its primary activity is playing hockey, but it also has an active social role.

Location

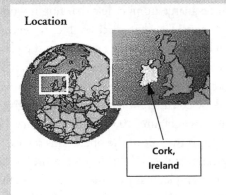

Cork, Ireland

Factbox
- University College Cork, Ireland.
- Founded in 1845.
- 12,000 students.
- Almost 100 student clubs and societies.
- A large number of sports clubs.
- Men's hockey club run by a committee of seven.

The Hockey Club is very typical of many clubs and societies throughout colleges and universities. The club plays matches and tournaments and has its own web pages within the website of University College Cork. The club has an active social life, its members taking part in a whole range of student activities. Its committee organizes frequent events, both small and (relatively) large scale, for its members and their friends and partners.

The choices of activities to end the 1999/2000 academic year produced a list of possible events which included a quiz night, a charity horse race night, a buffet with disco, a formal dress ball, an American style prom, dinner at a local restaurant or a fancy dress party. As the Hockey Club is a relatively informal kind of organization, these choices were bounced around members of the committee and the team and their friends. There was no major formal process involved in deciding which event to have. The informal process simply involved the major stakeholders (the team and their friends) in the decision-making process. The choice made was the result of a general consensus about what event they wanted, in this case a formal dress ball, which members of the committee, together with a few helpers, organized.

The kind of process involved here is very typical of voluntary organizations. The limited market may mean that in-depth research is not required. However, the larger and more diverse the market, or the more unknown the style of event, the more likely will be the need to do a survey or at least pilot research work to ensure the event is what the market is interested in.

Based on this case:

If you are a member of a club, society or association, what is the major event in the organization's social calendar? How is this event organized and who by, and how are the choices made about what kind of event it will be? Can the process be said to involve any research or confirmation that the event is appropriate? If you were the chair of a committee planning an event which the public had to pay to attend, what steps could you take to ensure your proposals would meet what the public wanted to participate in?

Related website for those interested in University College Cork and its student life: www.ucc.ie/about

For events with a volunteer style of organization and volunteer staff, the matter of achievability is important. Has anyone within the organizing committee got relevant expertise? If so he or she must be used to best effect. People with financial backgrounds may best be suited to financial issues, people with design backgrounds best suited to design issues. In addition, volunteer organizations should not only look at members' jobs, but also at personal interests – creative people and good organizers are needed for special events. Clues about people's background, hobbies, interests and expertise need to be sought and could yield useful experience. However, volunteering is hard work and not everyone wants to do it. In the end, they may not have time to participate in the event and may be called upon to deal with all kinds of occurrences or emergencies that they may not be familiar with, or equipped to cope with.

Equally important is knowledge of previous activities. Is the event a regular one, say every year, and if so, who knows what has gone on in previous years? However, we need to recognize the boundaries of volunteer expertise. The person who has attended the annual flower show of a town down the road might be the only one in a volunteer organization who would know anything about 'how to organize' a flower show, but the limitations of this approach must be understood: I might go to the bathroom regularly but it doesn't make me a plumber. Going to a flower show (or any other event) as a visitor does not necessarily tell you anything about what goes on behind the scenes, how the event was organized or what efforts went into putting it on. This is the issue of expertise and when to know you need some. All kinds of special events have to start somehow, and the expertise to run them is often built up over many years, or at least the knowledge about where to obtain the expertise is. This expertise is key when issues of health and safety, legalities or technology are important to an event.

The operations screen, then, is all about what can be achieved. From the original list it will have been possible to eliminate some of the activities on the basis that they are too difficult or complicated, or because there isn't the time, the staff or an appropriate venue. This can be done by using an events screening form (see Figure 5.6), which will help to formalize the screening. Several events might be written up, in order to identify any major problems and possible unforeseen issues in terms of licensing, regulations, permissions or approvals needed.

The financial screen

Almost all special events will have a budget of some kind, even if that 'budget' is only an approximate figure of what the organizers or clients can afford, based perhaps on similar events. For many events, the financial issues are cost-orientated. For a wedding there is no discernible financial revenue to be set against the balance of what might have to be spent. In this case, the 'organizers' (the parents of the couple to be married and the couple themselves) will have some idea of how much they can afford and if several ideas are being considered (for example) for the reception, the deciding factor might be the cost.

OUTLINE EVENT DETAILS:

Purpose of event: _____

Suggested location: _____

Is the proposed event: A one-off event? ❏   Expected to take place annually? ❏

Have you checked that the venue or location is available?   Yes ❏   No ❏

DETAILS OF THE ORGANIZER OR CHAIR OF THE ORGANIZING COMMITTEE:

Name:_____   Phone number:_____

E-mail:_____

Address:_____   _____

_____

FUNDING OF THE EVENT:

How do you expect the event to be paid for?_____

_____

What are the major costs of your event, and have you included insurance?

_____

_____

(A summary of the outline budget should be attached to this form).

ATTENDANCE AT THE EVENT:

How many people do you expect to attend? _____

How many other people will be there? (include organizers, crew, players, ushers, staff, etc.) _____

LICENSING, PERMISSIONS, EMERGENCY ISSUES:

Will you be liasing with any of the following services to establish their input to the event?

Police ❏   Fire ❏   Ambulance ❏   Red Cross ❏

Licensing Authority ❏   Town Council ❏   Other (specify)_____

Will the event have any implications for local residents, e.g. noise, site set-up, parking, access, crowds?

_____

_____

Will you need any specialist help with the event or other professional advice or input?

_____

_____

Signed:_____   Date:_____

Figure 5.6   *Events screening form. Kindly provided by Tendring District Council.*

Not all events are 'cost only'. Often there is a financial reason for putting an event on – fund-raising or economic regeneration. There are events which are expected to make sufficient money to cover costs and break even, or make a small surplus – often the case with local volunteer events such as an annual town carnival. The carnival committee will be concerned with putting on a good show at a reasonable cost, and generating enough of a surplus to start next year's carnival properly.

Assuming that the event has to make money (say for fund-raising purposes), or at least cover its costs, then the financial screen is all about identifying which possible events from the shortlist could achieve this. Two or three possible events might be compared with an outline budget. For this to happen, the organizers will need to come up with some basic financial information, both in terms of revenue (how many people might attend, what can they be charged, what other ways revenue can be raised during the event, etc.) and in terms of costs (the likely costs of the location or venue, the staffing, the materials, the decor, the consumables, the insurance, the power, the food and drink, etc.), and from this whether a profit or surplus will be made. In some projects, especially large-scale ones, there are both capital costs and running costs. Think of the Olympics – the capital costs are about building the facilities, the infrastructure, the accommodation, etc., and the running costs are about actually operating the games. Will the revenue cover both of these, or, in the case of the capital costs, will some other benefit be the outcome? Could the athletes' accommodation be turned into flats and sold afterwards? Could the stadium replace one which is old and needed replacing anyway? Crucially, will the event being planned take place within the appropriate budget?

In short, the purpose of the financial screen is to take the shortlist of possible events, preferably no more than two or three, and prepare an outline budget for each one, to help the decision-making process. A little later, as part of the detailed planning, the outline budget can be turned into something more detailed and accurate. For care in preparation, the outline budget should really underestimate revenues and overestimate costs.

Progressing the Idea

In many respects, choosing the event, through the process outlined above, is the easy part. The sequence of brainstorming then filtering ideas to see if an event is appropriate can be quite enjoyable. Serious financial and operational feasibility testing, if this were a major project, would then follow on from the screening phase. The clients or organizers would also have some feel for the acceptability of the event, given their knowledge of the market or who might be attending. In addition, with any event involving a significant budget or complicated organizational issues, a risk analysis might have to be undertaken (see Chapter 10). How vulnerable is the project financially and operationally? What issues might constitute a risk? Are there factors related to fire, health and safety, crowd control, security, hazardous materials or activities which have to be considered?

Having found the preferred concept, the organizers might then wish to review the proposal again in the light of the objectives: does the proposal still meet the objectives? Hall (1992) and Richards (1992) sought to identify a range of possible objectives for events:

- Development of public involvement in the arts, sport or other leisure activities.
- Fund-raising for a special project or charity.
- Starting a new event to create a tourist attraction, extend the tourist season or make better use of a resource.
- Introducing a new idea to the market.
- Attracting more visitors to a venue or tourist destination.
- Focusing attention on a specified subject or project.
- Creating a sense of community, involving the community or strengthening its goodwill.
- Advancing and promoting the community for the public benefit.
- Supporting community or organizational objectives.
- Promoting political and cultural exchange.
- Encouraging participation in, or support of, an organization.

It is common for events to have additional objectives, such as to educate, or to make money, or to leave a useful legacy. To take the idea forward there would have to be some building on the initial objectives, with a draft of the proposal containing the overall objective broken down into several aims and then into the component parts or component plans for the event. Even relatively simple events may have several component parts. How will these be put together? Who will be doing the organizing and who is responsible for what? Where will the event be held and has more than one venue been approached? When will the event happen and are suitable dates and times available? What materials, supplies and equipment might be needed? What transport, parking or access? Why is the time schedule for achieving this important, and what are the deadlines?

All these questions will have to be answered. More work can be done later, but even if this is put into a few pages of notes it will be a useful start and the planning can then be built from the initial ideas. The most important aspect of this pre-planning phase is to have enough time, not only to work up the detailed plans properly, but also to determine whether the event is achievable in the time available. In general, volunteer organizations may require more time to deal with complex events than professional or full-time organizations, but, equally, those professional organizations are likely to have a far more realistic appreciation of the amount of work involved and the likely time it will take to achieve.

There may well be a 'critical path' (see Chapter 10) of timing issues which will determine whether a project or event can be done in the time scale, which the unfamiliar organizer may think is easy, but might not be. Consider building projects as an example. Builders are often seen as overrunning the time 'allowed' for a project, but frequently this is owing to an unrealistic appreciation of the complexity of the job, the need to get planning permission, the logistical problems, the delivery of long lead time special materials, etc. Much the same is true of special events, which might seem very simple at first glance but can become horribly complicated once someone actually sits down to write out all the parts. Nor is there any guarantee that what appears to be the 'critical path' of a project will be so. Suppose we are organizing a special prize ceremony for the best rose grower in the district. The organizing committee wants this to get some good local publicity, so has decided that the presentation should be made in the famous gardens of a nearby stately home by the mayor. Several factors impinge on the timing: the event needs the stately home, the mayor and the local media (assuming there is to be no other activity after the ceremony). The critical path will emerge from one of the three elements:

- How long to book the stately home? Are the possible dates available?
- How long to get a slot in the mayor's busy diary, and will this match the availability of the stately home?
- When is a good day for the local media?

For example, the lead-in to the 'critical' path may be the last of these. Not all days are good days in media terms. If the local newspaper is published on a Friday then it might be looking for good local stories several days before, probably on Monday or Tuesday (not Wednesday or Thursday, as the staff have to write up a story and get the photos done in enough time for their own print deadline). This gives a framework for which would be the best days to do the event. In all probability, both the booking of the stately home and the mayor's diary have long lead times. Whichever is longest (after preliminary enquiries) will have to be done first; everything else can then follow.

As a generality, the larger and more complicated an event, the more detailed the planning process will need to be and the longer lead times will be. The key lead time is often booking the venue, as popular venues are booked months, sometimes years, in advance.

Summary

At the beginning of the feasibility phase, a large number of ideas or concepts for an event could be identified. These various ideas were then put through a series of screens (marketing, operations and financial), whose purpose was to filter out those ideas that were not really viable. Having done this, the organizers should now have, at the end of the process, a small number of events to choose from; it is even possible that just one event may have made it. In fact, if the process is done in a very formal way, against set criteria for each part, there might be no ideal outcome, only the 'nearest fit'. Where there is more than one possible event, what advice can be given as to which to choose? Well, the objectives can be looked at again, and if there is still more than one special event on the shortlist, choose the one that would be most enjoyable – and have a good time!

Reference List

Badmin, P., Coombs, M. and Rayner, G. (1988) *Leisure Operational Management, Vol. 1.* Harlow: Longman, p. 106.

Camacho in Richards, B. (1992) *How to Market Tourist Attractions, Festivals and Special Events.* Harlow: Longman, p. 101.

Costa, J. and Teare, R. (1996) 'Environmental scanning: a tool for competitive advantage'. In R. Kotas, Teare, R., Logie, J. and Bowen, J. (eds), *The International Hospitality Business.* London: Cassell, pp. 12–20.

Goldblatt, J. J. (1990) *Special Events.* New York: Van Nostrand Reinhold, pp. 31–7.

Hall, C. M. (1992) *Hallmark Tourist Events.* London: Belhaven, pp. 100–17.

Kakabadse, A., Ludlow, R. and Vinnecombe, S. (1988) *Working in Organisations.* London: Penguin, pp. 152–83.

Richards, B. (1992) *How to Market Tourist Attractions, Festivals and Special Events.* Harlow: Longman, pp. 103–5.

Seekings, D. (1996) *How to Organise Effective Conferences and Meetings,* 6th edn. London: Kogan Page, pp. 21–9.

Tribe, J. (1995) *The Economics of Leisure and Tourism.* Oxford: Butterworth Heinemann, p. 170.

CHAPTER 6

Events Planning

Aims
- To examine the planning process for events and highlight the need for effective planning.
- To consider the mechanisms for ensuring the effectiveness of the planning process.
- To consider operations, financial and marketing related planning activities

Introduction

Events are, by their nature, non-routine. The techniques used to organize and manage them, though, are not. The purpose of this chapter is to consider one of the most important aspects of events management – the planning process. Planning is vital to the success of events, because of their complexity, their unusual requirements (which may be considerably different from the regular or routine activities of an organization) and the possible unfamiliarity of those organizing an event with what is required. However, care may be needed as, occasionally, some organizations get so locked into the planning process they never get to the doing part ('analysis paralysis'), or the plan itself becomes a cage from which they cannot escape. A plan will not survive its first contact with reality, however good it is. Some change, however small, will be needed. Nevertheless, a plan is a guide and tool to measure progress against, and should not be lightly disregarded.

It can be argued that it is the planning process itself which is the real key to what will happen. In having to sit down and prepare a plan, you have to think ahead about the event you are going to undertake, and therefore identify the elements and issues which need to be sorted out. For this to work well, there has to be a systematic approach, because, unless you break the plan down into smaller component parts, something important could easily be missed. The planning process, consequently, reveals both problems and opportunities. It should serve to get people involved and act as a mechanism to search the environment for information.

Planning has a number of benefits. These include better coordination, the creation of a focus, the experience of thinking ahead and the provision of a device (the plan) for effective control of the progress and outcome of the event. However, planning is time-consuming and necessarily involves thought and effort. Things may still go wrong, but as Reiss (1995) noted, 'this is a reason to plan, not to fail to'.

The Planning Process

The diversity and individuality of events can make them very labour-intensive, because of the effort involved in undertaking a non-routine activity. This is not simply a matter of how events are operated on the day, it is also a management and organizational issue. The management input to any event will be far greater than that of a routinely manufactured product (with a routine product, once the initial development phase is over, management becomes essentially a supervisory function based around quality control, because all you are really doing is repeating the manufacturing process, again and again). Planning events, for the uninitiated, or for the organizer new to it, is therefore rather more important and time-consuming than the equivalent processes for other goods and services. The example of a wedding is useful in understanding this. The actual wedding itself may be a ceremony of no more than an hour followed by a reception and a buffet, but the planning may well have taken several months, involving large numbers of people: families, friends, the venue management, the caterers, the florist, the dress hire company, the musicians, the car company, the religious authority or civil registrar and so on. This complexity of planning is typical of events in general and is part of a whole cycle of interrelated activity covering planning, action and control. The increased importance of planning is due to its key role in helping to deal with the uncertainties of events.

Planning is the process by which the manager or organizer looks towards the event to discover what various courses of action are available to arrange it, and which course of action would be the best. This is not to say that a plan is going to appear the moment someone sits down to think about it. The manager, organizer or planning committee may have run many events; they may have run none. The advantage of having done it before is not only the experience but also records and previous plans. On the other hand, with a new event, the plan, to start with, may be no more than a vague hunch or an organizer's intuition about what might be appropriate. However, this can

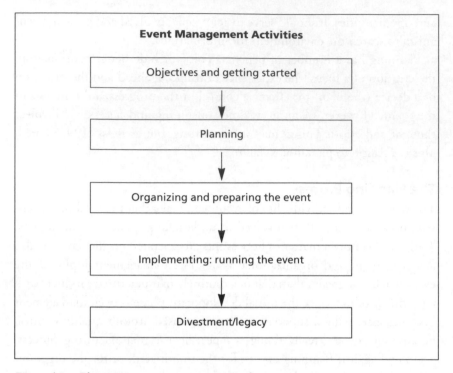

Figure 6.1   *Planning as a management activity for an event.*

be worked up very quickly into something more useful and relevant – a plan is essentially a predetermined course of action based on given objectives.

The objectives have to be carefully thought through. They have to be sufficiently precise and clear to ensure that the purpose of the event is obvious to all those involved in it, from the chair of the organizing committee or clients, right down to staff or volunteers at the operational level. Clarity at the beginning also helps the planning process and acts as a way of getting everyone to pull in the same direction. The objectives should not be too complicated, perhaps consisting of only one or two primary objectives, though these can be broken down into a number of detailed aims – perhaps not more than six, as otherwise you are just obscuring the point, and simplicity is best at this stage.

Objectives, Environmental Search and Information Gathering

The objectives are the starting point for the planning of any event. What is the event intended to do: to celebrate, to entertain, to fund-raise? Given this, and some view of the feasibility of the event after the screening process,

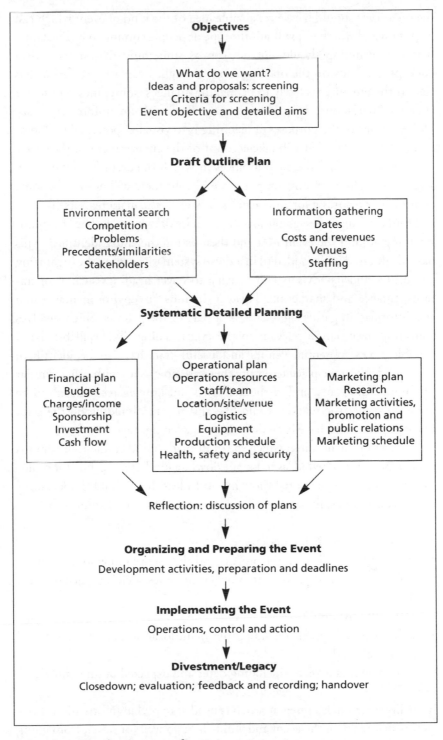

Figure 6.2   *The planning process for events management.*

the organizers should have a reasonable idea of the kind of event which can be put on and whether it will suit the type of people coming to it (the 'target market'). Planning should not be seen as something that starts with a concept and ends on the opening hour, though. Even after the event has started the organizer is likely to be making changes, sometimes very major changes, in response to problems or to deal with an unforeseen crisis. However, one of the purposes of planning is to visualize potential problems and to have a plan that will take account of the environment of the event, the stakeholders and the circumstances in which the event is taking place, and what might go wrong; or, put more simply, there will need to be some contingency planning for emergencies, as well as the main plan itself.

From the bare bones, an outline plan can be drawn up, perhaps by brain-storming around the event idea and then listing the issues identified. This basic draft can then be added to in a more systematic way, by the organizing committee and its advisors and helpers; to cover headings such as opera-tions, finance and marketing. This can include an 'environmental search and information gathering' phase, or a part of the process which involves collecting information relevant to the event. Things like available dates, suitable times, potential venues and useful staff have to be identified; checking has to take place to ensure there are no clashes with other, similar or competitor events; and, if the market is not known, research has to be done into what the market would like and pay for, building on the pilot research that might have been done at the screening stage.

In terms of the headings which the draft plan should contain, the draft is really a place for initial ideas to be put down, a kind of scrap-box for brain-storming and all your initial thoughts and ideas, but should, importantly, cover six key issues, in order to give it some structure and form:

- *Why* is the event being undertaken?
- *Who* will be involved in the process and the event (and who will not)?
- *What* will take place and what information or research is needed to make decisions?
- *How* will it be done?
- *Where* will it happen (including the main location and any additional locational needs)?
- *When* will it take place (including dates and expected outline times)?

In addition, an environmental search is needed to pull in information about factors that relate to the event and will help it go well (or save it from going badly). It is part of the mechanism, like the screening process, by which an organizer seeks to identify potential problems at an early stage. Once all the ideas and information have been 'thrown in', it can then be reorganized to give it some proper structure. Always keep the first drafts, though, as sometimes they may contain material which might be thought of as not terribly important, until, one day nearer the event, a bug re-emerges.

Case Study 18

The reopening of the Scottish Parliament

On 1 July 1999, the Scottish Parliament met for the first time in almost 300 years. It had been abolished after the joining of Scotland with England and Wales had removed political power from Edinburgh in 1707 and made Westminster the only UK parliament. The re-establishment of the parliament was met with considerable enthusiasm in Scotland.

Location

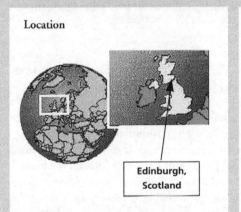

Edinburgh, Scotland

Factbox
- Reopening of the Scottish Parliament, Edinburgh.
- First parliament in Edinburgh for almost 300 years.
- Ceremony combined old and new elements.
- Parliament opened by Elizabeth, Queen of Scots.
- 'The Scottish Parliament, which adjourned on 17 March 1707, is hereby reconvened'.

The environment and circumstances of the planning stage

The nature of the opening of the Parliament was a matter of some controversy during late 1998 and early 1999 in Scotland. There was a feeling that the ceremony would be too short and modern, and that the event would fail to include the heraldic flag-bearers of Scotland, who are traditionally associated with royal Scottish ceremonial events. In public, the reason being given for this was that the ceremony needed to be 'modern', but the scathing publicity in the Scottish media given to the failure to have the flag-bearers present suggests that the organizing committee was taken by surprise.

The committee initially failed in two ways: first, they had insufficient experience of Scottish public feeling; second, they had not undertaken an environmental search properly. It was thought that the committee originally had no idea of Scottish traditions, because the reform had been initiated in London, and the committee's 'starting point' had been London, not

Edinburgh. There was, therefore, little recognition (owing to inexperience and too little research) that a Scottish parliamentary tradition existed, let alone how it had worked. However, the committee (fortunately) was actually listening very closely to public opinion in Scotland, and these issues were addressed carefully and in time.

The stakeholders

The people and groups most concerned with the opening were its organizing committee, the political parties (notably the Labour Party, under whom the reform had been promoted, but other parties as well, including the Scottish National Party), Queen Elizabeth and the royal household, the Scottish Office (a government department), the national and local media, the people of Scotland, the army (as escort to the royal family), the heralds and ceremonial officers of Scotland, the Duke of Hamilton (as Scotland's senior lord, responsible for the crown jewels of Scotland) and a very large number of people and groups involved in the ceremony, such as the orchestra, schoolchildren and poets.

On the day

The outcome was an event which was very well received (Engel, 1999). In the modern (and temporary) chamber of the Church of Scotland, the ceremony was opened with a fanfare played by the Royal Scottish National Orchestra, following which the royal procession entered, with the Duke of Hamilton carrying the Scottish crown on a purple velvet cushion, followed by the Queen (Scottish protocol is that she is not Queen Elizabeth II of England, but Elizabeth, Queen of Scots), and then the Lord Lyon King of Arms and the Heralds ('more Heralds than were needed to put on a Hollywood movie', the newspapers reported). This was followed by the opening speeches, and, this being Scotland, by some poetry and spontaneous singing by the Scottish MPs.

The ceremony was hailed as a major success, not only in style but also in tone. It fulfilled the need to open a modern parliament, but also recalled the traditional way in which the old parliament, 300 years before, had been opened, thus fulfilling its objectives.

Based on this case:

Why is finding out about the environment and circumstances of your event important? How can you identify the stakeholders (those people and groups that would take part or be interested in some way) for an event? Why is doing this important, and what might happen if you do not identify them all? Why is clarity of objectives key to running a successful event, and were the objectives for this event clear from the start?

Related website for those interested in the Scottish Parliament: www.scottish.parliament.uk

In many ways the environmental search or information gathering process is also a search for opportunities (as well as problems). For example, another event in the same area of the same type might be seen as competitive, but could be complementary. The organizer or, in the case of a very large event, a professional researcher is looking for information about demand for the event and the market; any competition; availability of technology, equipment and supplies; financing and sponsorship; organizations and the availability of staff; local cultural or social issues and precedents; and time issues in planning. This information can then be included (or put aside) and helps the organizers to plan and identify what else is needed, but will also help in the organization and running of the event. Sometimes, however, the process of 'environmental searching' does not take place properly and results in some major problems or gaffes, which embarrass the organizers.

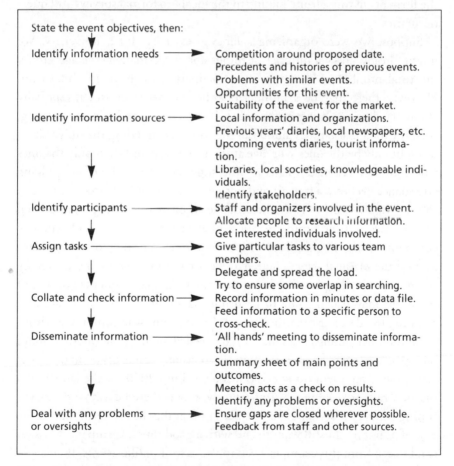

State the event objectives, then:

Identify information needs ⟶ Competition around proposed date.
Precedents and histories of previous events.
Problems with similar events.
Opportunities for this event.
Suitability of the event for the market.

Identify information sources ⟶ Local information and organizations.
Previous years' diaries, local newspapers, etc.
Upcoming events diaries, tourist information.
Libraries, local societies, knowledgeable individuals.
Identify stakeholders.

Identify participants ⟶ Staff and organizers involved in the event.
Allocate people to research information.
Get interested individuals involved.

Assign tasks ⟶ Give particular tasks to various team members.
Delegate and spread the load.
Try to ensure some overlap in searching.

Collate and check information ⟶ Record information in minutes or data file.
Feed information to a specific person to cross-check.

Disseminate information ⟶ 'All hands' meeting to disseminate information.
Summary sheet of main points and outcomes.
Meeting acts as a check on results.
Identify any problems or oversights.

Deal with any problems ⟶ Ensure gaps are closed wherever possible.
or oversights Feedback from staff and other sources.

Figure 6.3   *Information gathering and environmental searching for events management. Source: adapted from Costa and Teare (1996).*

Demand and Operational Planning

For many events, the issue of demand may not seem directly relevant – for personal events in particular, it might be thought that demand does not significantly feature as a factor in the planning process, except to know roughly how many people are coming or to be invited to an event, such as a wedding or birthday party. But, for almost all events, demand and the potential market are an issue. General public events can be difficult to plan for. What sort of people are interested, how many might attend, when would be a good date or time to put the event on? It can be difficult to assess this effectively, especially when no similar event has been run before. With many types of events, on the other hand, the potential number of attendees may be quite specific, or specific enough for the event manager to get a feel for the requirements. This can be checked by some research, in the form of anything from 'talking to the locals' to formal surveys and questionnaires.

Suppose we were organizing a fancy dress party for a university. We might already know a number of things about the market: the age group, the total number of students, their inclination to dress up and so on. However, there may be a number of other factors to consider, especially about the date or timing of the event. If the event is to be in the evening, then the total market may not be all the students attending the university – it might only be the ones who live at the university, and then only the ones who have not yet made plans for the suggested date. Therefore, judging attendance becomes a fine art and both experience and research are needed to get it right. From an assessment of the whole market, the potential total of attendees and the timing, various other factors can be considered. The competition may be significant. More than one event may be taking place around the planned date. There may be a band in town or the university rugby club may be planning its annual party. As a consequence, timing of the event may become key to ensuring maximum take-up of tickets, by avoiding the dates of the other events. In addition, searching the environment for other timing issues may still be needed, on the basis of other things taking place, such as examinations or revision, some other major local attraction, a big event on television, such as Euro 2000, or the launch of a big new film at the cinema. Importantly, might there be a finance-related timing issue – the students may be better off at the start of term than at the end of it (but might still want to end with a good time). Comparative issues can be seen from this example, even in the case of public events. If an event is perceived as expensive then it may only be appropriate to have it at a vacation time when discretionary income might be available in the case of tourist events, or at a time of the month when many people get paid in the case of local or community-based events.

Moving on to some of the detailed issues of the planning process, the event will require a whole range of resources. It is easy to regard these resources as simply being staff and equipment. In practice, the single most important resource for event managers is time, because the brief for an event may allow only a very limited time scale. Sometimes the brief (which is a specification or contract for an event, sometimes given by companies or organizers, for commercial and many other types of events) does not allow a realistic time scale to do it properly without incurring very high costs of management time, staffing and resources to 'throw at it' in order to get it done. Professional events managers may turn down some briefs on this basis. There has to be enough time to plan the event properly, to meet deadlines and cut-off points and to achieve the set-up, run the event and break down afterwards.

Case Study 19

The opening night of the Millennium Dome, Greenwich

The Millennium Dome, at Greenwich in London, took three years to build. The total cost of the building and its operations was some €1,200 million. It was opened at a ceremony on the evening of 31 December 1999, running into the early hours of the morning of 1 January 2000.

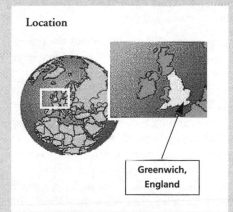

Location

Greenwich, England

Factbox
- Millennium Dome, Greenwich, England.
- Cost: in excess of €1,200 million.
- The Dome contained 14 zones.
- Much of the cost was covered by companies sponsoring the Dome and by Lottery grants.
- The opening night was 'a disaster'.

The Dome was the culmination of a plan, first suggested in 1994, to celebrate a Christian (religious) event for 2000. Initially it was thought that Birmingham, in the English Midlands, would be the site. However, as the idea began to be adopted by government, the concept changed from being religious (once the site was selected as Greenwich in east London), to having the purpose of regenerating a large area of derelict land on the Greenwich peninsula, over-looking the River Thames. In this form it had been intended to be a trade exhibition, rather like the Festival of Britain of 1951, and its forerunners such as the Paris Exposition of 1889 (mentioned in an earlier case study), but the idea gradually changed from a trade exhibition to an exhibition celebrating 'time' and the phases of life as its theme. The final outcome was the 'Dome', containing 14 zones (such as the mind zone, the journey zone, the home planet zone), representing various life experiences. Each zone attracted consid-erable sponsorship from national and international companies. For example, Ford sponsored the journey zone with almost €19.5 million of support (Nicholson, 1999).

The opening ceremony, despite every intention to make the event successful, was a shambles of haphazard ticketing, ineptly managed security and unfortu-nate late arriving guests. The effects were not only tremendous stress and anger on the night itself, among those struggling to get to the event, but also massive public relations damage to the image of the Dome and the organizing company. The cause of this shambles was inadequate planning and a lack of awareness on the part of the New Millennium Experience Company (NMEC) of scheduling, especially of the ticketing, together with the apparent lack of a thought-out time scale for the activities of ticket processing and security checks. Ten thousand people had been invited to the opening ceremony. A few days before the event, only just over half the tickets had been sent out. At this point, it was discovered that there would not be enough time to send out the remaining tickets by post to the invited guests. What compounded the problem was a lack of a sense of urgency that this was a major material issue and, if not handled well, would result in serious damage.

NMEC showed no apparent significant managerial concern about the ticket-ing problem until the issue began to appear in the newspapers a few days before, by which time it was too late to get the tickets out. Consequently, guests were told to get themselves to Stratford underground railway station in east London on the night, where special arrangements would be made to get them on to the Underground, which was running special trains to the Dome station at Greenwich. The Dome had been designed with almost no car parking. Access was by public transport only; this poor infrastructure was also a major cause of low visitor numbers from the opening night. Indeed, car parking was often designated at public transport hubs – one such designated car park being at Luton Airport, some 70 kilometres from the Dome. (In August 2000, with the Dome having had further grants and loans of over €100 million, in addition to its original costs, and with continuing low visitor numbers, a car park with a capacity of 1,000 car parking spaces was opened at the Dome site, too late to save the peak summer season.)

As the ceremony was performed by the Queen, together with the Prime Minister and the Archbishop of Canterbury, and with a large number of VIPs present, there was tight security. In practice this meant that every single guest was supposed to walk through an electronic security gate to make sure he or she was not carrying anything dangerous. The impact of 4,000 people turning up at the Stratford underground station, where there were four security gates (only one of which was working properly), had not been thought about properly or checked. As the 4,000 ticketless but invited guests began to turn up at Stratford, in their best evening wear, dinner jackets and ball gowns, the outcome was complete chaos. In no way could 4,000 people get through one gate (Watt and Wells, 2000).

Management locations on the opening night:

Senior management in Greenwich at the Dome

↑

Supervisors at the Dome

↑

Junior contact staff

↑

Operations at Stratford

As the situation deteriorated and with an apparently blasé attitude on the part of the NMEC management (most of whom were already at the Dome and could not understand the magnitude of the chaos at Stratford, partly owing to the filtering effect of layers of management and limited communications, as well as the distance), some efforts were made to get the guests to the Dome in time for the main ceremony, scheduled for midnight. Special buses were brought in, and in the end attempts at 'security' were stopped, in an effort to get people to the Dome. By 10.40 p.m., when the 4,000 unfortunate guests were at last beginning to arrive, all the food and drink (including 10,000 bottles of champagne) had been either consumed or removed and further chaos ensued while people tried to find their seats. In this maelstrom the atmosphere of happiness intended for the evening was largely ruined, though the ceremony went ahead.

The following day, the Managing Director of the NMEC dismissed the chaos as unimportant. Unfortunately for the company, among the 4,000 invited guests who had been put through the mess at Stratford were several national newspaper editors and their wives, the Director-General of the BBC and a number of the major sponsors. The company and the event were trashed in the media, and it and the government had to apologize. Within a month, and partly owing to 'lower than expected attendances' at the Dome, the Chief Executive of the NMEC had been replaced – the price of inattention to detail in planning and lack of conviction in management. To avoid jibes about Disney, the NMEC had avoided seeking advice from the amusement park industry, which had the necessary experience of large-scale outdoor events.

The new chief executive, appointed after the disaster, was from Disneyland Paris, Pierre-Yves Gerbeau, an expert in visitor park attractions and ticketing.

Based on this case:

Identify the key mistakes which NMEC made in its organization of the opening night of the Dome. What are the likely background reasons for these mistakes? What management tools or systems, used in event management, would have prevented the initial ticketing failure? How did the shambles of the opening night organization impact on the public and media image of the Dome as an attraction? Was this the only reason for lower than expected numbers of visitors to the Dome, or did the Dome have infrastructure and content problems too? What is the accounting convention known as 'sunk costs' and what might its relevance be to the Dome?

Related website for those interested in the Dome: www.mx2000.co.uk
Related website for those interested in media commentary on the Dome: www.guardianunlimited.co.uk (you will have to search this site).

Event managers need to be aware of key timing issues. The lead times of various event-related activities are often underestimated; hence the difficulty of getting so many tickets out for the Dome. But there are many other lead time issues, from marketing and the production of brochures to the lead time of booking the right venue. Many venues will be booked up well over a year in advance. Popular dates and times of year often take the uninitiated by surprise and almost the first activity in planning will be to identify suitable venues and dates. Bookings can be made provisionally but will usually be subject to a deposit, even if the venue is the village hall. For events which are self-funding this may result in a chicken-and-egg type problem – what to do first, confirm the venue or sell tickets. This is usually resolved by having a cut-off date by which the event will be confirmed and the venue be paid for, by selling a limited number of tickets early on. If the event is cancelled, no money is lost before the booking cut-off date and refunds can be given to those who booked early.

Financial Planning

The plan should be starting to take some shape. The organizers should have been able to quantify the size of the event: how many people are coming, whether there is any competition and whether it is convenient in relation to the competition. Identifying any competition may also have given some feel for prices people are willing to pay. However, price should not really be determined by the competition, but by what it will cost to put on and whether it has to be profitable (the issue of budgeting is dealt with in more detail below). This issue of pricing is very important. Inexperienced organizers typically underestimate the various costs. It is absolutely essential to sit down and list all the items required and cost them properly – 'a few balloons' may turn into a budget for decorations and theming of several thousands of euros.

There is a tendency on the part of everyone to say 'Oh well, it will cost about . . .', without actually checking. When someone actually gets around to checking the real amount comes as a shock. A good example is discos – someone on the organizing committee always 'has a mate' who does a disco and it will be 'really cheap'. No it won't! The 'mate' either will not be able to do the date or will take various liberties with the organizers, who will find out after the event that they could have had a cheaper disco by getting several quotes from firms in the phone book. The other serious mistake made at this stage is for organizers to start off with a ticket price they have picked out of thin air: 'Oh, I think tickets should be . . .' This method, based on no reasoning whatsoever, is almost guaranteed to land the event in serious financial difficulties. If you decide the ticket price before the costing has been done, you end up cutting back on all the things that make the event special. The ticket price has to be based on accurate costings and only then considered in the light of competition and what the market will pay, which should also be based on some realistic data, not on what the organizers 'think' the market will pay, which often underestimates reality. A further financial issue which should be included with the budget and cash flow statements is a calculation about the break-even point of the event. Say ticket prices are €10 and costs are €500. This means, for the event to break even, that 50 tickets have to be sold. What if the venue only seats 45? (You couldn't make a profit.) In essence, once the full costs of the event are known, the ticket price can be calculated, with an awareness that enough tickets have to be sold to cover all eventualities.

There are other, more hidden, cost risks involved in event management. Breakdown and bottleneck costs can be very severe, and not apparent until they occur. The ticketing problems of the Millennium Dome could be thought of as having breakdown costs, with there being not only negative financial outcomes, such as having to pay compensation for the breakdown, but also the costs of damage to the company's reputation, which might turn out to be so severe that the company might not recover. These breakdown or failure costs can be thought of as falling into three categories: cost risks related to quality, management and standards; cost risks related to the expense of putting on the event; and cost risks related to the effective timing and scheduling of events. A tension exists between these issues. For example, for the quality of an event to be assured, both adequate time and money have to be put in; if this is not done, the outcome may not be as intended. This was the case with the Dome opening night. There was the failure of not having planned enough time and given enough resources (such as expertise, management and staffing) to despatch 4,000 tickets. The breakdown resulted in a quality failure and a cost failure (the simple cost in terms of getting people to the Dome by special buses, and the terrible later cost of the public relations damage). What action could have been taken to deal with the problem is open to debate, but it should have been possible, for example, to courier tickets out to more than one place for distribution, to arrange for people to meet at more than one place for their onward transport and to have more than one operating security gate at these different locations. Doing this would have cost money to sort out, quite a lot of money. But it would have saved the reputation of the NMEC. The lesson is to pay enough attention to the services being provided for the event and what the guests are saying. In this, perhaps the cost of solving a problem as it develops may be less than the cost of trying to put the damage right afterwards.

Marketing Planning

All events require marketing planning. We might think some events that are not intended as public activities, such as those open only to our immediate family and friends, might not need marketing. But think what you do when you invite your friends to a party. You want to make it sound good so people will come; you are, in effect, doing some marketing. So the issue of how to market an event does become significant, even if we are only 'marketing' within a group of friends, neighbours or a small organization, rather than to the public as a whole. Arguably, we are looking at several marketing-related activities: research (if a public event, who make up our market, what will they pay, what are their interests, how will they get to us, etc.?); internal marketing (within the organization, with respect to both people involved in preparing the event and people within an organization that the event would be for); and/or external marketing, for public events, or for events where some external public relations would be a benefit.

Assuming the event organizers wish to obtain some publicity or public relations coverage, it is necessary to plan the marketing activities that would produce this. For some kinds of activities, such as product launches, the budget available for the promotion of the event might be very large indeed.

For other events, such as a village fête, there might be a modest budget, so the marketing might have to be based on effective public relations rather than advertising or expensive promotional tools. In working up a marketing plan, the event organizer might have to identify what the available budget was. There are essentially two ways of doing this. One way is to say, 'Well, here is the income, marketing can have so much' (after which the marketing team will get a fright and probably have to see what they can get for the money). The preferable way is to look at the event objectives and work up a marketing budget based on what needs to be done.

The next stage will then be the planning of the marketing effort in terms of time. We can call this a marketing action plan, or even a launch plan for the event. This plan is a schedule of activities leading up to the event (some activities may take place afterwards, such as getting pictures of the event in the local newspapers). The marketing team will need to identify the key lead times for each activity. Suppose a 'programme' is required. It will be important to find out not only how long it will take to collect the information to include in it, but also how long the programme will take to print, how long it will take to be proofed and checked, how long it will take to be delivered. Many marketing teams have come unstuck with programmes or brochures because a vital piece of information is not ready ('Oh yes, the committee is meeting next week to decide that.' 'But we need to get the proof to the printer today.' 'Oh sorry, you'll just have to wait.' 'But . . .'). In consequence, the key to the marketing programme is to allow enough time and to know who is making relevant decisions and when. Things which often appear simple are not, or take much longer than expected. Comments such as, 'I rang up the radio station to tell them about tomorrow's fireworks. They said they needed to know three weeks ago in order to get it into the right schedule' are very typical for the inexperienced organizer. It is essential to find out, genuinely, how long marketing and public relations matters will take, and then plan accordingly.

There are many lead time issues which relate to the marketing function. These include: printing of tickets, posters, menus, programmes, banners, etc.; ordering of equipment (often the more specialized the longer the lead time); advertising and promotion (even local radio may need two or three weeks notification of an event to ensure it is given good coverage); liaison issues, where relevant, with police, highways departments, health and safety and so on, especially where large numbers of the public may be attending. In essence, the longer the lead time available before an event the better, although this is not to say that it is impossible to put on an event very quickly, but to do so may need professional or expensive help.

Outline marketing plan: August / September 2001, weeks 1 to 4. To raise money for the church bells.
Middleburg Sports Day to take place on Saturday 8 September 2001, including a sack race, three-legged race, tug of war, knockout games and 'guess the weight of the big church bell'. Various traders and stalls.

Week	**1** M	T	W	T	F	S	S	**2** M	T	W	T	F	S	S	**3** M	T	W	T	F	S	S	**4** M	T	W	T	F	S	S
Write plan, check costs, etc.	**X**	**X**	**X**																									
Make sure Mayor Beaumont is booked to open the event					**X**																							
Send sponsorship request letter to local businesses								**X**	**X**																			
Promote event competition in the town newspaper, public notice boards, library and halls										**X**	**X**																	
Design a poster										**X**	**X**																	
Write media release										**X**	**X**																	
Send media release																**X**	**X**	**X**										
Put up posters in key places																**X**	**X**	**X**	**X**	**X**								
Vicar to go round local businesses to follow up sponsorship letter																								**X**	**X**			
Post out invitations on mailing list																								**X**	**X**	**X**		
Open Sports Day																											**X**	
Work out what money was made for the bells fund																											**X**	
Have a glass of Alsace with Mayor Beaumont																											**X**	
Make a note of any problems for next event																											**X**	

Figure 6.4   *Marketing lead times: Middleburg Sports Day.*

Getting It Together

At the point at which the organizers have got all the information, have written the plans and sorted out the major issues, there should be a pause. This pause may happen naturally between the planning and the event, or it may have to be built in. It is needed because there should be sufficient time to reflect on the progress of the event so far, because of the need to check the status of the plans and because time is needed for discussion and feedback on the plans and for people to respond. This is one of those points when everyone should meet to see what else has been done, to discuss what still needs to be achieved and to participate in further arrangements and final checking. Organizers must handle this phase sensitively. It is not necessarily there for organizers to tell people what will be done; it is for jointly and openly exploring progress, and is a characteristic of good events planning – an opportunity to pause and listen.

Throughout this process the event will be getting closer and closer, there will be deadlines to deal with and, in due course, the event will take place. With careful planning, modest (or major!) success should be the result. After that, a short 'wash up' session should take place, for feedback on the event, to write up the accounts, complete the records and make any notes of importance to the planning of any future event.

Summary

Planning, and the planning process, plays a key role in the organization and management of special events. Planning is a tool that organizers can use effectively, or sometimes badly. Even the simplest of events, such as a birthday or dinner party, will need to be planned, or given at least some forethought. The larger and more complex events become, the more detailed and systematic the planning will have to be. Care, time and effort at the planning stage of an event will yield many benefits, the most important of which is ensuring the most positive outcome to the event.

Reference List

Costa, J. and Teare, R. (1996) 'Environmental scanning: a tool for competitve advantage'. In R. Kotas, Teare, R., Logie, J. and Bowen, J. (eds), *The International Hospitality Business*. London: Cassell, pp. 12–20.

Engel, M. (1999) 'Opening of Parliament', *Guardian*, 2 July, p. 5.

Nicholson, A. (1999) 'The theatre of the age', *Sunday Telegraph Magazine*, 5 December, pp. 11–45.

Reiss, G. (1995) *Project Management Demystified*, 2nd edn. London: E&F Spon, pp. 27–43.

Richards, B. (1992) *How to Market Tourist Attractions, Festivals and Special Events*. Harlow: Longman, pp. 21–43.

Stokes, D. (1995) *Small Business Management*. London: DP Publications, pp. 210–11.

Watt, N. and Wells, M. (2000) 'Falconer apologises for Dome fiasco', *Guardian*, 3 January, p. 1.

CHAPTER 7

Financial Management and the Budget

Aims
- To provide an introduction to some of the financial planning, control and budgetary issues in running events.
- To consider budgetary organization of events in terms of break-even, monitoring and recording of revenues and costs.
- To discuss additional financial issues such as raising income, public funding, concessions and sponsorship.

Introduction
Financial planning and good financial control are important aspects of the event management process. Even if we are only organizing a small personal event, we need to know how much can be spent. For the vast majority of events, there will be both income and expenditure. The careful monitoring, recording and control of these incomes and expenditures is a significant concern of clients, organizers, coordinators and finance officers at events of all kinds. For the professional finance officer, this chapter will seem only the most general outline of what has to be done, but for the person new to the job of volunteer treasurer or financial officer of an event, it should prove at least a helpful starting point. The purpose of the chapter is not to deal with the entire financial management subject as it relates to this area; for this the reader may wish to look at Hussey and Hussey (1999) or, for the serious, Kotas (1999). The recording of the financial aspects of events, ranging from the purchase of items to the final budgeted accounts, is potentially much more complicated than the summary here, and good financial control is important to the success of events, even those not intended to be profit-making, but there are many useful accountancy practice books (as noted) and software applications available for those who wish to expand their expertise.

For events which are revenue generating, as well as those where the recording of outgoings against a client's budget is needed, we can begin to see the necessity of normal accounting processes, rather than simply being able to list the costs on a sheet of paper. Even the scouts with their 'car wash' fund-raising can serve to illustrate the fact that events exist whose primary purpose is to make money with a minimum expenditure (a few buckets of warm water, some sponges and a large number of happy, if rather wet, scouts, being all that is needed), but for which it is still essential to know what money has been made. So, while we might have events which are entirely cost-orientated on the one hand, or events which are entirely income-orientated on the other, there are a very large number of events which require both these things and have to be financially managed in an entirely conventional way, with careful assessment of potential income, expenditure and profit (or surplus or break-even) depending on the type of event.

In all cases some effort needs to go into providing an overview of the financial aspects of the event, at the planning stage, during the event itself and at the end. In the case of the wedding or the scouts car wash, this might simply comprise a list of what has been spent or what has been made (though it is better to do two lists – what is planned and what actually happened, forecast and actual). Clearly, if at the wedding it was planned to spend €5,000 but €10,000 were spent, someone had to find the money. Equally, if the scouts planned to raise €1,000 from washing cars but only raised €500, then perhaps the new roof and redecoration of the scouts' hut might have to become just the new roof. The function of financial control is to tell us what happened. Financial control also takes place before and during the event. Beforehand, a budget will be needed so that the organizers can judge whether the event is likely to be a success, and afterwards as a guide to check whether the event could be judged as successful against its financial objectives. Additionally, we will look at ways in which the potential income for an event can be increased, and also at the public funding of events and at sponsorship.

Objectives and Financial Planning

The setting of objectives is of importance for the entire event, but it is also the key to what has to be done financially. Event organizers may be faced with a range of financial choices depending on what has been decided about the objectives (see Chapter 5, regarding the financial screening process). Care, time and effort will need to be expended at an early stage to ensure good financial management of the event, and that all the possible kinds of expenditure and income have been identified. Small personal events, whose objective is the enjoyment of the participants, may have little in the way of financial management, except an awareness of the total of what might be spent in general terms. For very large events on a regional, national or international scale, the financial aspects may have to become the subject of financial feasibility studies based on a range of possible techniques, from cost–benefit analysis to assessing the tourism multiplier of the total event project (Hall, 1992). These techniques are, however, rather beyond the boundaries of this book and we will concentrate on the more common aspects of financial management in terms of budgetary organization and control, which are most appropriate for the middle range of events.

One key to the effective financial management of events is the appointment of someone responsible for it, in the same way that members of an organizing committee might be responsible for bookings, organization,

---

Leisure Event

International city athletics competition

- Primary objectives: to develop sporting talent in athletics; to bring a large number of visitors to the city to watch or participate; to improve the city's image.
- Financial objectives: to make enough money (surplus from the event) to rebuild the city stadium; to provide some additional housing once the competitors have left, based on the financing of the athletes' village in conjunction with developers.

Cultural Event

Village fête

- Primary objective: to hold an enjoyable annual celebration for the village.
- Financial objective: to make enough money to break even and to buy a new bench to put beside the village pond.

Organizational Event

Sales managers' team building day

- Primary objective: to improve the team skills of the sales department.
- Financial objective: to keep within the budgeted cost allowed for staff development.

Personal Event

Family wedding

- Primary objective: to celebrate the wedding and have a good time.
- Financial objective: to keep cost less than €5,000.

Figure 7.1 *Various example events and their objectives.*

staff and publicity. It is somewhat typical of events (particularly those that rely on volunteer staffing, as many do) for their financial aspects to be relatively poorly understood, especially in terms of cash flow (that is the relative timing of income and expenditure). Many events organizers do not fully appreciate the financial implications of the decisions they are making and are consequently surprised, when the accounts are done, by how little profit has been made or how big a loss has been incurred. Even apparently unrelated decisions can have a major impact on revenue. A good example of an impact might be the decision about the timing of an event. If the timing decision is wrong, perhaps where the event clashes with a similar one at the same time, then the target market might not be able to attend both, with a consequent loss of ticket sales, income and other revenue, which may result in a forecast profit becoming an actual loss.

It is also useful to understand the links between the original setting of the objectives and following those through into the financial management and budgets. It is no good saying, in the objectives (as in the example in Figure 7.1), that a key objective is to raise enough money 'to rebuild the city stadium' if it is not known how much that would cost, and whether the budget for the event will actually be able to cope with it. Similarly, it is no good saying that the objective for a wedding is to spend less than €5,000, if this is not written into the budget properly, or if someone goes out and blows €4,500 on the pre-wedding party, leaving only €500 for the whole of the actual wedding ('Oh, nobody told me we only had €5,000'). The objectives and the financial management are intimately linked. It is essential that the organizers make the links clear.

Cash flow issues also tend to be serious, particularly for events that involve pre-booking, such as a gala fund-raising dinner. Some expenditure or investment may well have to take place before any income is generated or tickets are sold, thus exposing the organizers to risk of financial failure. Venues for events often have long lead times for bookings and require money up-front to hold or confirm the reservation. When this is the case, the treasurer (or finance officer of the organizing committee) will have to ensure that sufficient money is available to pay for the various costs before the deadlines, or risk losing the booking and the event. This will also mean careful attention to issues such as debt collection and credit periods. (For example, if an agent has agreed to take so many advance tickets for an event, when do you, at the event, get paid for them. If the period between booking the tickets and payment is too long, your event might go bankrupt in the meantime, because you have to pay money out but have not got enough cash coming in.)

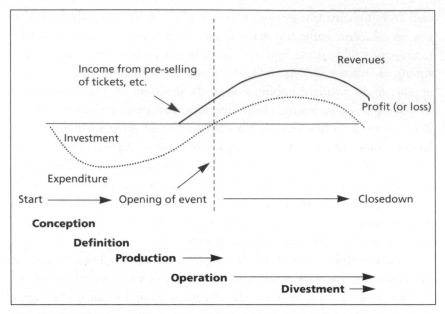

Figure 7.2   *Cash flow at events. Source: adapted from Morris (1994).*

Suppose a town festival committee has booked a marquee for a medieval banquet as the climax to its annual town pageant. Although the festival might not take place until August, the marquee company, the caterers and the musicians may all want a booking fee. Altogether these booking fees might add up to €1,000. The capacity of the marquee is 250, and the booking deadline is the end of June. So, in a very basic way, the financial manager will have to find €1,000 from existing funds (if the event has been run before and generated a surplus in previous years); or, in the case of there being no existing funds, will have to get 250 deposits of €4 per person (or equivalent) to cover the booking costs by, say, a week before the end of June, to have a chance of the event running; or from other methods, such as sponsorship, donations or borrowing (e.g. a bank loan, bearing in mind that this would have to be repaid with interest). This might be only the first of several financial deadlines and serves to illustrate that cash flow and deadlines could mean the difference between whether an event runs or not.

Creating the Budget

For commercial organizations, senior management or a company department might do the preparation of a budget for an event. However, in the case of many events, run by volunteers, committees, individuals or families, who may have no experience of how to make an event work in financial terms, the preparation of a budget might involve several people, or a volunteer with some financial or organizational background to suit the task. For the person new to the financial aspects of running an event, the planning of a budget may not be as easy as it first appears. A great deal of information has to be collected, which might not be obvious at the start. However, the time and effort put into careful preparation of a budget is extremely important to the success of the event, and to the financial and general control of what is going on. Common budgeting mistakes include:

- Ignoring the objectives of the event when setting the budget.
- Plucking a figure out of the air for ticket sales *before* finding out how much the event is going to cost (a serious and regrettably frequent mistake).
- Not involving everyone concerned in the budget planning and failing to identify the full range of costs accurately.
- Being over-optimistic about demand for the event or failing to find a venue with enough capacity to do it properly.
- Overlooking subsidiary issues such as the costs of ensuring safety and security, or the effect of having to add tax.
- Not having enough capital or start-up funds to get the event off the ground, given the need for deposits or advanced payments of various kinds.
- People spend money but don't get receipts or invoices, so the money is lost and you have no control evidence that they actually spent it.

The budget for an event may be no more complicated than a list of revenues and costs on one sheet of paper, or it may be vastly complicated. Either way, it has to be determined with the objectives of the event in mind. It is no good setting a budget, in which a large profit is forecast, if the event is supposed to be for public entertainment and only intended to generate a small surplus or break even, because making a large profit might result in having to charge too high a ticket price. So what is the objective financially? Is the event intended to make money or simply cover its costs? If it is to cover costs only, what is the headline amount which can be spent, specified by either the clients or the organizing committee?

The ticket price issue is also a frequent source of heated debate, sometimes before any attempt has been made to identify costs. This is such a common mistake, partly because organizers wrongly see it as the most important issue. Yes, the ticket price might be an important issue, but it simply is not good enough bouncing along saying 'we must make it cheap or no one will come'. This is usually based on someone's private opinion, not on a carefully budgeted assessment of the costs, let alone an objective view of what the target market would really pay. In essence, costs need to be listed first and accurately (not just 'my mate said it would be the same as the one they did last year at the football ground'). Quotes or actual prices need to be obtained for all aspects of the activity (how much the football ground would cost, with a quote from the ground manager, not from 'your mate'). In some cases there would need to be more than one quote. From there, the expenditure can be assessed and then, and only then, should a ticket price be estimated, bearing in mind the numbers expected to come (McDonnell *et al.*, 1999).

In the case of certain types of events there might also be differential pricing of tickets (e.g. at sporting events where the best seats have a higher price). Differential pricing also allows us to provide a range of tickets at a range of prices; for example, family tickets, group tickets, full price or off-peak tickets. This needs careful understanding. It is about the marginal costing of the event, sometimes called cost–volume–profit analysis (Hussey and Hussey, 1999).

Suppose our estimates of what the target market will pay show that only half the 1,000 people we expect to attend will pay the full price of €10. What do we do? Perhaps we might have to cancel. On the other hand, we might find that the other half are willing to pay €8 for tickets. Does this help, even if we have said the ticket price must be €10? It depends. It depends if the €8 will be enough to cover our marginal (variable) costs, *and* enough people come paying the full price to cover our fixed costs. In the case in Figure 7.3,

			For one person:
Maximum capacity of the venue:	1,000		
Ticket sales at €10		€10,000	€10.00
Variable costs:			
Buffet	3,000		3.00
Staff	2,500		2.50
Consumables	350		0.35
Total variable costs	€7,850		€7.85
Contribution		€2,150	€2.15
Less total fixed costs			
Hire of marquee		900	
Net profit (loss)		€1,259	

Figure 7.3 *Marginal costing at an event.*

the variable costs per person are €7.85, so the lower ticket price will cover variable costs and make a small contribution of 0.15 cents to the fixed costs. Whereas the full price tickets make a contribution of €2.15 to the fixed costs. If 500 people pay the lower price, the total contribution towards fixed costs will be 500 × 2.15 = 1,075 and 500 × 0.15 = 75, total contribution to the fixed costs of €1,150. The fixed costs are €900, so the event will still make a profit of €250.

Clearly, this depends on the entire 1,000 people coming a buying the tickets at these prices, or a larger number paying the higher price. If too many people paid the lower price, the event would make a loss, as it would do if too few people came.

You will have noticed that we didn't use the word discount in this example. Forget 'discount' – it gives you the wrong idea. The marginal costed tickets still have to cover the variable costs and pay something towards the fixed costs, and we still have to sell enough full priced tickets to cover our total costs. This is why you can go to, say, a leisure centre or a theme park at an off-peak period and pay less than you would at a peak period. It is about having differential ticket prices for different times, for different target markets (see Chapter 9) and different groups, in the knowledge that not everyone will pay full price. Airlines do it too. You might have got the last two seats on a plane at €50, when everyone else has paid €500 a ticket, but that is because the airline is covering its total costs, and might as well have two people with cheap seats, rather than two empty ones. On the other hand, if everyone paid €50, then the airline probably couldn't afford to taxi the plane along the runway. This is also true of events, and can allow you to do some creative ticket pricing, perhaps to get in larger numbers of people in target markets that you hadn't exploited before.

Quotations should be made on like for like basis, and the criteria decided (do you want the cheapest quotation, do you want the best quality of good or services, etc.?).

A major issue for event organizers is knowing how many people will attend, in order to prepare a reasonably accurate budget. The estimates of attendance may be based on surveys of the market, attendance at similar or previous events, knowledge of the limited size of the available customer base and so on. From the point of view of budget preparation, an organizer might want to be optimistic about attendance. Given the potential problems about booking deadlines and deposits, it is important to be realistic about how many tickets can be sold and whether the venue can be filled, or whether the budget should estimate to break even if, say, half the venue is filled. Optimism is very nice, but the acid test is often when the organizing committee or sales team go out and try to sell tickets and find that 'no one wants to buy them yet'. There are ways in which this kind of response can be influenced, such as by asking for a deposit (once people have committed some money they are generally likely to buy the whole thing when the time comes) or by offering discounts for advance purchase (rather like advance purchase airline tickets). Break-even is a key issue and sometimes not terribly well understood. Say an event will cost €500 to put on, and the venue will accommodate 100 people. At first glance you might say, well, we need to sell 100 tickets at €5. But if you did this, you would make a loss even if 99 out of the 100 tickets were sold. You have to consider what your realistic break-even is.

Other difficulties arise owing to unforeseen costs or subsidiary issues, a common one being whether tax (e.g. VAT) has to be added to ticket prices. For most small-scale or family events, this is irrelevant, but for big events it would have to be checked with the correct government department (in the UK, for example, this is the Customs and Excise), as there is a minimum threshold for payment.

For those new to events budgeting, the outline budget form (Figure 7.4) will help you understand what is needed and what information is still missing. It will also show you that once you have identified all the costs, your first ideas about how much to charge as an entry fee or event ticket may be completely wrong. Most important of all, it may also be evident that there is no margin of safety in running the event between its revenue and its forecast costs. In simple terms what we mean by this is that there have to be enough people attending and paying to cover the costs and to make sure there is a profit or small surplus. (Although there are few types of events which are not intended to make a profit these are less common.)

Suppose our total costs are €1,000. We forecast that 100 people will attend, and the ticket cost would therefore appear to be €10. This, however, is not a safe position to be in – if even 99 people come to the event it will still make a loss. So the budget should be worked out based on the idea that more people will come to the event than are needed to cover the costs – for example 125 people at €10, or, that the ticket price is higher – for example, 100 people at €12.50. In this respect, it is also necessary to take into account not only how many people we expect to attend, but whether the venue capacity is appropriate. If the venue will accommodate 75 people but we need 100 people to attend in order to cover our costs then the event is not viable at that venue. It is possible, on the basis of various cost estimates, for the organizing committee or finance officer to prepare some comparative outline budgets to help the decision-making process, where an issue such as the venue needs to be compared with others.

Proposed event: _____   Date today: _____

Date of event: _____   Days to go: _____

Forecast number of people expected: _____ (paying guests/paying visitors)

Capacity of the venue: _____

List of costs

Venue hire: Total amount: € _____

Deposit amount: € _____   Deposit due by: _____

Staff/labour.

Number of volunteers needed: _____ Number of paid staff needed: _____

Total staffing cost inc. staff feeding: € _____

Example overheads:	Total amount €:	Best price quotation given by:
Advertising	_____	_____
Printing/posters/tickets	_____	_____
Signs/place cards/menus/programmes	_____	_____
Custom t-shirts/uniform/badges	_____	_____
Equipment hire	_____	_____
Food	_____	_____
Drink	_____	_____
Entertainment	_____	_____
Music	_____	_____
Decorations	_____	_____
Linen/linen hire	_____	_____
Prizes/complimentary items	_____	_____
Floristry/plants	_____	_____
Security/crowd control/guides/info point	_____	_____
Insurance	_____	_____
Refuse removal/cleaning	_____	_____
Power/heat/light/air conditioning	_____	_____
Ticket distribution/stationery/postage	_____	_____
Licence/licence application	_____	_____
Audio-visual/sound	_____	_____
Phones/mobiles/radio links	_____	_____
Photographer/video company/press kit	_____	_____
Other items	_____	_____

Total of all costs <u>including venue and staff</u> € _____

Total costs divided by number of paying guests (including venue hire, staffing and any other items not listed here but known, expected or planned):

€ _____ (costs per person)

Profit/surplus required?   € _____ (profit per person)

List any additional deposits or prepayments required:

_____

_____

Figure 7.4 *Outline budget form (for quotations).*

Venues:	Luigi's Garden Bistro	Rolf's Bar & Marquee	Rumôurs Nightclub
Venue capacity:	60	100	120
No. of guests expected:	50	50	50
Costs:	€	€	€
Venue hire	0	1,450 (marquee)	500 (deposit)
Staffing costs (door/costs)	0 (included	0 (included in meal)	100 in meal)
Printing	50	50	50
Menus and place cards	50	50	50
Food	1,250 (sit down meal)	1,000 (sit down meal)	750 (buffet)
Reception drinks	300	300	300
Band	500	500	500
Raffle prizes	100	100	100
Total estimated costs	2,250	3,450	2,350
Ticket price if 40 people attend:	£45	£69	£47

Figure 7.5   *Example of comparative outline budgets for a proposed company party.*

This first attempt at providing an adequate outline budget will help us to identify what further information is needed to prepare a more detailed budget forecast. The detailed budget can be based on a given number of people, or we can have alternatives showing worst case and best case. It is necessary, probably crucial, to have a good idea of the point at which the event will break even and make a profit. For this we have to bear in mind that some costs are fixed and some are variable (Wilson and Chua, 1988; Hussey and Hussey, 1999). For example, for whatever number of people attend, the cost of hiring a marquee for an event would be fixed – let us say €1,450. The marquee will still cost this whether one person attends our event or whether 100 people attend our event. On the other hand the cost of the food might be variable in relation to the number of people. Let us suppose a sit down meal costs €20 per person. In the case of the meal, if one person attends the cost is €20. If 50 people attend the cost is €1,000 and if 100 people attend the cost is €2,000. This is a variable cost.

In terms of expenditure and costs it is essential that we have properly calculated the total costs and have included everything in the list of costs which might be involved. It is very important to take care to ensure that all the costs have been checked and that the list is genuinely complete.

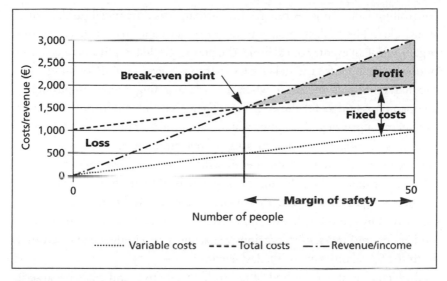

Figure 7.6   *Break-even chart.*

Budgeting

It would be very easy to use the common financial term 'budgetary control' at this stage. However, 'control' often concentrates financial managers' minds only on costs or expenditure and, clearly, in event management terms, revenue generation and the 'whole' picture are equally important. If the event objective is about quality rather than profitability, then over-concentration on costs might well damage the success of the event because cheap materials might be bought rather than good quality ones. We have already noted that certain types of events can be more revenue led than cost led.

A budget is a forecast or plan that helps to regulate the operation of an event (or any business) over a given period of time. In the case of a business such as a hotel, the budget might be an annual one. In the case of an event, because events are one-off and time-limited, the budget will normally be for the time period of that event. A budget is also a management tool by which responsibility for various activities (e.g. sales or the control of costs) can be seen in much the same way as the general event plan. The budget, as it is both a forecast of what is intended to happen and a record of what is happening (or, after the event, of what had happened), acts as a means of comparing the forecast with the reality and sets targets which the organizers can strive to achieve (Richards, 1992, 49–64).

The advantage of having a budget is that it is a detailed forecast of what should be happening financially, and as such it helps planning; though, as with any other element of a plan, it should not come to be the one controlling factor in it. A budget is just that, it is a financial guide, not a straitjacket. The budget should result in better coordination between the organizers of an event. For example, the budget could be split into a revenue budget, as a target for the ticket sales staff to achieve; a publicity budget for the marketing staff to keep to when they are spending money on publicity; an operations budget for the events manager to ensure that he or she has not overspent on printing, decorations, staff, equipment or other resources. The budget is intended to act as a measure of performance between that which is forecast and the actual outcome for which the respective organizers have been responsible – often this forecasting may be difficult for events because of their unique nature, and the forecast may simply be an approximate estimate. On the other hand, some events may have occurred before, in similar circumstances, or in previous years, and a new budget can be created from the actual outcome of the last event.

Budgeting is also a method of controlling expenses and costs because it should help to establish clear lines of responsibility about who can or cannot spend money. Related to this, the budget should also make managers aware of costs and revenues, so that they do not get over-enthusiastic in spending money or in failing to exploit an opportunity to make money or generate revenue from some aspect of the event. For example, it might be very nice to have a media celebrity open a carnival or present the winners of a sports competition with their prizes, but most media celebrities charge a major fee for appearing and if this has not been budgeted for, it should not be done – it might result in an event which should have made money making a loss.

The budget, because it is helping the planning process, should also seek to ensure that the resources that the organizer has are most economically used, thus helping to keep costs in control or helping to ensure a profit or surplus is made. For example, there is no point hiring twenty ushers all day if they are only going to be needed for the first ten minutes – costs like this might well show up in the forecast as being out of line with the rest of the budget. The budget can be made more or less detailed depending on the needs of the organizers or clients. For a small event, it might be enough to include minor costs (cost of ushers, for example) in the budget line about staffing. On the other hand, we might want to have full and complete details of all items. To do this, the general budget, with its list of incomes and costs, can be broken down into extra information, as shown in Figure 7.8.

(Summary) Event Budget

Event:_____

Date of event: _____   Date of this budget: _____

Attendance (paying guests)   Forecast: Actual:
_____   _____

Income/revenue	Budget €:	Actual €:
Ticket sales	_____	_____
Catering	_____	_____
Income from concession stand rental	_____	_____
Raffle	_____	_____
Other (specify) _____	_____	_____
Total income	€_____	€_____

Expenditure:	Budget €:	Actual €:
Venue hire	_____	_____
Staff/labour	_____	_____
Advertising	_____	_____
Printing/posters/tickets	_____	_____
Signs/place cards/menus/programmes	_____	_____
Custom t-shirts/uniform/badges	_____	_____
Equipment hire	_____	_____
Food	_____	_____
Drink	_____	_____
Entertainment	_____	_____
Music	_____	_____
Decorations	_____	_____
Linen/linen hire	_____	_____
Prizes/complimentary items	_____	_____
Floristry/plants	_____	_____
Security/ crowd control/guides/info point	_____	_____
Insurance	_____	_____
Refuse removal/cleaning	_____	_____
Power/heat/light/air conditioning	_____	_____
Ticket distribution/stationery/postage	_____	_____
Licence/licence application	_____	_____
Audio-visual/sound	_____	_____
Phones/mobiles/radio links	_____	_____
Photographer/video company/press kit	_____	_____
Other items	_____	_____
Total costs	€_____	€_____
Surplus (profit)/deficit (loss)	€_____	€_____

Figure 7.7   *General budget form (summary)*

Detailed Budget Income and Cost Breakdown

Event: _____

Date of event: _____   Date of this budget: _____

Attendance   Forecast: Actual :

    Paying visitors/guests   _____   _____
    Complimentary/hospitality visitors   _____ _____
    VIPs   _____   _____
    Press   _____   _____

Opening balance (at bank):   €_____

Income/revenue   Budget €:   Actual €:

Ticket sales
    Individual   _____   _____
    Family   _____   _____
    Group   _____   _____
    Discount/elders   _____   _____
Catering
    Restaurant food   _____   _____
    Restaurant drink   _____   _____
    Arena coffee bar   _____   _____
    Arena hospitality area extras   _____   _____
Income from concession stand rental
    Ice cream stands   _____   _____
    Retail stands   _____   _____
Raffle
    Saturday raffle   _____   _____
    Sunday raffle   _____   _____
Other (specify): parking   _____   _____
Total income   €_____   €_____

Expenditure: Budget €:   Actual €:
Venue hire   _____   _____
Staff/labour
    Staff wages   _____   _____
    Staff feeding   _____   _____
    Staff insurance   _____   _____
    Staff uniforms   _____   _____
    Volunteers feeding   _____   _____
    Volunteers gift bags   _____   _____
    Volunteers sashes and armbands
Advertising
    Local radio 6 adverts (10 second)   _____   _____
    The *Telegraph* 3 adverts (1/8 page) _____ _____
    Banners (2)   _____   _____
    Newspaper inserts (10,000)   _____   _____
    Artwork for leaflets   _____   _____
    Leaflets (10,000)   _____   _____
    Etc.   _____   _____
Etc.
    Etc.   _____   _____
    Etc.   _____   _____

Total costs   €_____   €_____

Surplus (profit)/deficit (loss)   €_____   €_____

Closing balance (at bank):   €_____

Figure 7.8   *Detailed budget breakdown.*

Who Spends What

We have prepared our detailed budget, it has been approved by the clients or the organizing committee and the serious preparations are about to begin. People will want to go out and spend money, but before they do, it is vital that we have a control system in place to record who is spending what, when and how. Each part of the budget needs to have someone responsible for it (not just the finance officer who wrote it). The revenue part of the budget may be the responsibility of the marketing department, together with their own expenditure. For example, the advertising expenditure budget might be €1,000, but in giving the marketing department this amount to spend, we expect them to attract 500 people to the event, paying for tickets at €10 each. Therefore, the marketing department must have their own clear targets about how their money is best spent to attract the 500 people. Similarly, if we expect the catering department to make money, say, €500 on beverages, they need to have some idea of what kind of beverages they are going to sell, and how many they will have to sell and at what price and profit to make the expected €500.

An important issue is who is allowed to spend money. If a department has a budget, normally it will be the department head who has the authority to spend this budget. The key question is how much and who else can authorize it. Events management depends on the ability of managers and events organizers to solve problems, often very quickly. If they do not have the funds to do this, or the ability to have decisions taken quickly, then the event may fail. (The ticketing fiasco at the Millennium Dome opening night is an example. The inability to deal with the problem of not being able to get enough tickets out to enough people may well have resulted from the ticketing manager not having the authority to spend enough money to get the tickets out in time, the result being a public relations disaster.) In normal circumstances, many items for events are pre-ordered, and for this to take place properly not only are purchase specifications needed (which describe what sort of item is being ordered in detail, so you get what you ordered on the day – for example, 500 blue stacking chairs, not 250 green armchairs), but also purchase order numbers for any item above a given amount. In this way expenditure can be properly recorded (Wood and Lightowlers, 1985).

Similarly, for small items, petty cash may be needed and a system will have to be set up to issue this (which is small amounts of money for those items which have to be paid for in cash, say at local shops, as well as minor items and things which are too small to be bought in bulk). Normally, an amount of petty cash (perhaps €500) might be held by the event coordinator and issued on petty cash vouchers, so that people can be sent out quickly

---

Middleburg Events Company
Festival Park Street
Middleburg
00 44 (0) 1786 123456

To: Order Number: 48519
Red Dragon Furniture Hire
Ty Gwyn
Fford Uwd   Date: 14 August 2001
Abertawe, Wales
SA5 6RE

Dear sir/madam,
Please supply and deliver the following items to the address and on the date
stated below:

Quantity	Size	Description	Cost
500	Standard	Stacking chairs (Type 2000) Blue only	€5,600 (inc. VAT)

Deliver to	On
Mr Kevin McDonald	28 August 2001
Events Co-ordinator	(Before 1pm)
At: Middleburg Music Festival	
Festival Park	
Middleburg	

Yours faithfully,
Anna Murray
Purchasing Officer
Middleburg Events Company
(anna@middleburg.co.eu)

Figure 7.9   *Purchase order form.*

for things which are needed. At the end of the event, the various petty cash vouchers and receipts, together with the major receipts and invoices, will be collated to help make up the final accounts.

The budget is also a mechanism for showing what is going wrong. If the budget shows a forecast expenditure of €1,000 on seating, but the real cost is €2,000, you need to find out why, and do so quickly. The reasons might be legitimate and necessary, and you might have to adjust the rest of the budget to take account of the problem, perhaps by increasing prices or cutting back on something else. On the other hand, the reason may not be legitimate and you will have to take very rapid action. Someone may be defrauding you, or theft taking place, or any number of other problems, which the divergence between the budget forecast and the reality might show.

Petty Cash

Petty cash requested for:	Amount issued
_____	€_____
_____	
Issued to (signature):	Date:
_____	_____
Print name:_____	
Authorized by (signature):	
_____	
Receipt attached for items	Cost: amount used
	€_____/____cents

Figure 7.10   *Petty cash voucher.*

Income for Events

So far we have assumed that income is derived from people coming and buying tickets. It is also important to bear in mind that there might be other sources of income or revenue besides the ticket price and income. These sources may be other revenue-generating activities, or sponsorship-related activities. However, it is important to bear in mind that a large number of events, especially corporate events, have a predetermined budget as part of the event brief, as the event is not intended to raise money, but to perform some other organizational function. Therefore income (or revenue) is simply a matter of the use (or application) to which the budgeted figure might be put.

Special events are such diverse activities that it is often difficult to generalize about them, especially in financial terms. Subsidiary income is often needed for events, even those where there is a defined ticket price. For example, we might wish to run a charity fund-raising race night and charge tickets at €15. This ticketing might raise a good amount, above and beyond what was needed to break even. But more money might also be generated for charity by having other things going on besides the races. There could be a raffle, or an auction of pledges, there could be games such as 'hit the whisky bottle' (with a large denomination coin – whoever gets the closest wins the bottle, and the rest of the coins are collected for the charity), there could be a cash bar, in addition to, say, wine included in the ticket price. A little careful thought can identify many good, simple, money raising activities, thus helping to increase the income of an event. (Control needs to be exercised over loose cash, though. Money should be recorded properly if going through tills. If being collected in some other way, say for charity, it needs to be collected in sealed containers, which should only be opened with at least two people present. In this way it can be counted and recorded legitimately.)

This is not to say that the financial manager of an event should not be actively seeking external or additional ways of raising money to support an event. In fact, the generation of revenue is often a key failure of many events, especially volunteer events, because it is, wrongly, seen as less important than financial control. It is easy to see who is responsible for cost control within budgets, but the raising of additional or extra revenues is often overlooked: no one is made responsible for ideas to raise additional income or to carry those ideas through, and consequently opportunities to raise extra income streams are lost. The following list suggests some sources of additional revenue:

- programmes, brochures, guidebooks;
- catering, fast food, sales stalls;
- retail, souvenirs, merchandising;
- corporate hospitality areas, lounge suites, chill-out area, crèche;
- photography charges, photography sales, video;
- car parking, transport services;
- concessions, stalls, stands, pitches, franchises, rentals, contracting;
- raffles, lottery, tombola, games;
- broadcast rights (usually major sporting events only);
- the use of 'membership' type subscriptions to encourage repeat visits (where appropriate).

Events vary considerably in how they are funded. It is important to recognize that many events have more than one source of income or revenue. In fact, there might be as many sources of income as there are costs associated with the event. Equally, we should not necessarily regard the term 'income' as meaning revenue. The 'income' for operating an event may simply be a budgeted amount that an organization has to spend, funded by the organization itself. Similarly, events put on by government or councils may depend on a budgeted amount which is funded by tax nationally or locally (the purpose of taxation being to provide public services) of which events, such as sporting, cultural, ceremonial or tourist events, might be an example (in the same way that refuse collection, street lighting and hospitals are public services paid for by tax). Certain types of events can require start-up funding. This can be sought from all kinds of bodies that might have an interest in the event, not just government, councils or agencies, though there are official bodies (and some sponsors) that often have limited funds for this type of activity (but many calls on them) (Richards, 1992, pp. 101–10).

Leisure Event

International city athletics competition

Funding: Possible range of funding, including government agencies such as a Sports Council, local government funding for sporting events, support from sports sponsors and broadcasters, together with income generated from ticket sales, concessions selling food, drink and sports-related merchandise.

Cultural Event

Village fête

Major income might be from entrance tickets, parking, renting pitches for the various stands, money raised from a raffle and various games, as well as sponsorship of activities on an organizational or individual basis and charitable donations.

Organizational Event

Sales managers' team building day

No direct income as such. The event will be paid for within a particular budget determined by the organization and operated by the sales department itself (for staff training) or a related department, such as personnel, according to the appropriate organizational objectives.

Personal Event

Family wedding

No direct income as such. The event would be paid for by the people getting married, and their families, with donations of presents and other useful things 'in kind', e.g. friends decorate the church, or help making a buffet, or contribute flowers.

Figure 7.11   *Types of event funding.*

Sponsorship and Public Funding

One of the common misconceptions about the design of events is the view that an event might easily attract sponsorship. In practice the attractiveness of any given event to potential sponsors will be very limited. The time and effort which the organizers might waste trying to get (elusive) sponsorship could well be better used elsewhere, perhaps in developing secondary income streams for the event, such as catering or retailing, as mentioned above (Hall, 1992). The most important aspect of sponsorship is for event organizers to remember that potential sponsors have to get something out of the event – they are extremely unlikely to provide money for nothing. Therefore, it is important to keep in mind what the event would do for a potential sponsor (Watts, 1998). There are several points to this. First, the event and potential sponsors should be looking at the same target market. It is no good trying to get a hearing aid manufacturer to sponsor an annual student ball. Second, there is the issue of media exposure: what are the publicity and public relations plans for your event, and will the sponsor benefit from them? Third, will the sponsor get some direct benefit besides media coverage – for example, some places at a table in the gala dinner, free admission to the event for the sponsor and a colleague or partner, complimentary VIP seats in the hospitality box. Without some or other of these benefits to give to potential sponsors, events organizers will have significant problems attracting sponsorship. Sponsors will be looking not only for hospitality opportunities, but also for events which raise their image (for example, as organizations which actively support their local community) or support some other marketing objective. In short, to get sponsorship an event organizer must fall (conveniently) into a sponsor's own plans. Sources of sponsorship, grants and other income include:

- 'in-kind' arrangements, mutual benefit exchanges of goods or activities, volunteer work or donations;
- grants from local, regional or national government or the European Union;
- grants from charitable bodies, development agencies, arts, leisure or heritage bodies;
- lottery grants or subsidiary (matching) funding;
- fund-raising activities related to the event;
- commercial borrowing (from banks, etc. – this will have to be repaid with interest);
- commercial sponsorship from local or national companies;
- funding from trusts or other philanthropic bodies, often listed in national directories of funding agencies and trusts.

Sponsorship is not the only potential alternative income source for an event. Much depends on the type of event for what might be obtained from a range of sources. Local authorities or other funding agencies might be willing to put money into an event (for example, a sporting or tourism event) if an appropriate and suitable case is made to do so. But such a case must comply with the objectives of the funding body. It might be that there is some kind of social or other benefit to holding an event which the funding body could be interested in. The event might, for example, attract large numbers of tourists; or have an arts impact for which arts trusts and foundations might consider grants. It should be noted, though, not only that funding from public bodies requires time and care in applying, but also that the response of many public funding bodies is notoriously slow (Pick and Anderton, 1996).

The proposal for funding would have to say much more than 'This will attract a lot of tourists who will spend money in the town while they are here.' Measurement and quantification of the benefits will have to be stated. How many visitors will it attract? How many visitors per €1,000 spent? What will the visitors spend while they are at the event and how will this benefit local businesses and local people? Will there be a positive outcome in terms of public image? These are the types of questions that will have to be dealt with, very often, in order to get public funding (see also the case study on the French Grand Prix at Nevers for further details of the quantification of benefits for events).

Summary

The financial implications of organizing even a relatively simple activity or celebration are significant. A knowledge of finance is an especially useful attribute in an organizing team or committee. Not only have the obvious issues of cost control to be addressed, but a good understanding of the sources of revenue and income, and the mechanisms for adjusting ticket prices, as well as subsidiary revenue streams such as catering and retail, is increasingly useful. Careful monitoring and recording of purchases, expenditure and income is an integral part of the financial officer's responsibilities, as is the setting up of systems and procedures to ensure cash and other monetary control.

Reference List

Hall, C. M. (1992) *Hallmark Tourist Events*. London: Belhaven, pp. 50–9, 148–56.

Hussey, J. and Hussey, R. (1999) *Business Accounting*. Basingstoke: Macmillan.

Kotas, R. (1999) *Management Accounting for Hospitality and Tourism*. London: Thomson Business.

McDonnell, I., Allen, J. and O'Toole, W. (1999) *Festivals and Special Events Management*. Milton, Queensland: Jacaranda Wiley, pp. 166–88.

Morris, W. G. (1994) *The Management of Projects.* London: Thomas Telford, p. 245.

Pick, J. and Anderton, M. (1996) *Arts Administration.* London: E&F Spon, pp. 78–87.

Richards, B. (1992) *How to Market Tourist Attractions, Festivals and Special Events.* Harlow: Longman, pp. 49–64, 101–10.

Watts, D. (1998) *Event Management in Leisure and Tourism.* Harlow: Longman, pp. 52–9.

Wilson, R. M. S. and Chua, W. F. (1988) *Managerial Accounting.* London: Van Nostrand Reinhold, pp. 99–114.

Wood, F. and Lightowlers, P. (1985) *Purchasing, Costing and Control in the Hotel and Catering Industry.* Harlow: Longman, pp. 3–14.

CHAPTER 8

The Event:
Preparation, Logistics and Support Services

Aims

- To discuss the preparation phase for events, including logistics.
- To identify the range of support functions for events.
- To consider the key components of celebrations, including the creation of the appropriate ambience and atmosphere.

Introduction

The preparation and development phase for events is not necessarily separate from the planning phase – the two mostly run hand in hand. However, the business of getting an event ready involves considerable time, effort and hard work. At the point where the event is starting to be implemented, the number of people and the quantity of resources involved will begin to increase with the workload. The pace of preparation and development will also increase once the venue has been identified and orders begin to be placed for equipment, facilities and services. The logistics of ensuring that all these items arrive in time for the event in their proper place, in good condition and in the style or format that was ordered represents a considerable effort on the part of the event coordinator.

The support functions for events, such as food and drink, music and entertainment, technical and related activities and services, can be very complicated depending on the size and importance of the event. If you consider the sheer complexity of the preparations for even a modest family wedding it becomes evident how crucial careful logistical preparations are. Different types of events will require different support functions, which can be supplied directly by the organizers or contracted out. Where support functions are contracted out, the need for careful specification of the service being purchased is particularly relevant for event coordinators.

Getting everything in place for an event is not only a matter of the behind-the-scenes efforts in terms of logistics, organization and preparation, it is also crucial to the atmosphere and ambience which will be created. Events may be simple or complicated; in the modern world it is more difficult to impress an audience with an event, because the general public are very much more used to seeing events in the media and attending events. This means that the efforts put into creating an attractive ambience at a venue, in circumstances that might make its staging quite difficult, may have to be very considerable indeed. This stage of the process may have to take into account not only the venue and its environment, but also the design, decor, lighting, music, colour scheme and a whole range of other incidental but relevant factors. Nevertheless, we must bear in mind that at the vast majority of events it is the guests or visitors themselves who will help to create the atmosphere, simply by their presence or by their participation and involvement. The issue for the event organizer in creating an event which is well organized and enjoyable is to work smarter, not harder. To do this, a range of techniques are discussed in this chapter and in Chapter 10 (on project management) to help to ensure the event runs efficiently.

The Preparation Phase and Finding the Venue

At this point in creating an event we may not yet have identified the venue, let alone what other facilities and services we will need. But hand in hand with planning there will be the early exploration of issues such as what our key requirements are, including those factors critical to success. These might include the location of the event, the range of potential venues available, ease of access and the ability to ensure that all the necessary items of equipment, resources, personnel and visitors can get to the venue easily. So the preparation phase of the process will consist not only of venue finding but also of logistics. Logistics is the discipline of planning and organizing the flow of goods, equipment and people to their point of use. Logistics is important to events because of the need to concentrate resources on a particular location for a particular time (even if that event is multisite and taking place over a fairly long period of time). Without careful planning of this activity, the item which we need in order to undertake an event may not arrive correctly.

In logistics terms our supplies are not simply products and services; they also include the flow of customers and customer services. For example, when we choose a venue we must ensure that our potential customers, visitors or participants are able to get to it easily, using their typical mode of transport, and also that there is suitable and adequate access, for them, for supplies and in case of emergency. The Millennium Dome opening night served to highlight several logistical problems, including the supply of tickets, the unnecessary queuing and the lack of car parking at the Dome site itself. We can see from this example that logistics does not refer only to on-site activities.

Venue finding is probably one of the most important aspects of the development phase of an event. In some cases an event organizer might know exactly which venue to choose. In other cases the choice of venue may be extremely limited, especially in rural areas. In general, however, a reasonable choice of venue will be available. The first question an organizer will normally ask is: what location is required (bearing in mind the objectives of the event) and, then, what are the available venues within that location (bearing in mind any criteria that we have set up about selection, in the screening process)? Early on a number of questions have to be asked about the potential venue (and assuming we know something of the type of audience for the event and the event itself, as this will inform our judgement about the venue). For example, if our event were to be a national sales exhibition, then the venue would probably have to be large and central to the whole country. If our event was to be a town carnival, then the venue might cover several locations in the town as well as suitable areas for the assembly and dispersal of a carnival procession. Organizers may themselves have a good local knowledge, but if not, a visit to the area will be necessary to look around. Alternatively, a professional venue finding agency can be used; these are quite common and can be identified in the telephone book under 'conference/event organizers'. Normally an agency or organizer will come up with a shortlist of three or four possible venues. These venues will have to be visited and a checklist made about the particular requirements of the event in terms of the venue (Seekings, 1996). Whichever venue best matches the criteria, bearing in mind price considerations and the professionalism of the venue management, should be chosen (see Figure 8.1).

The site visits are useful, and the organizer needs to have a reasonable idea of the event requirements before visiting venues (go with a poor idea of what you need, and you give yourself problems later). These visits should be arranged via venue managers, or, for larger sites, the venue sales team. Where a professional venue finding agency has been used to identify possible venues, the agency may also be able to provide an organizer with a professional to help to inspect venues, for a small fee. It is important for organizers to have made out a list of questions to ask each venue before going, in addition to the checklist of criteria. Much depends on the event. Is a band required during the party? Is a stage needed? Will sound equipment be needed? And can the venue provide these?

Event_____   **Date:** _____
Name of venue: _____   Address: _____
Phone number: _____   _____
Fax number: _____   _____
General manager: _____   Event contact: _____
GM's e-mail: _____   Contact's e-mail: _____

What are the objectives of the event in relation to the venue?
_____

What factors are critical to the success of the event in relation to the venue? (What do you need?)
Factor 1_____
Factor 2_____
Factor 3_____

Does this venue satisfy these factors?
Factor 1: Yes ❑   No ❑   Factor 2: Yes ❑   No ❑   Factor 3: Yes ❑   No ❑

Site inspection: venue environment and location
General environment (e.g. leafy countryside, city centre) _____

Access	Good	OK	Poor	Comment
By road (car and taxi)	❑	❑	❑	
On foot/cycle	❑	❑	❑	_____
By bus/tram	❑	❑	❑	_____
By rail	❑	❑	❑	_____
Nearest station: _____				
By air	❑	❑	❑	_____

Nearest airport: _____
Identify any access problems related to loading/unloading/mobility impaired visitors/limitations of parking:
_____

Site inspection: venue facilities and services
Capacity of main area: _____   Capacity of support areas: _____
Capacity of parking: _____   Capacity of kitchens: _____
Area (sq. metres) main: _____   Area (sq. metres) support: _____
Is internal access for entry and exit of visitors, loading and the mobility impaired adequate?
_____

Is a scale plan of the venue available? If so, obtain one. If not, measure main features.
State ceiling height: _____m   State access door height: _____m
State access door width: _____m
Has the venue power? ___ How many power points?___ Lighting/dimmers ___
Has the venue gas? __ Air conditioning? _____ What sort of heating? _____
Attach a copy of the fire procedure to this checklist. In relation to the needs of your event, what other specialist facilities/services are available (sound system, presentation equipment, etc.) *or* are missing?
_____

Comment on your impression of the venue and the venue management
_____
_____

Figure 8.1   *Venue finding checklist. (See also website: www.conferencesdirect.co.uk)*

First impressions are important. The first impression an organizer gets may well be the same first impression that visitors and guests get. Organizers should pay attention to all their senses. What does the site look like? What are its surroundings? Is it attractive? What can be heard? Is it quiet, noisy, is it under a flightpath, does it have good acoustics? (Clap your hands to hear the echo or listen for dead areas in sound transmission.) What does it smell like. Is it neutral, does it smell of stale food? Does it have scented gardens? Are the toilets clean and fresh? Touch the furnishings and some of the equipment. Do these feel clean? Do your shoes stick to the floor or the carpets?

At your first visit you are probably not going to be able to taste anything, but if food is an element of your event, then once you have made a selection of venue, you may wish to try samples of the food you have selected, especially if the event is large or involves VIP catering, in order to see if the kitchen is up to the job. On your visit, try to make sure you see all the areas your visitors will use, not only the main room, site, arena or hall, but also the entrances, corridors, car parks, toilets and food service areas. Are these places well kept? Is there evidence of activity, cleanliness, good maintenance? These things are all indicators of an active and capable management at the venue. The more capable they are, the easier your job will be.

Logistics

Once given a venue, the event coordinator or logistics officer can address some of the major licensing and official preparation activities, such as permits and insurance (see Chapter 10). In logistics terms, services which have a long lead time of provision must be considered early on. The event may have special power requirements or it might need additional utilities laid on (e.g. telecoms, gas, water, sewerage, waste removal), which have typically long lead times to arrange, especially if groundwork has to be undertaken to put them in. The logistics officer has to be conscious of those event activities which have the longest lead times and have to be dealt with first. A logistics plan, showing these various needs and putting them into order, may have to be prepared.

It is useful to recognize that the nearer the event deadline is, the less able we will be to make big changes without having to spend enormous amounts of money and effort to make the changes. In short, there is a cut-off point at which the contractual arrangements have to stand (which varies depending on what supplies or services are being provided and how long they take). Logistics officers will need to draw together a potentially wide range of support functions for an event to work properly.

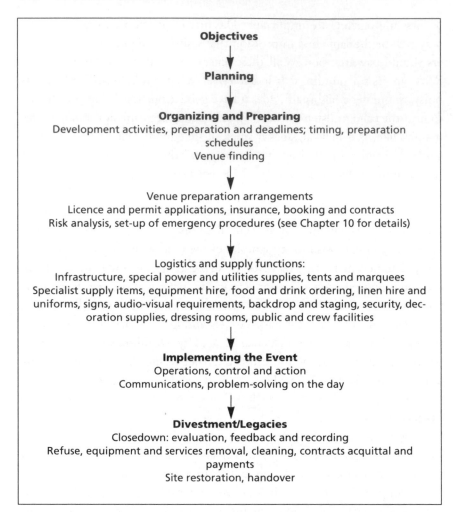

Objectives

↓

Planning

↓

Organizing and Preparing
Development activities, preparation and deadlines; timing, preparation
schedules
Venue finding

↓

Venue preparation arrangements
Licence and permit applications, insurance, booking and contracts
Risk analysis, set-up of emergency procedures (see Chapter 10 for details)

↓

Logistics and supply functions:
Infrastructure, special power and utilities supplies, tents and marquees
Specialist supply items, equipment hire, food and drink ordering, linen hire and
uniforms, signs, audio-visual requirements, backdrop and staging, security, dec-
oration supplies, dressing rooms, public and crew facilities

↓

Implementing the Event
Operations, control and action
Communications, problem-solving on the day

↓

Divestment/Legacies
Closedown: evaluation, feedback and recording
Refuse, equipment and services removal, cleaning, contracts acquittal and
payments
Site restoration, handover

Figure 8.2   *The events management process: organizational and logistical activities.*

The key to the implementation part of the event, i.e. running the event itself, is good communications. It is helpful to commit ideas and important issues to paper. With a large number of people to manage, it is impossible for one person to communicate 'in person' with them all. Therefore, many forms of communication can be used to help to ensure that people know what to do: briefings about plans, the event programme, the emergency procedures, etc. must take place. The logistics officer, working with the marketing officer and the overall event coordinator, must also organize pre-event meetings and use tools such as site maps, bulletins and newsletters to help to get across major issues to staff, crew, artists, volunteers and helpers.

Case Study 20

Festival of St John, Oporto

Oporto, situated on the River Douro in northern Portugal, holds a number of attractive and colourful events during the year. Its biggest event is probably the long summer festival in June, celebrating the festivities of a number of saints, including St Anthony, St Peter and, largest of all, St John. These kinds of festivals are common in many parts of Europe and are extremely historic and traditional.

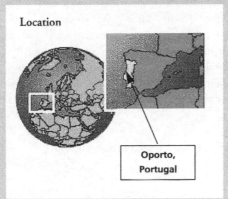

Location

Oporto, Portugal

Factbox
- Festival of St John, Oporto
- Has taken place for over 500 years.
- Is religious in origin.
- Local people make large numbers of *cascatas*, which are dioramas or models that refer to St John, using miniature figures.

Staging the festival is a combination of local informality, with people decorating their own houses, courtyards and streets, and formal organization in the form of practicalities provided by the city authorities and by the religious authorities related to St John's Eve. Local people build miniature theatrical scenes (dioramas) with figures to celebrate some aspect of the saint's life. These are displayed all over the city, which is decorated with flowers and plants, especially with leeks, basil and bunches of other aromatic plants. At the peak of the festivities, the summer solstice, people flood on to the streets in the evening in their best costumes for the traditional celebrations.

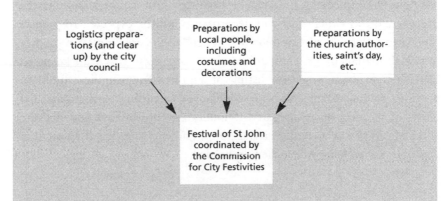

Logistics preparations (and clear up) by the city council

Preparations by local people, including costumes and decorations

Preparations by the church authorities, saint's day, etc.

Festival of St John coordinated by the Commission for City Festivities

Preparations therefore involve three main groups: local people, with traditional efforts, such as model-making (*cascatas*), decorating residential areas and dressing up; the city council, to coordinate the activities, promote the event and deal with the clear-up afterwards; and religious officials, for the formal activities associated with St John in the city's cathedral and churches. The department responsible for the coordination of these efforts is the Commission for City Festivities.

Based on this case:

The advance preparations for the festival of St John at Oporto are extremely informal, and led by local people. How do they know what to do, and how have such traditions been maintained over many centuries? The logistical preparations for the event do not, at first sight, involve any great complexity. Why is this, and is this approach suitable for other types of events? Oporto is a world heritage site. Do the preparations for the festivities and the festival itself help to attract visitors to the city in large numbers, or would visitors come anyway?

Related website for those interested in Oporto: www.portoturismo.pt

Supplies, transport and distribution

We have said that logistics is the discipline of planning and organizing the flow of goods, equipment and people to their point of use. Therefore logistics includes activities such as ticketing and enquiries (in cooperation with the marketing department), arrival and departure of visitors, the flow of people, equipment, suppliers, artists and crew around the venue. Within this, the preparation, opening and running of an event (whether it is a wedding reception or a coronation) depends on getting all the elements to the right place in time for a range of deadlines. This can be a complicated process and individual staff and departments will be expected to prepare their own order lists of requirements. Where events are being run by professional management companies, these organizations will keep on computer database a general listing of supplies and suppliers used for previous events, which can be easily adapted according to the particular needs of the one being prepared. Supplies can be ordered and delivery checked, usually at a central arrival point, and the supplies distributed as required to the places where they are needed.

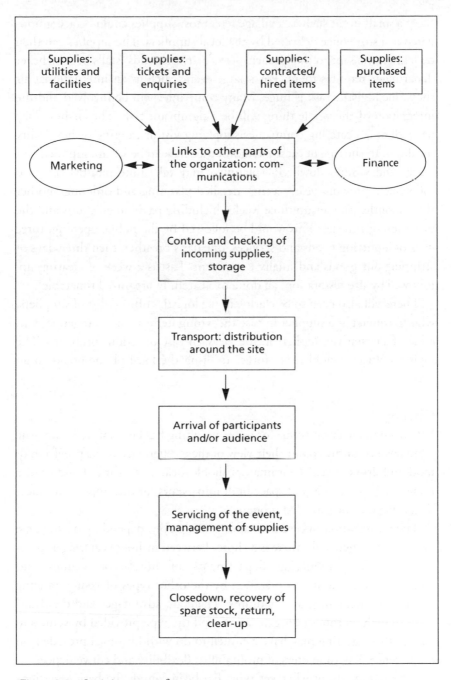

Figure 8.3   *Logistic sequence for events.*

At a small event such as a village fête, most supplies could be accommodated in a store once delivered by the local suppliers. The supplies can then be laid out or sent to the kitchen, service areas, stands, stalls or whichever department requires them. For a large event, such as an international air show, the logistics task is huge. Many companies will be involved and the integration of the whole thing will be a significant task. The airshow may have 20 or 30 catering companies supplying visitor catering or hospitality pavilions. In the case of these pavilions, they have to be set up, supplied regularly, and wound down. Pre-planning may take nine months (perhaps following a previous year's event); detailed planning and ordering another three months; site set-up three weeks, including pavilion erections and the provision of utilities. This would be followed by the public opening, three days of inputting goods and services, one day's breather, then three days of stripping out goods and finally equipment. Last is a week of clearing up, followed by site restoration, all done to a carefully organized timetable.

There will also need to be clarity, in the logistics officer's list of suppliers, who to contact at a supplier in case the wrong items turn up, together with a list of alternative suppliers in the areas, in case of serious problems. The logistics officer should never forget to bring the local phone books to an event!

Catering

When a suitable event venue for those attending has been created, one issue which will certainly colour their view of their experience is the provision of food and drink. Event coordinators should bear this in mind and ensure there is sufficient time and space built into events for this important aspect if catering is to be provided properly.

The organization of catering varies considerably, depending on the type of venue, but, generally, there is a choice between in-house catering as practised by the banqueting departments of hotel-type venues and contracted-out catering as practised by the other types of venue, ranging from public halls to sports stadiums. There are advantages and disadvantages to both methods of organization, and the type provided by venues to handle their catering may have as much to do with historical precedent in those venue as with matters of profitability, flexibility and convenience.

When a caterer, of whatever type, has been found, the basic questions and the starting points to determine what the visitor will have are the same. These are questions of the number of people, of refreshment times, of the budget and of the visitors themselves. It could be argued that one of the chief failings of catering provision at events is an insensitivity towards

Item	Size/type	No.	Supplier	To go to	Received/checked
Furniture					
Stacking chairs blue	Standard 2000	450	Red Dragon	Park arena	❏
Stacking chairs blue	Standard 2000	50	Red Dragon	Catering tent	❏
Office chairs blue	Operator	10	Red Dragon	Park office portacabins	❏
Round tables	1 metre	6	Red Dragon	Catering tent	❏
Square tables	1metre	6	Red Dragon	Catering tent	❏
Trestle tables	2 metres	2	Red Dragon	Catering tent	❏
Trestle tables	2 metres	2	Red Dragon	Park office portacabins	❏
Trestle tables	2 metres	1	Red Dragon	Park entrance gate tent	❏
Utilities					
Mobile toilet block	M/F Type 20	1	T. Crapper & Co.	100 metres west of catering tent	❏
Power	3 phase	2 lines	Mid Electric	Arena stage	❏
Power	8 socket supply	1 line	Mid Electric	Catering tent	❏
Mobile chiller room	32 cubic metre	1	Coolfridge Hire	Back of catering tent	❏
Tents and shades					
Marquee white	Deluxe 50 metre	1	Grand Tents	Catering tent as marked out	❏
Tent white	Standard 5 metre	1	Grand Tents	Park entrance tent as marked out	❏
Equipment					
Plates white	Dinner 25 cm	450	National Equip	Catering tent	❏
Plates white	Side 10 cm	450	National Equip	Catering tent	❏
Etc.	Etc.				

Figure 8.4 *Middleburg Festival equipment receival form.*

the type of people attending. There is a tendency towards standardized and rather predictable menus, which, while convenient for chefs and sales coordinators, may be inappropriate for certain types of visitors. The public attending events are better educated in food and drink than at any time in the past. The range of services on offer is essentially built around continuous provision throughout the event, rather than the traditional presentation of breakfast, lunch and dinner. The layout for cafeteria-type services also needs to be given careful thought. Bear in mind that people are inherently used to lining up in queues to do things. In an unfamiliar situation (such as at a new event) they will naturally revert to this method. Therefore, planning catering outlets at events to be 'free-flow' may be counter-productive – people may be confused and irritated, especially if there is a log-jam at the cash desk (see Figure 8.5).

In cases where there will be a large number of people at an event, queues at catering outlets can be relieved by having smaller outlets which deal only in drinks and small food. This helps to take the weight of demand off major

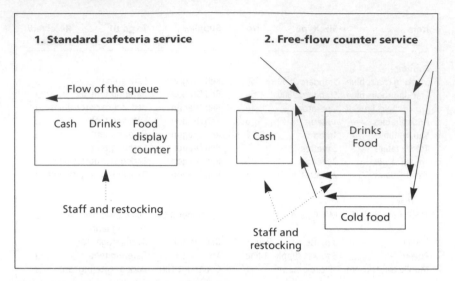

Figure 8.5   *Alternative cafeteria flow services.*

food counters. The same kind of rules apply to cafeteria service as to buffet service. Think carefully about how many people your counter can handle at once. Add more counters or small outlets to ease the crush.

Buffets are popular at events, and there are commonly two types: finger buffet or fork buffet. With the former, guests would normally stand, with the latter, guests would normally sit. The buffet food may be hot or cold or both. The timing issue is an important one. Many people will politely queue at a buffet, and this takes time and must be taken into account when laying a buffet. More than one direction or side of a buffet table should be available. It will take the average diner 20 seconds to load his or her plate. Multiply that by the number of people and you will understand why more than one buffet queue is needed for a large event. It should also be borne in mind that buffets are often understaffed. This leads to chaos, inability to restock and inability to clear tables. The normal buffet service ratio is one staff to 30 diners. This can be raised to 35 if serving international delegates. They are less likely to queue, and may simply descend on a buffet table. This must be taken into account when laying out the buffet. For international delegates the buffet should not, generally, be laid out in a linear fashion, but similar dishes can be laid out in various sections of a buffet, for variety.

Where events may feature a particular element, such as a gala dinner, organizers should ensure they have provided a seating layout for the event which will best suit the client (Shone, 1998; see Figure 8.6). For a full service meal, the typical service ratio is one staff to between ten and fifteen

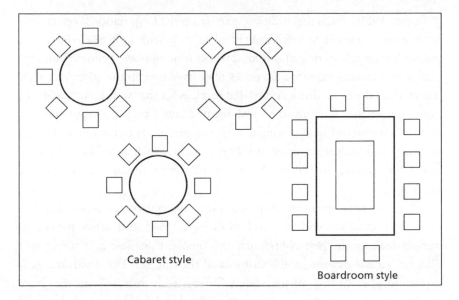

Figure 8.6 *Examples of seated meal plans (there are many others).*

diners, plus one member of drinks staff (for wine service) to every thirty diners.

Menu composition and the range of food provided are significant in terms of the menu available, but are also about what a venue may offer within its capabilities. For example, a range of individually priced dishes may be suggested to the organizer (given what the venue can provide), who then chooses a selection to suit the likely visitor profile. This is based on the view that organizers know something of the style, likes and dislikes of the public. However, not all do, and organizers often pick dishes they themselves like, only to find that visitors criticize their poor judgement. Menu composition is, therefore, not simply a technical issue, but also a serious question which organizers can ask themselves. What are our potential visitors like? What are their demographics? What are their most popular styles of eating?

The chief 'back of house' players in catering operations are the head chef and the bars manager, in the sense that they are responsible for food and drink costings, pre-planning, ordering and preparation of food and drink. Nevertheless, it must be remembered that the initial enquiry and first meeting between the venue and the organizer will probably take place with the venue sales manager or sales coordinator, though some organizers will ask for the chef to be present, to find out what the venue's caterers are able to produce.

The alternative is to contract out the catering to a specialist organization

(Warner, 1989). Such organizations vary from the large national operations with many contracts to small individual caterers with only one contract or *ad hoc* business. Catering of this kind is common in many venues. Contractual arrangements vary. Some venues may have one approved caterer who provides all the food, drink and related services for that venue. Alternatively, some venues may have an 'approved' list of caterers they are happy to work with, these caterers being familiar with the venue, its operation and management and typical requirements. Some venues, such as public halls, may allow any caterer, including the event organizers themselves, to do the catering.

The advantage of contracting-out is that the organizers do not need to concern themselves with the technicalities of food and drink provision, simply making the best contractual arrangement possible and acting as a link between the client (or the visitor) and the caterers. The disadvantage is some loss of control: a contract caterer interested in cutting costs may have no incentive to provide a quality service. A related disadvantage is less well known, but probably more serious – loss of flexibility. An in-house catering function is, in practice, highly flexible and can provide peripheral activities which contractors do not (e.g. provide an 'on the spot' VIP dinner for a key client). The chief problem is that contracts are often badly written, ignoring a wide range of needs, some of which may only occur occasionally but are nevertheless vital, and which a contractor will charge extra for. Issues involved in the determination of menus and refreshments include:

- The number of visitors attending and expected to buy refreshments, and how many refreshment opportunities a visit to the event might represent.
- The number of staff or crew who have to be fed and at what times.
- Details about the visitor group themselves: who they are; typical food interests; age group; male/female balance; special dietary needs (e.g. vegetarians).
- Whether there is a budget for refreshments, or whether food is exclusive of the ticket price.
- The expertise and ability of the catering staff.
- The type of catering facilities, storage capacity and equipment available at the venue.
- Whether the food/drink is brought in from outside and how it is brought in.
- What utilities and mains services are available at the venue.

The number of visitors attending and the number expected to eat may not be the same. At some kinds of events visitors may bring in their own food; for example, to a summer evening open air concert. For the caterer it is also of importance to have approximate numbers up to two weeks prior to the event and final numbers two days in advance, in order to enable accurate food, drink and equipment ordering. A deadline must be enforced for bookings where the event has elements such as sit-down gala dinners as opposed to continuous through-the-day catering. The time of refreshments should also be checked between the organizers and the caterers on the day.

Visitors and some sections of the public attending events may be traditional in their tastes, but they are no longer uneducated in food. Travel abroad, ethnic and specialist restaurants at home and wide ranging food programmes and articles in the media have engendered a far greater range of tastes within the public. Venues and even hotels are not always in the forefront of change when developing menus, nor perhaps would the public necessarily wish them to be; but it is essential that the food presented at an event is of a suitable standard, and appropriate to the type of people at the event. Sometimes it is not, partly owing to insufficient attention to the type of customer or visitor, sometimes partly owing to the lack of competitor analysis and complacency on the part of venues; what in other industries would be called benchmarking. Older banqueting managers and caterers may recall the days when it was *de rigeur* to go out and eat in competitor establishments, or at similar events. This is extremely rare among modern managers and the quality of event food sometimes suffers from the lack of knowledge of what competitors are providing, or a lack of awareness about how competitors' efforts might reasonably be exceeded.

There are other common weaknesses in event dining, some of which are training related. Event dining often relies on casual staff, even on volunteers, and this is a particular difficulty. Such staff may have limited food preparation knowledge or poor hygiene training, or may have gleaned their meagre knowledge of food and drink service from other staff or from *ad hoc* demonstrations by the head waiter(ess) or head cook. Some considered effort needs to go into training, even if, for waiting staff, this only amounts to a half-hour briefing before service about the food, the drink, who to serve first and how to look around for diners trying to attract staff attention. Nevertheless, where professional caterers are present, either in-house or contracted, the standard of staff training is generally very good.

Meals are often intended as the highlight of an event, sometimes in the form of gala dinners or theme dinners to provide a fitting end (Goldblatt, 1990). Regrettably, they are sometimes badly done, with poorly cooked food, indifferent service and poorly presented staff. Style and content at many events is as important in this environment as it is in the fine restaurants of great hotels, and guests often expect the same standards of service at an outdoor event as they would receive in a fine restaurant. The problems in delivering this for outdoor event caterers may be extremely severe: anything from having no mains services, electricity, drainage, etc. to having to bring in fresh water in sealed containers and fresh food in chiller lorries, or even having no proper access to muddy fields where outdoor events are being held except by farm tractor or golf buggy (Konopka, 1995).

A further issue is the feeding of staff and crew, especially volunteers. The feeding of staff should be a charge supported as part of the budget. How many staff and crew need to be fed? With what? At what time and by whom? When will the staff dining room be open, if there is one? Do staff and crew pay for reasonable refreshments in such a dining room? If not, where and how are the staff and crew to be fed? Is food and drink for volunteers entirely free, or subsidized, as part of the contribution for their help?

On a final catering note, it is far better to plan activities (such as food restocking) as a matter of professional routine than to allow something to go wrong and have to expend inordinate effort putting it right. This can be called the 'salt pot' syndrome. If a function is badly prepared and not checked, then there are things in there waiting to create maximum disruption: the missing salt pot will be discovered by a guest about to consume his or her main course, who will, rightly, demand one at the busiest point of service, causing widespread disruption. In scenes from a comedy, typically there will be no salt pots in the function area, and the staff will have to go to the washing up area to get one, a location where, mysteriously, there will be no salt pots. This will necessitate the slowest washer up in the entire site having to search for, wash, dry and fill a fresh salt pot, taking the maximum care, because it is now a 'special' salt pot, and thus taking the maximum possible time. The guest's food, now cold, will have to be returned to the kitchen, and the guest will have to wait for it to be heated up. In the meantime the rhythm of service for the whole function will have been destroyed (Slack *et al.*, 1998). This kind of unprofessional shambles can often be seen in catering tents where staff have not been trained to maintain the flow of key supplies as they go along; or where there are a depressing number of staff behind a counter, but none of them are actually serving, to the considerable anger and distress of a large number of potential customers watching them do anything and everything except serve. Poor managers and lazy staff may regard good preparation as a nuisance, but it is, in fact, the bedrock on which all else is built.

Drinks services

Bars for events are essentially of two types: paid and cash. Paid bars are those where the client or organizer has arranged for some element of payment for guests, let us say for VIPs, to have free drinks, because the company or association is paying. In some cases, organizers may specify that guests may cover their first drink by this method, but such arrangements must be made clear, with strict monitoring applied. It is far better to serve a predetermined aperitif (e.g. juice, a spritzer or a fizz) than to attempt to monitor who is 'just' having the first drink. The alternative method is to set a bar limit, which the organizer will pay for, and after which delegates pay for their own. Again, this method has severe limitations and could result in an undignified scrum at the bar to get as many free ones as possible before guests have to pay. It is far easier, and much more normal, to have a cash bar. Guests pay for what they have.

Bars at events should normally be staffed at a ratio of one member of staff to every 75 drinkers (for example, at a pre-dinner reception). These ratios can be subject to some variation; for instance, experience of a particular event may conclude that guests on previous visits have been particularly heavy drinkers, thus requiring a strengthening of the service. The importance of this latter point is that the manager responsible for the food and drink service at an event dinner (or lunch or breakfast) must be flexible. It is far too easy to assume that a preset standard will do for all functions; this is an easy approach, but leads to lack of attention to the detail of staffing and potentially serious mistakes such as under- or over-staffing.

There is also the related issue of drinks served during a meal. The most common method is for organizers to include an allowance of one or two glasses of wine or juice with a meal for guests. Thereafter, diners may buy their own wine on payment to the sommelier (wine waiter/ess). Similarly, liqueurs are usually dispensed on a cash basis. Drinks service tends to go on the basis of one bottle of wine (75 cl) to six persons; with a common ratio of three to one in favour of white to red, in Northern Europe, depending on the type of guest. Spirit service is of the order of 28 (25 ml) measures to a bottle. Jugged iced plain water should always be put on the table before the meal arrives. There is a belief that diners will not drink alcohol if water is put on the tables. This belief is fallacious, and it always results in tables asking for water and service being disrupted to get it. Such disruptions reflect an amateur approach.

Finally, the following points in food and drinks services should be considered:

- Have licences for alcohol and food sales (e.g. from stalls) been applied for and granted?
- Is there sufficient space for food, drink and equipment storage, preparation and service?
- Are these areas easily accessible, and do they have the necessary utilities and comply with hygiene regulations?
- What are the set-up, opening, closing and departure times?
- What cleaning and clearing arrangements are there? What arrangements or equipment have been put in place for cleaning emergencies?
- Are there selection criteria for a mix of catering providers, and what arrangements are there for them to pay for their concession, pitch or stall areas?

Technical facilities

The technical services that events coordinators and venues are expected to provide are becoming increasingly sophisticated, to the extent that event coordinators may choose to outsource the hi-tech needs of clients to production or multimedia companies. The larger and more important the event, the greater the likelihood of the need for specialists, though a contributory difficulty is that venue managers may not be sufficiently knowledgeable of the capabilities of production companies and of contemporary technology, which develops extremely quickly.

Video projection of various kinds is available and is often used in conjunction with other media. Multimedia can include video, computer-generated text and graphics, transfer of pictures from digital cameras and the insertion of sound or video into presentations. Similarly, rapid development in communications has seen increasing use of video-conferencing and, at large-scale events, satellite links from one continent to another, enabling presentation of a speaker in, say, Frankfurt, to be made on a video wall in Bilbao. There is also the issue of the image a client may wish to foster among the audience. Consequently, there has been a significant adoption of theatrical scene-building techniques to provide backdrops for events. Large-scale integrated staging and backdrops are mainly the province of production companies. (See next section.)

The other frequent technical issue is that of sound and the need for sound reinforcement, in all but the smallest events. Sound reinforcement is provided by the use of microphones, amplifiers and loudspeakers. Technical skill and careful preparation can provide a presentation of considerable effectiveness. In terms of the soundtrack there are issues of copyright for music and video and also, in venue terms, the quality of the facilities and the acoustics of the design. The development of the technology to entertain an audience has moved extremely rapidly, from the point at which, twenty years ago, the highest level of technology would have been a 35 mm film projector of the kind used to project cinema films to a whole range of presentation methods ranging from the laser projector to the video wall.

If venues have suitable equipment available, the venue management and technical staff should request that presenters come and test their material at least a week prior to the event. This particularly applies to computer presentations. Not all systems are compatible and minor glitches such as cabling problems or insufficient attention to text size for projections are as much a problem as compatibility (or lack of compatibility) of the equipment and software itself. It is unreasonable to expect that hi-tech presentations will work first time unless the speaker and venue are regular partners. In addition, the level of technical skill required to solve the simplest of equipment problems is not always available on the spot. Increasing sophistication of communications is also permitting advances in how, and where, events can be held. However, the resources required to do this may have to be brought in specially.

Backdrops and staging

While technical support may be thought to be essentially aural or visual reinforcement (additional sound or lighting systems), it is increasingly the case that event organizers (on behalf of a more sophisticated public) are looking for a standard of event which is extremely high, and are willing to pay for it. The backdrop, or staging, is a major concern. It not only provides the location of a screen but is also the place where a corporate or marketing image is demonstrated (Goldblatt, 1990). The backdrop may, of course, be simple: a contained screen with banner and a little special lighting. On the other hand, the backdrop may be a matter of considerable technical expertise incorporating stage design elements (Holt, 1993). These elements may range from the preparation and construction of stage flats (Thomas, 1991) to back projection and theatrical style lighting. Gobos (light projectors) are often used for backdrops. These projection screen designs which can be provided from a range of prepared formats, such as cityscapes or starfields or, more commonly, be purpose made with a logo or theme to use as a backdrop.

It is also more common for large-scale events to use video walls composed of a bank of TV monitors. This has been a feature of special events at concerts and gigs for some time, to enable very large (often outdoor) audiences to see the performers. Where backdrops are constructed and set up by a production company, the company may work regularly with a particular venue (as most of the large venues have links with local production companies), but where this is not the case the production company will have to undertake preparatory site work to assess factors such as available space, power, structural capacities and access to the hall or arena in order to do the job properly. The company will also work closely with the event coordinator or logistics officer to ensure everything gets to the right place when it is needed. For this, a production schedule will be drawn up (see Figure 8.7).

Lighting

The lighting of venues has a number of purposes. In terms of function rooms themselves the main purposes are to provide ambient lighting, highlighting of artists and lighting of backdrops, and to enhance the atmosphere. In the other areas of venues the lighting has to provide adequate background illumination in both public and support areas, and provide some decorative illumination, particularly in VIP rooms, dining areas and foyers. The final lighting issue is one of provision for safety, particularly in terms of exits and traffic routes in and around the venue or site.

Diffused illumination is necessary in the public areas of a building. Corridors, toilets, foyers and reception areas should be well lit, though not harshly so. This is necessary to enable the proper functioning of these areas, to ensure safety and security, and to maintain a pleasant general ambience. Consideration must also be given to lighting control systems, dimmers and sensor switches. Typically the scalar illumination of public rooms should be of the order of 200 lux, with corridors and background areas at approximately 100 lux (Lawson, 1995).

Emergency lighting is essential, and a legal requirement, in public buildings. Typically this is provided by secondary battery powered light lasting up to two hours, activated by the fire alarm system or a power failure. Exits should be clearly illuminated and the emergency lighting adequate to allow means of escape. In some modern buildings floor lighting strips are provided along exit routes, similar to those in aircraft floors to direct people to emergency exits. Security lighting is also necessary for areas containing expensive equipment, such as computers. Externally, particularly in car parks and around the building, good lighting is needed to ensure visitors feel secure. Lighting should be provided right through the venue, from the various public areas to the place of final exit.

Middleburg Festival Production Schedule 2001

Start at	Production	Finish by
Preparatory work		
Monday 27 August		
08.00	Coordinator's briefing at Park House, welcome volunteers, coffee	08.30
08.30	Site checks of Festival Park	09.00
09.00	Mark out parking, arena, market, marquee and tent sites	11.00
11.00	Hold meeting with emergency services, council representatives and others	12.00
12.00	Lunch on Park House terrace, delivered by Anna's Bakery (at 11.30)	13.00
13.00	Coordinators to assist afternoon deliveries of tents, utilities, portacabins, etc.	17.00
17.00	Hand over to night security man (and complete any outstanding set-ups)	17.30
Set-up and rehearsals		
Tuesday 28 August		
08.00	Coordinators' briefing at Park House, coffee	08.30
08.30	Coordinate arrival of supplies, check arriving items, direct to correct area	12.00
12.00	Lunch on Park House terrace, delivered by Anna's Bakery (at 11.30)	13.00
13.00	Organize volunteers to set up arena, market, catering and entrance tents	16.00
16.00	Check completion of set up, arrival of supplies, chase outstanding items	17.00
17.00	Volunteers' tea on Park House terrace, delivered by Anna's Bakery (16.30)	18.00
17.00	Issue volunteers with T-shirts, badges, site maps and answer any questions	18.00
18.00	Test all services, list items not working for attention Wednesday a.m.	19.00
19.00	Middleburg Festival Orchestra rehearsal	22.00
22.00	Hand over to night security	22.15
Festival event		
Wednesday 29 August		
08.00	Coordinator's briefing at Park House, coffee	08.30
08.30	Attend to outstanding problems, get volunteers to their posts, check signs	09.30
09.30	Check Festival market	10.00
10.00	Check Middleburg Band is ready near Venetian Bridge	10.10
10.10	Welcome Mayor, provide coffee in Entrance Tent	10.25
10.25	Go with Mayor to Venetian Bridge for opening speech and tape cutting	10.45
10.45	Festival opens, band plays light music, festival market opens	10.45
12.00	Volunteers and band lunch (rotation) in Catering Tent	13.00
14.00	Afternoon concert by Middleburg Band	16.00
16.00	Parade by Middleburg youth organizations	17.00
17.00	Various music soloists and small groups scheduled to play in Catering Tent	19.00
19.00	Guests' arrival for main evening concert	19.30
19.30	Main evening concert in arena, seats and picnic places	22.00
19.30	Festival market closes down	20.00
20.00	Volunteers' dinner on Park House Terrace (supplied by Catering Tent)	21.00
21.00	Catering Tent closes after concert intermission	21.10
22.30	Coordinator hands over to night security	22.45
Closedown		
Thursday 30 August		
08.00	Coordinators' briefing at Park House, coffee	08.30
08.30	Suppliers arrive to remove utilities, tents, return equipment	13.00
12.00	Volunteers' lunch on Park House terrace, delivered by Anna's Bakery	13.00
13.00	Volunteer litter pickers, site cleaners complete clearing	15.00
15.00	Hand over site to park keeper; site repairs and lawn restoration begin	17.00

Figure 8.7   *Example of a logistics production schedule.*

Sound and communications

Historically, the 'sound system' at venues was, at best, a microphone and a couple of loudspeakers, and if you were lucky an amplifier and a mixer. This tends to be inadequate for current needs. Consequently, provision of professional sound systems is often necessary. Not only is there the issue of the audience being able to hear the proceedings, there are also the issues of the need for sound reinforcement to go with visual tools, video and multimedia presentations, to accompany the set and to provide atmosphere, as well as the whole range of aural stimulation for an audience at an event.

Notwithstanding copyright law (for which there are various requirements, including payments for public entertainment and public performance), music may be taken from CD, minidisks or whatever system is available. Major venues are usually equipped to provide modern sound equipment, but while almost every home has a CD player, not enough hotels or municipal venues are so equipped. Organizers wishing to incorporate good quality sound often have to hire in the equipment to provide it. Companies providing equipment are able to supply packages which include not only public address (PA) systems but also complete music systems. Given the complexity of these things, a package, including the hire of a technician (again an element few venues are able to provide), is often necessary.

The loudspeaker system may, in some cases, be built into a room such as an arena or large hall, but is often in the form of quite large portable loudspeakers. These would normally be set up between presenters and audience, and would also be quite high up, at least above head height for a seated audience, to reduce the amount of sound absorbed by the audience. Most loudspeakers will be stand- or floor-mounted, but in purpose-built venues they can often be ceiling-hung from gantries designed for them. There are some issues of aesthetics to be borne in mind and increasingly loudspeakers are screened by some means such as lightweight curtaining, floral displays or careful illumination around them, so that they are in relative seclusion.

Where an event is extremely large, and takes place in an arena-type venue, there may also be a need to allow communication between more than one technician and between coordinators. For this purpose it is preferable to provide a communication ring. While this can be done using 'walkie talkie' radios or mobile phones, there is a danger of these interfering with other systems and of failure in an emergency. In consequence the communications ring must be a land line. Sufficient time must be allowed for crews to set up extensive systems in the case of a large event and to obtain frequencies for events radio communications, if these are needed. The logistics

---

Contact Listing
Add contacts to the list as you make them (in alphabetical order)

Telephones: M, mobile; W, workplace; H, home

                                                  Date/time of this list: 24/03/2001 14.05

Internal Contact Network

Name	Job	Base Location	Phone	Radio
Jo Example	Event Coordinator	Site Office	07720 123456 (M)	Yes
			01234 234567 (H)	
Marc Sample	Volunteer Leader	Catering Tent	None	Yes
Mike Specimen	Stage Technician	Stage	01334 654321 (W)	No
Etc.				
Etc.				

External Contacts and Suppliers

Name	Address	Phone	Fax	E-mail
Catering equipment:				
National Equipment	Arboretum 12 Castle Hill Middleburg Scotland SG1 3PQ	01786 123456	01786 123457	jock@necatering.com
Furniture:				
Red Dragon Hire	Ty Gwyn Fford Uwd Abertawe Wales SA6 5RE	01792 123456	01792 123457	rhys@reddragon.co.eu
Marquee hire:				
Etc.				
Etc.				

Figure 8.8 *Logistics: communications contacts list.*

officer should, when planning the provision of communications, prepare a contact listing, for both internal and external contacts. This acts as a kind of event phone book and saves trying to track down contacts from bits of paper, and should be built up as the event is being created (see Figure 8.8).

Amenities, cleaning and clearing

Cleaning and clearing are issues sometimes neglected in the servicing of venues, sites and events. It is essential that when there is a break in the programme, or at any other convenient point, the opportunity is taken for minor rubbish clearing, bin emptying, replenishment of consumables and other stock. This should be planned to happen at regular intervals and can be regarded as 'preventative' action. Cleaning equipment and materials must be available and accessible to the support staff. It may be a simple case of needing to clear up a broken glass. On the other hand, a guest may have over-indulged at dinner and in the bar and proceeded to throw up in the grand manner on the way to the lavatories, resulting in multi-coloured vomit all over the corridor. Delay in responding to these crises, major and minor, is typically due to lack of equipment, material and forethought.

In terms of the provision of amenities, the general rule is to provide one toilet for every 75 people (of each gender). This can be increased for VIP events. Portable toilets, for example, can be hired in blocks. Different standards of facility can be also hired, as well as shower blocks if required. It is essential to provide servicing for event toilets and supervision to ensure that effective cleaning is being done. There are admitted difficulties of maintaining cleanliness in facilities that are not only used for ablutions, but may possibly be used by drug users or by people having sex in them. Nevertheless, proper systems for servicing and supervision are just as necessary for cleaning and amenity provision as any other support service. As with most other activities, this can be contracted out if necessary.

Creating the Ambience

Ambience is often significant to the creation of a good event. An event with the right ambience can be a huge success. An event with the wrong ambience can be a huge failure. At a personal event, such as a birthday party, the ambience may be created by the people who are there, without the need for anything else – good company among friends can make an excellent event.

Case Study 21

Glastonbury Festival

In a number of large fields on Worthy Farm, in Somerset, owned by Michael Eavis, nestling in the rolling green English countryside, 100,000 people gather to listen to bands playing anything from hip hop to jazz. This is Glastonbury, put on by Michael Eavis, a large number of volunteers and some paid staff almost every year at the summer solstice (not quite every year, because sometimes the land needs to be given a rest). This is a farm and it has real cows. In fact, at the first festival, the admission price included free milk for the 1,500 people who attended it then, in 1971.

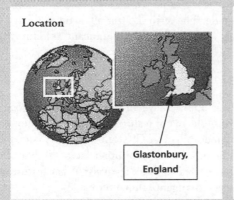

Location

Glastonbury, England

Factbox
- Glastonbury Festival, England.
- Attracts 100,000 people over three days.
- Employs some 1,700 during the event (excluding volunteers and pre-event contractors).
- Admission price in 2000 was €140.
- Famous for its informality and its mud.

Glastonbury has, over the thirty or so years of its existence, become internationally famous. It has played host to hundreds of bands and individuals. It is 'peculiarly British' in the type of people it attracts, a cross-section of the music loving public. It is relaxed in a hippy, new age kind of way. It is well known for the nature of its portable toilets and, in rainy summers (this is England), its seas of mud. Although there are headline bands each year, the programme is not especially fixed, but might contain over 50 bands or acts over the three days, who play on several sound stages throughout the farm area. There is a tendency for much of what goes on to be impromptu, and because of its rural situation it plays all night (to the annoyance of a few vocal local residents).

The general theme has tended to be dance music, which makes for an enjoyable social environment. The social inclusiveness of the festival also means that considerable charitable funds are raised for Greenpeace, Oxfam, CND and other local and national charities. The audience is catered for by the provision of facilities such as the festival markets, which include over 700 stalls in five or so main market areas, which are laid out in pre-sold pitches, in effect a way of licensing stalls. These markets are grouped together around key services such as water, electricity and toilets. Camping, in the open, in tents, vans, motor caravans, caravans and flashy winnebagoes (big motor homes) is a feature of Glastonbury, and the campsite fields have various facilities, including campsite cafés. In the evenings the warm glow of campfires in the summer dusk contributes to much of the atmosphere of the festival, also created by its location, in a beautiful valley extending towards the Tor (rocky hill) at Glastonbury.

The festival has also had a number of impacts. Its informality (as well as the sound) did not go down well with some locals, to the extent that in 1981 the local Member of Parliament tried to stop the festival by creating a law (via the British Parliament) which meant that all festivals in Britain had to be licensed by the local authority. The intention was to stop the Glastonbury Festival, but the local authority approved the licence, and continues to do so. The festival has become sufficiently important that it also played a major role in a recent overhaul of the UK event safety guide. The festival, after all, attracts a large number of visitors and participants and contributes a significant amount of money to the local area and to those local businesses associated with it.

Based on this case:

In what way does the setting of Glastonbury have an impact on the atmosphere and style of the festival? Identify the major features of the surroundings and the communal lifestyle which predominate at Glastonbury. Is the atmosphere solely due to the type of music or are a range of other factors in place? Can these factors be successfully transferred to other festivals? What features make the Glastonbury Festival unusual in organizational terms?

Related website for those interested in Glastonbury: www.glastonburyfestivals.co.uk
For media material consult the *Guardian* website on: www.guardianunlimited.co.uk
You will have to search the latter.

Some events may need a little help to go well. As at a birthday party, there might be the need for decorations, music and games, as well as food and drink. But it is relevant that the presence of these things does not, in any way, guarantee that things will go well. One can have a wonderful environment, expensive themed decor, large amounts of excellent food and drink and the event could still not be quite the success the organizers intended. One of the roles of an events coordinator is to try to ensure the event succeeds by careful attention to detail and by trying to encourage the desired outcome. Berkley (1996) illustrates some components in trying to create atmosphere at an event, as do Bateman and Hoffman (1999) in their discussion of the physical environment of service operations. In rather simpler terms we can consider the staging and ambience of an event to comprise a number of interlinked factors (see Figure 8.9).

The physical setting of an event, which deals with various design and staging activities, is primarily intended to look after the surroundings of the event and the visitor's responses to the surroundings. Visitors respond to physical stimuli on their senses of smell, sight, touch, hearing and taste. The physical responses to a pleasant meal environment are well understood, and much the same applies to an event environment.

An event environment is probably quite complicated, in certain situa-

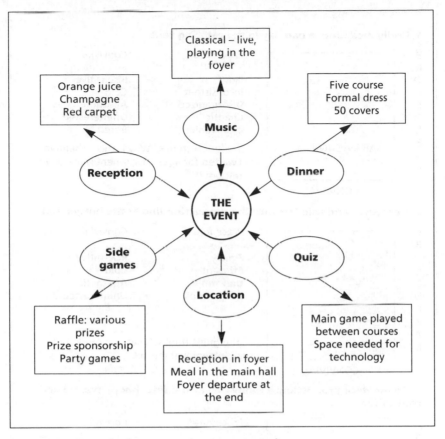

Figure 8.9   *Example of component elements at a quiz dinner.*

tions. Suppose we are organizing a medieval theme night. In order to be effective, the planning and execution of the theme night will have to appeal to all the senses, so as to provide a believable themed environment which would be convincing to the guests. This environment might require the careful selection of a suitable venue, as it would be easier to adapt a suitable building than to create a total medieval experience in a marquee (though this could be done, with enough time and resources). After this, all the elements of the theme could be prepared, ranging from the decor to the costumes.

The physical elements, of surroundings, backdrops, props, layout, equipment, personal artefacts, etc., go towards making up what Bitner (in Bateman and Hoffman, 1999) refers to as the 'holistic environment'. This environment, together with the cognitive, emotional and physiological responses of the guests (as well as staff, crew, artists and musicians) helps to make up what people feel about the event, and will also help to determine

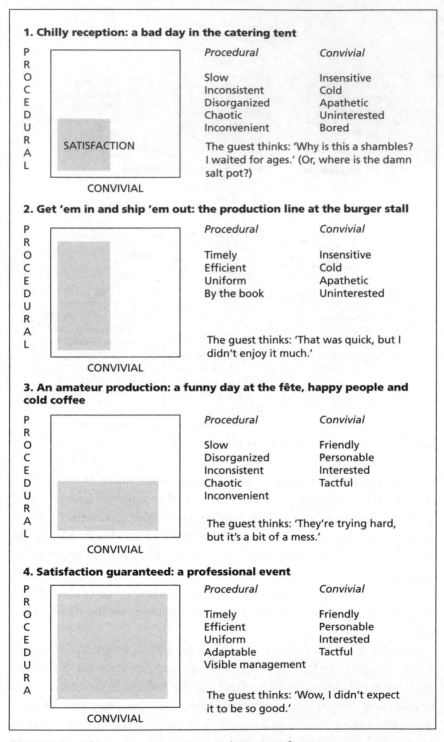

1. Chilly reception: a bad day in the catering tent

Procedural	Convivial
Slow	Insensitive
Inconsistent	Cold
Disorganized	Apathetic
Chaotic	Uninterested
Inconvenient	Bored

The guest thinks: 'Why is this a shambles? I waited for ages.' (Or, where is the damn salt pot?)

2. Get 'em in and ship 'em out: the production line at the burger stall

Procedural	Convivial
Timely	Insensitive
Efficient	Cold
Uniform	Apathetic
By the book	Uninterested

The guest thinks: 'That was quick, but I didn't enjoy it much.'

3. An amateur production: a funny day at the fête, happy people and cold coffee

Procedural	Convivial
Slow	Friendly
Disorganized	Personable
Inconsistent	Interested
Chaotic	Tactful
Inconvenient	

The guest thinks: 'They're trying hard, but it's a bit of a mess.'

4. Satisfaction guaranteed: a professional event

Procedural	Convivial
Timely	Friendly
Efficient	Personable
Uniform	Interested
Adaptable	Tactful
Visible management	

The guest thinks: 'Wow, I didn't expect it to be so good.'

Figure 8.10 *The event service experience and visitor satisfaction.*

how guests interact socially at the event, how they respond to staff and whether they stay and enjoy themselves.

In addition to the setting of the event and its surroundings are the service factors as perceived by the guests. Many events are run by amateurs and volunteers, and this may be a key part of the experience. If the client is paying a professional to put on a medieval theme evening, he or she is likely to have certain expectations of the event and its service standards. If, on the other hand, the event is a cooperative one, put on by volunteers and amateurs in their spare time, and by their own efforts, the expectations of the event and its service standards may be different. Service at events might be thought of in terms of procedural characteristics and conviviality characteristics, as exemplifed in Figure 8.10 (I am grateful to Rudi Drost of the Colchester Institute for expressing this concept in relation to events).

Summary

This chapter has discussed the preparation and support activities for events, including logistics and the ordering and supply of goods, equipment and the other supplies needed to ensure everything is ready at the correct time, and in the correct place. All these elements have to be assembled in a way that will help the event coordinator to create the right kind of event, not only in terms of the efficiency of organization itself but also in terms of its ambience and atmosphere, so that visitors to the event will regard it as having been enjoyable to attend and well run.

Reference List

Bateman, J. E. G. and Hoffman, K. D. (1999) *Managing Services Marketing*, 4th edn. Fort Worth, TX: Dryden, pp. 135–49.

Berkley, B. J. (1996) 'Designing services with function analysis', *Hospitality Research Journal*, **20** (1), 73–100.

Goldblatt, J. J. (1990) *Special Events*. New York: Van Nostrand Reinhold, pp. 65–8, 73–7, 107–17.

Holt, M. (1993) *Stage Design and Properties*. London: Phaidon, pp. 36–51.

Konopka, C. (1995) 'The big event', *Caterer and Housekeeper*, 18 May, 64–6.

Lawson, F. (1995) *Hotels and Resorts*. Oxford: Butterworth Heinemann, pp. 295–8.

Seekings, D. (1996) *How to Organise Effective Conferences and Meetings*, 6th edn. London: Kogan Page, pp. 94–6, 135–207, 304–6, 333–5.

Shone, A. (1998) *The Business of Conferences*. Oxford: Butterworth Heinemann, p. 93.

Slack, N. (1998) *Operations Management*, 2nd edn. London: Pitman, pp. 703–6.

Thomas, T. (1991) *Create Your Own Stage Sets*. London: A&C Black, pp. 54–87.

Warner, M. (1989) *Recreational Foodservice Management*. New York: Van Nostrand Reinhold, pp. 11–17.

CHAPTER 9

Marketing and Public Relations for Events

Aims

- To explore some of the key marketing issues of events management including budgetary and timing issues.
- To suggest appropriate marketing and public relations techniques that events organizers can use.
- To consider some of the marketing needs for both new events and repeat events.

Introduction

As with many aspects of events management, the breadth and range of types of special events gives rise to the problem of trying to generalize about how to market events when those events are intended to fulfil very different objectives and may be targeted at very different markets. The key to how an event will be marketed is the target market itself – what kind of people will attend, where they live and how they can be influenced to attend. Marketing is not simply about pushing out a few posters and hoping for the best. We need to know as much as possible about the target market and to be able to split that target market into convenient segments in order to understand what techniques we can use to make them aware of the event and attract them to it. We also need to consider issues of differential pricing for the different target market segments. People have limited discretionary income (the money they can spend freely on things that interest them, sometimes referred to in a general way as 'disposable income') and limited time. This being the case, events are competing for the public's attention, money and time, against all kinds of other activities and attractions, from eating out to engaging in sports and hobbies.

Careful marketing planning, and effective marketing itself, are required for those activities which will help to ensure the success of what we are doing. As with other activities, there will be finite money, time and staff available for marketing, and these resources need to be planned carefully and used effectively. In the initial stage marketing was one of the filters, or screens, through which various event ideas could be put, to identify ideas which were appropriate. This filtering process should have given the events organizer a firm basis to work on, and a starting place to consider some of the more detailed aspects of marketing, beginning with research. Research will be required about the target market, as well as a thorough assessment of the competitive environment the event is operating in. Once these things are known and objectives have been set, work can begin on the budget and on the marketing schedule.

One of the key functions of the budget will be to obtain the most effective marketing impact for possibly limited money. Not all marketing is expensive; indeed, some types of activities, such as public relations (PR), may have quite modest costs and be as effective as large-scale, expensive advertising campaigns. The budget, therefore, has to relate to what needs to be done, and can either be calculated as a percentage of the overall budget or built up from 'zero' based on what is needed to be done and how much that will cost. Some commentators suggest that events need to have quite a substantial marketing budget compared to normal kinds of products, perhaps as much as 10 per cent of the total event expenditure, as opposed to 3–4 per cent for most other goods and services, because of their short duration and unique profiles compared to other types of goods and services, which are much longer lived. Of all the marketing planning activities, the marketing schedule is the one most likely to surprise people new to the job. The lead times for preparing some marketing activities can be shockingly long. You could not, for example, just bang out a brochure in a day or two. You have to decide what you need to say in it, you have to find suitable pictures or graphics to put in it, it has to be laid out to look attractive, assembled, proofed, checked, returned, amended and checked again. This all takes time if the end result is going to be professional.

The chapter also looks at events marketing in terms of the considerations needed for new, or 'one-off' events, as these will need more detailed research and preparation work, due to the uncertainty of the target market and the questionability of the success of the event, where a new concept has not been tried before. This can be compared with the marketing of repeat editions of an event, where the event has run previously, perhaps for many years, and where a great deal of experience has been accumulated about it. In these cases the market and its participants or visitors may be well known, although, especially where an event has been organized by volunteers, the information recorded might not be especially complete or particularly detailed. A case is therefore made for the kind of information that a marketing officer would find useful to record for the marketing of further editions.

The Target Market

The term 'target market' refers, in the main, to the people who would be coming to a particular event. (Though we should bear in mind that, for some events, there is a target market which could be watching it on TV, or via the net, or follow it as a recreational interest, e.g. sports events.) In the most general way, we can see that the 'target market' for a rugby tournament would be very different from the 'target market' for a heritage pageant or a motor show – different people like different things. The issue for the events organizer is how much is known about the potential target market for a given event, and whether this can be used to some kind of marketing advantage. In addition, it might be wrong to think that an event could only have one target market, this may not be the case. Take the case of the village fête. The main target market might be people who live in the village itself, a secondary market might be those who live in the surrounding area and another secondary market might be tourists who happen to be visiting the village on the (we hope) sunny summer day when the fête is being held. Key questions about the target market include:

- Is your event targeted at the general public or at a specific group?
- What sort of age or lifestyle group will your event attract?
- Will your event appeal to special interest groups?
- Can you identify these different segments to attract?
- Are the different segments likely to be responsive to different prices?

When we ask questions about the potential market, the answer will help us to decide what has to be done next. For example, if the answer to the question 'Is your event targeted at the general public?' is 'Yes', then the next step is to consider how this knowledge helps us. It helps us by providing some focus around which to work, what techniques can be used and what marketing approach might be best for that particular target market, given the resources we have. An appreciation of the limitations of the concept of the target market is also important. The larger an event is, the more likely it would be to attract a more diverse range of people, for which more comprehensive market segmentation might be needed (Swarbrooke, 1995). There might also be 'stakeholders' in the activity and opinion leaders who could be regarded as separate or discrete target markets themselves, at least from the point of view of public relations.

Part of the process of identifying the target markets for an event involves knowing where your visitors are going to come from. This is easy if you are organizing a student ball, as the catchment area is the campus – the students and their friends. Similarly, if you are organizing a wedding anniversary party, catchment is not really an issue, because the 'target market' is simply the friends and relations of the happy couple. However, for many events an understanding of the catchment area is useful for the marketing officer. The target market might have been determined for, say, a horticultural show to consist of gardening enthusiasts and that part of the general public in the 55 plus age group who are retired and enjoy gardening. If this is a village show, the catchment might be quite small: people from the village and mainly those within walking distance. But for a larger show or event, a typical travel time of one hour might be seen as reasonable to define how far visitors might travel to visit the event, to be involved or entertained. The more important the event, the larger its catchment (as a general rule). Questions about the catchment area include:

- Where does most of your target market live?
- From how far away will people come to your event?
- What is the most likely distance (or time) people would travel to your event?
- Can you say how many people in your various target markets are in each catchment?
- How will these various groups travel to your event?

Travel distances in the catchment area are influenced by the time it takes to get to and from the event from various population centres. An hour's travel time on a motorway may cover 100 km, but an hour's travel time on a country road might cover only 30 km. These limits in terms of time, rather than simply distance, are what will determine the outer limit of the catchment area for the event. From this information it is then possible to calculate the size of the catchment area in population terms from census information, or from other sources, such as from local newspaper 'rate and data' information (local newspapers often keep information on the population structure and social groups of their area, in order to help to sell advertising space) or from companies that provide market research assessments or local council economic development departments. Combining this information about, say, social group size and catchment in the area should give an idea of the total potential size of, say, the working population, or that section of the population in a particular age group. However, not all information is necessarily collected in a way which makes it useful for event marketing officers to use easily. Nor will all the people in the target market in your catchment area attend your event. Attendance will be influenced by a whole range of things, from effective (or ineffective) marketing to personal preferences or the opinions of friends.

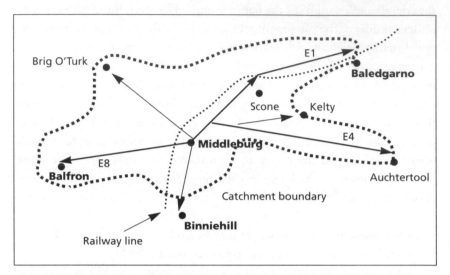

Figure 9.1 *Example of a catchment area: the Middleburg Music Festival.*

More detail can be added to the catchment, as a better picture is built up. For example, if the special event is opera, a large-scale map can be drawn up showing areas of upmarket housing (given a presumption that opera goers would live in those districts, which is not necessarily correct but serves to illustrate the point). Clearly, different towns, and different areas within a town, have different population compositions, and a thorough knowledge of the target market and the areas in which they live will help to focus the marketing effort on those areas.

Case Study 22

Marketing catchment areas: Lake Vyrnwy, Wales

Running is a very popular sport, with large numbers of road races, marathons, multi-terrain races and related activities such as triathlons taking place throughout Europe. There are a very large number of clubs associated with the sport, which has also quite a lot of sponsorship activity attached to it. The Reebok DMX Lake Vyrnwy Half Marathon is an extremely popular event attended by some of the best runners around a good course, known for its fast, scenic route.

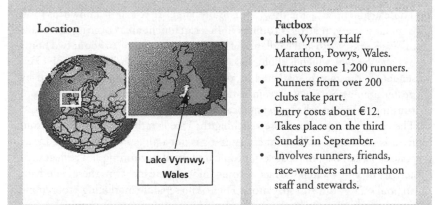

Location

Lake Vyrnwy,
Wales

Factbox
- Lake Vyrnwy Half Marathon, Powys, Wales.
- Attracts some 1,200 runners.
- Runners from over 200 clubs take part.
- Entry costs about €12.
- Takes place on the third Sunday in September.
- Involves runners, friends, race-watchers and marathon staff and stewards.

The race takes place during the afternoon, starting at 1.00 p.m., with the fastest runners being able to get around the course in about an hour and ten minutes, and the average time being an hour and a half to two hours. The race has over 12 classes, depending on age and sex of the runners, with a number of awards for the various class and overall winners. The race is organized by the Oswestry Olympians, which organizes various other races and competitions in North and Mid Wales. For example:

Race	Location	Type of race	Type of participants	Date
Park relays and 10 km	Oswestry	Relay race	Schools years 5 and 6	1 July
Mynydd Hill run	Trefonen	Recreational run	Under 18s short run Over 18s long run	29 May
Gobowen pentathlon	Gobowen	Pentathlon	Club members Individuals	4 August

The target markets for this type of activity are:

- amateur and professional runners;
- members of running clubs;
- recreational (occasional) runners;
- individuals interested in trying the sport, but not wishing to do a whole marathon;
- race-watchers and sightseers;
- friends and family of the runners.

The catchment area for this race is quite large. It is a well known race, in popular scenery. It attracts runners from a catchment area covering the whole of Wales, the North and Midlands of England, a drive time of about two hours to Lake Vyrnwy, which is about 20 km west of Oswestry and Welshpool. Consequently, the race is marketed locally and regionally in newspapers and by poster promotions, as well as in national running magazines and by flyers to running clubs and other relevant locations (such as leisure centres) in the area. The catchment area for those watching the race is rather smaller. Apart from friends and family of the runners, running is not a huge spectator sport on the scale of soccer, but, nevertheless, people interested in running as a recreational activity do go to watch the race. Because of its scenic location, there is perhaps an hour's travel time for spectators. There is no separate marketing programme for spectators.

The issue of catchment and travel time must also be seen in the light of accessibility. If we were to say that catchment was an hour on motorways, this would cover a far larger area, because you can go further and faster on a motorway than would be the case on minor roads. This means that catchment areas are unlikely to be circular, but will vary according to the quality of roads and access to the place concerned. This can be seen in the shape of the example catchment pattern in Figure 9.1.

Based on this case:

Take a map of Wales and the surrounding area. Consider the road network around Lake Vyrnwy. How does this affect the potential catchment for runners? If this race was held in central Birmingham, how would the catchment compare and why? Consider an event you have recently attended: what different types of people were there and how could they be classed into various target markets? How would this information be useful?

Related website for those interested in the Lake Vyrnwy Half Marathon: www.allweb.co.uk/olympians/lake

How Do You Influence the Target Market?

There are several reasons why a knowledge of the target market is important to the events organizer. The most important of these is that a knowledge of the target market enables some thought to be given to how to promote the event to them, as well as knowing what kind of activities they would enjoy, or what kind of publicity material they might respond to, e.g. what things they read, what they watch on TV or things in their lifestyle which the marketing officer can use as a marketing mechanism. This also helps us to understand the likelihood that they would come to our event. In all probability, our marketing plan will have to contain a range of activities to raise awareness of the event, but also to convert possible visitors into definite visitors. In what ways can you influence the market, so as to get people to attend? Consider:

- What are their media habits; what newspapers, magazines, etc. do they read?
- Can you use direct mail or newspaper inserts to influence them?
- Do they watch TV, go to the cinema or listen to local radio?
- How can you influence them if they are not engaged by the media (not everyone is)?
- What public relations activities could you use for these groups?
- Who are the opinion leaders and how might they be influenced?

For the marketing officer who might feel that once you know who your target market is and what media habits and buying habits it has, all you have to do is to get the promotion or advertising right for them, a word of caution – there are a range of influences on why a target audience might or might not attend an event. Sometimes such reasons are straightforward. It might be the weather. On the other hand, for an event to be popular it might be necessary to have a critical mass of people showing an interest in attending. This critical mass might only develop through word of mouth via a reference group (that is to say, the people we know). For example, suppose the event is a student summer ball. Ticket sales might not have reached the break-even point needed by the break-even deadline, despite advertising in the student magazine, posters around the campus or other sales efforts. The reason for this could be that the reference group (other students) might not have shown a wish to go, perhaps because of other events planned on the same night, perhaps because of a lack of immediate interest or other reasons (Hill *et al.*, 1995).

In general, the determinants of why or whether a visitor would come to an event are very varied (and not just about whether we can advertise or promote our event in front of their noses), and some understanding of this process (the buying process) can help us in deciding how best to promote our particular event. In general, these motives can be seen as being relevant to the marketing of other activities and products, not just events (Kotler *et al.*, 1996). It is also useful for us to remember the points made in Chapter 2 about some of these motives being more important than others – primary and secondary motives – because we need to know how best to promote the event given what we know about why people will come to it. For example, a primary motive may be social, because the person knows that lots of his or her friends will go. A secondary motive might be to be entertained. This process is also influenced by other determinants, such as:

- Whether your friends might go (cultural, personal or other reference groups).
- What decision-making time is available, or what lead times before you have to buy a ticket.
- Whether the price is a major concern ('price sensitivity', high cost, low cost, total package and value for money).
- Whether the event will be good enough – the perceived quality of the event.
- Access factors, e.g. local, regional, national, international. Do people in your area go to this type of event? How easy is it to get to?
- One-off or repeat sales opportunities. Is this annual, biannual, occasional? Will the event happen again, or is this the only opportunity to go?
- Familiarity – people's knowledge and awareness. Have they been to one before, or something similar?
- Propensity to join in community activities (high, low).
- Inclination to join in the activity due to personal interest, education, entertainment, relaxation, status, etc.
- Considerations of personal enjoyment, arousal or other satisfaction from the event.

It can be seen that there are some differences in the buying process between, say, the purchase of the weekly shopping or new clothes and the purchase of a ticket for a special event. In the case of certain types of event, no purchase may be taking place. If you have been invited to a dinner party, you are not 'purchasing' the event – you don't buy a ticket, you go because you enjoy the company of your friends. This is true of many types of event: no buying decision is involved, only a social decision (although there is the hidden cost of the time and effort, which might be interpreted as buying factors). On the other hand, many special events, particularly in the sporting and organizational categories, will involve a buying decision – whether to buy the ticket, whether it will be value for money and whether the event will be enjoyable are all part of the buying decision in such a case.

A number of determinants can be seen as being specific to an 'events buyer'. 'Events buyer' is also a rather tricky term to use. The 'buyer' may be a whole family going for a day out, a group of people in a minibus going to a sports competition or one person buying a ticket for a beer festival. If you were the marketing officer for an event, it would be important to have an understanding of who was doing the buying: who gets the ticket and how would you influence him or her to buy the ticket (Russell and Cotton, 1999); what places you would advertise in; the benefits of the event you are promoting to the attendees, visitors, guests or participants; the price charged for a ticket; where people actually can buy the tickets.

For the marketing officer, perhaps a significant issue is what benefits a visitor or attendee gets from the event. This may also be related to the question of expectations. If the visitor to the event expects an excellent, well organized, enjoyable and good value event, then the level of satisfaction the visitor would have would be very high. On the other hand, if the visitor is led to expect these things, but gets none of them, then the outcome will be not only dissatisfaction, but possibly bad publicity for the organizers. Marketing, then, is not just about getting people in through the door; it is, at least in part, about ensuring they get the satisfaction from the event that they have been led to expect. Individuals' expectations include the following:

- What are the benefits of attending the event? Will it be enjoyable, entertaining, diverting, educational, stimulating or exciting?
- What will be the style and standard of the venue; distance to home; closeness to transport; convenience of getting there; parking; ease of arrival and departure; facilities?
- What will be the likely standard of the event? Will it be professionally done – even by amateurs or volunteers? Will it be well organized, will it be value for money or will it just be a jolly, convivial, if moderately disorganized shambles? (This last may be a *normal* expectation held by a potential visitor.)
- What will the people be like? Can we expect excellence, commitment, enthusiasm, knowledge (or otherwise) from staff, volunteers or other participants?
- What is the price (or value) in comparison to other uses for the money – other possible events, other days out, meals or other leisure or social activities?
- What range of activities is available – interaction, sights and sounds, inclusiveness?
- What is the reputation of the event if it has been held before?
- How easy is it to get information, get tickets or have questions answered?

Leading on from the issue of what motivates and influences people to attend or participate in an event, we have to recognize the difficulty of marketing what are essentially unique, one-off occasions to a diverse market; a market very possibly, of people who do not know they want to attend or participate.

In terms of personal events, there are no conventional marketing issues in getting people to a private party. These events are 'invited', not marketed. In fact, in some cases the problem is to stop people coming to events where they might not be wanted. Gatecrashers are an example of this. We can organize a party for friends, only to find they turn up with people we might not expect, perhaps even do not like, or that word has got around to people we would not want at our party. This happens not only at some types of personal event, but also at high profile public events, which involve celebrities or film stars. Various people might try to blag their way into the event by using all kinds of unscrupulous means: e-mailing the organizers to say they have not received the tickets they were promised (when no one said they could have tickets); trying to get in by hanging around, in the hope someone will recognize them and take them in; trying to buy tickets from touts; and so on.

For most events in the leisure, cultural or organizational categories, the issue will not be how to stop people getting in, but how to encourage people to be there. For a local charity fund-raising event, the issue will be how to get enough people in to have a good crowd and to be able to make some money for the charity concerned. For organizations selling products, there may well be a clear need to market the event, so that lots of people come to see the product and some of them might buy it. This is especially the case with events such as trade shows and exhibitions, but the need to market an event applies to a very large range of activities. The decision-making process for an event might look like Figure 9.2. There are some key marketing issues in this scenario. In promoting an event, it is necessary to create an awareness of the event among the target market. Here the method is posters, for a target market of students. The interest phase is about stimulating the interest of the target market. In any target market, people who are considering attending the event will be seeking a reference mechanism for confirming that the event is what they want.

For many people, the reference mechanism is word of mouth from people they know. One of the biggest difficulties facing the marketers of events is that for one-off occasional events, the word of mouth support may not exist, as no one has been to the event before or been able get a view of how good or bad it is. They then have to rely on external referents, such as

Attention
Saw poster at university for the summer prom.
Instinctive consideration of whether the date and the cost would be OK.

Interest
Talked to friends in the class (or other reference group) to see if anyone else
was interested.
If lots of people interested, do the benefits outweigh the cost (being a student
with limited money)?
Is there anything else going on?
If not, why should I go?

Desire
Primary motives for going: have a good time, get drunk, get laid.
Secondary motives for going: don't have to watch awful television in study
bedroom; food is free.
Reasons for not going: may be too difficult to get a ticket.

Action
Ticket seller knocked on the door, so bought a ticket.

Figure 9.2   *Event decision-making process for a university prom.*

the quality of the advertising material or the views of critics (like going to a
see a new play). In some respects, events marketers can try to generate word
of mouth support by targeting opinion formers, but this is problematic and
only suitable for certain types of events. Thereafter, what we are seeking to
create is desire for the product, through encouraging people to feel that the
event will fulfil their particular needs and by generating a positive 'buzz'
about the event. From here onwards, it should be easy. The prospective
attendee simply takes 'action' and buys the ticket, and the event, of course,
goes wonderfully well.

The Marketing Plan and Timing
The marketing plan, like the operational plan and the financial budget, will
be developed from the event objectives, in a number of stages (McDonald,
1995). Marketing techniques employed by events organizers vary, and the
range of approaches is extremely wide, because of the differences in the types
of events being put on and the different characteristics of the target markets.
Nevertheless, the nature of the event buying decision and the influencing
factors makes targeting potential visitors relatively complicated for certain
types of event, though not all – a village fête would have a relatively simple
target market in the catchment area (the village and immediate surroundings).

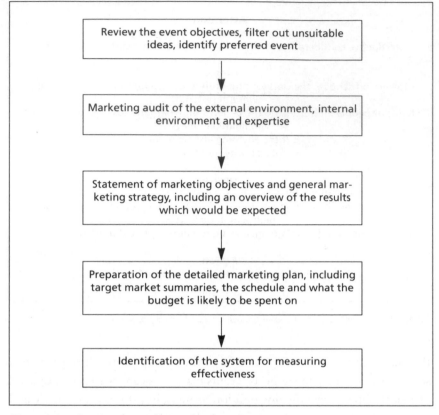

Figure 9.3 *Creating the marketing plan from the event objectives.*

The event marketing officer's expertise and resources in selling the event may not always be huge, often depending on volunteer effort and small budgets, and perhaps tending to rely on general awareness and word of mouth, or responses to enquiries, rather than expensive advertising. For this reason, public relations may play a greater role in promoting many events than paid advertising. However, this should not prevent some careful thought and planning about marketing as a whole activity.

Marketing for a New Event

Objectives and analysis of the environment

If the marketing of an event has to be started from a blank sheet of paper, the marketing plan will have to be written to cover six main elements (see Figure 9.4). Some of these should have been identified early on in the event planning process, and should be easy to summarize in the first few sections of the marketing plan. These are the sections dealing with the purpose of

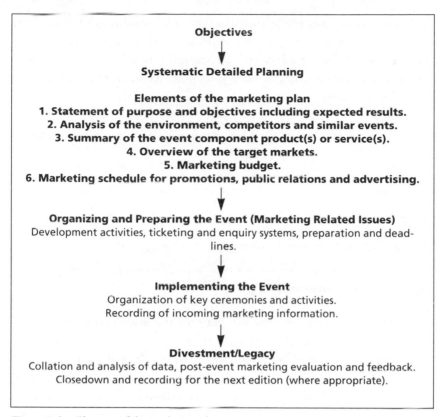

Figure 9.4   *Elements of the marketing plan.*

the event, which might be written as one line or sentence, and can then be broken down into several smaller objectives. To make this as simple as possible, there should be no more than perhaps five aims of the event (there might be only one, remember), because the more aims you have, the more difficult it will be to achieve them all properly. This section is followed by the analysis of the environment (which was covered in Chapters 5 and 6), which will show that some thought and research has been undertaken about the environment in which the event will operate, what competition there might be, what other things going on at the same time might take some of the potential target market away from your own event, and whether there have been or are similar events which could be seen not so much as competitors, but as complementary to your event.

Event components mix and target markets

The summary of event component products and services is a list of the respective parts of the event (which we might also call the product/service mix) that might attract different parts of the target market. In the case of the garden show, this mix might comprise: the main garden exhibition itself; seminars on gardening given by experts to visitors; the prize-giving ceremony for the best displays; the catering tent; the sales and retail stands; the prize draw competition to win a garden makeover from an expert; and the children's crèche.

	Exhibition	Seminars	Prize-giving	Catering	Sales	Draw	Crèche
Families	✔			✔	✔		✔
Pensioners	✔		✔	✔		✔	
Hobbyists	✔	✔	✔	✔	✔	✔	
Tour groups	✔			✔	✔		

Figure 9.5   *Event components and target market use.*

When you are preparing the summary of the event's components, the ability to cross-reference the products and services being offered against the likely target markets will help to highlight which parts of the event might turn out to be the busiest, but will also help the marketing and promotion effort, where that effort might be targeted at individual markets (rather than the general whole) by showing which elements of the event's components mix could be highlighted in specific literature or other promotional material for a given market segment or target. At this point in the marketing plan, the target markets can be identified and described in some detail, together with information about the catchment, and what kind of marketing tools will be used to influence each target market segment to come to the event, what media habits each target market has and what other promotions or public relations activities might also have an impact on their decision to attend the event. From this list, the most effective marketing tools can be identified, and as the marketing budget is assembled, these tools can be given priority as being potentially the most effective.

The marketing budget
The largest single cost in terms of marketing budgets for professionally run events is the staffing cost of the marketing department itself. Almost all larger professional events have marketing or sales teams or coordinators. The advantage that volunteer-run events have is that there is no staffing cost, but equally, for a volunteer run event, the marketing budget might be very small. The marketing officer's budget might include a range of items:

1. Print items: tickets, posters, brochures, leaflets, visitor maps (design costs, display costs).
2. Direct marketing: sales visits to opinion leaders, event organizers, agencies, mailings.
3. Advertorials: journal or magazine inserts.
4. Hospitality: familiarization visits, pre-event days.
5. Exhibition material for local promotion, stands, site models.
6. Paid advertising: newspapers, magazines, radio, TV.
7. Websites, CD-ROMS.
8. Payments for celebrity guests.
9. Press kits, photography and artwork activities (banners, signs, etc.).

In normal circumstances, the student of the events business would probably automatically think of advertising as the major marketing tool available to organizers – all you do is advertise in the right place and visitors or participants come flocking to you. Would that it were so easy. Advertising has its place and plays a significant role in raising awareness and helping to support an image for an activity. It is particularly relevant on a national scale for events organized in the corporate sector or by voluntary associations in the national market. However, the wide range of potential events can require a wide range of approaches, which may include not only advertising and public relations but also the use of a large range of other marketing tools.

Individual events can also attempt to entice the public, visitors, attendees, participants and even potential staff by providing pre-event activities or a series of awareness-raising promotions to help to familiarize people with the main event. It is also important to keep the target market 'warm', i.e. to call and talk to opinion leaders or invite them to familiarization or hospitality events. In this way, some of the target market or 'buyers' for an event can be influenced, or at least informed of the planned activities.

It is difficult to ascertain the effectiveness of the various methods, but personal contacts are often significantly important to marketing an event and do not show as a cost in a marketing budget, except perhaps as travel or hospitality expenses. In addition to paid advertising, which an event manager or organizing committee might or might not be able to pay for, many events rely significantly on good public and media relations, anything from word of mouth to imaginatively written press releases.

The marketing budget should be carefully prepared and costed. All the items that are needed should be included, with details of how many are required, as well as their size or type. In addition, for items such as brochures or leaflets, the cost per thousand (if this kind of number is needed) should be compared, to see which type is the most cost-effective. Wherever possible, in the costing process, more than one estimate or cost quote should be obtained.

The marketing schedule

In order for a special event to be marketed properly, not only must the planning and budgeting of the marketing programme have taken place, but also a schedule of activities needs to have been prepared. This schedule is intended to give the organizers an idea of the lead times for various marketing activities, and what needs to be done and when, to get the most benefit from the marketing effort.

In the preparation of a marketing schedule care must be taken to understand that many activities have long lead time. Brochures, for example, may take several weeks – the text has to be written, photographs provided, a draft assembled by the graphic designer or printer, this draft checked for error, corrected and then checked again before being printed. Similarly, for those types of media that a marketing manager may wish to use, it will be important to check the lead times. National monthly trade magazines might need two to four months' notification of an event to get it in, with editorial, TV and radio shows need up to six weeks' notice. Even a website might require not only several weeks intensive design work, but also its own advertising. Local media can work to shorter lead times, but it is best to find out whether they wish to have stories by a certain day and time of the week. A media kit or press pack can also be prepared at an early stage of the activities, which can include various fact sheets about the event, artist's impressions or (suitable photographs), a contacts list and information about sponsors, beneficiaries and key people involved. However, the first version of the press kit should not include admission prices, as the media might focus too strongly on these at too early a stage in the development of the event.

Marketing for Repeat Events and New Editions

Up to now, we have stressed that many events are one-off, unique activities. In some ways this is true, but all kinds of events are repeated, perhaps annually or biannually, or on some other time scale (the Olympics every four years). Even events that happen annually, in the same place and at the same time of year, may not be exact replicas of what has gone on before, perhaps because of a different organizing committee, different participants, different visitors or any number of changes in the operations and activities taking place. For this reason they are often called 'new editions'. Conse-

Marketing Budget Proposals

Event:

_____

Date of Event. _____   Date of this budget: _____

Target market segments:	Target numbers:	Ticket price:
Individuals	_____	€_____
Families	_____	€_____
Children	_____	€_____
Concessions / students / elders	_____	€_____
Groups	_____	€_____
Complimentary / hospitality / VIPs	_____	Nil
Press	_____	Nil

Expenditure:	Budget €:	Actual €:	Number/size
Research	_____	_____	
Staff: marketing office	_____	_____	
Staff: booking and enquiry office	_____	_____	
Volunteers: custom T-shirts, leaving gift	_____	_____	_____
Advertising: newspaper / magazine	_____	_____	_____
Advertising: radio	_____	_____	_____
Advertising: posters	_____	_____	_____
Advertising: other (specify) _____	_____	_____	_____
Direction signs	_____	_____	
Internal signs	_____	_____	
Printing: tickets	_____	_____	_____
Printing: brochures	_____	_____	_____
Printing: posters	_____	_____	_____
Printing: programmes, site maps	_____	_____	_____
Printing: menus, place cards	_____	_____	
Printing: other (specify) _____	_____	_____	_____
Uniforms / sashes	_____	_____	
Badges	_____	_____	_____
Celebrity costs	_____	_____	
Prizes	_____	_____	
Complimentary items / giveaways	_____	_____	
Marketing office hospitality	_____	_____	
Marketing office travel expenses	_____	_____	
Display stands	_____	_____	
Photography	_____	_____	
Video company	_____	_____	
Press kit	_____	_____	
Ticket distribution	_____	_____	
Postage / mail out costs	_____	_____	
Stationery	_____	_____	
Other items, e.g. website	_____	_____	
Total costs	€_____	€_____	

Figure 9.6   *Event marketing budget form.*

5–6 months before opening
1. Hold meeting to define objectives and to ensure coordination of various public relations activities with paid advertising. Establish timetable to match scheduled deadline opening date. Identify target market at a meeting with the organizing committee.
2. Prepare a media kit (information pack, contacts, etc.).
3. Order photographs, artists impressions, logo or design drafts. Begin website design.
4. Begin preparation of mailings and media lists.
5. Contact all prospective beneficiaries of the events and start listing VIPs and opinion leaders.
6. Book dates for press conferences at suitable venues (probably off-site to begin with).

4–5 months before opening
1. Send out initial press releases with suitable pictures to all media (local, regional, etc.).
2. Write a 'progress bulletin' or newsletter, for agents, media, VIPs and opinion leaders. This can also be used or adapted for internal marketing, i.e. to keep site and event staff and volunteers up to date.
3. Begin production of adverts, posters and promotional brochures.
4. Set up enquiry desk and advance ticket office.
5. Test and set up website.
6. Make final plans for the opening ceremony and associated events, including arrangements and invitations for VIPs and other invited guests.

3–4 months before opening
1. Launch publicity campaign to national media.
2. Send out mailings to all media.
3. Send second progress bulletin.
4. Arrange interviews with local media, trade media, gardening, design and leisure publications (not at the site, as it will not be ready or well presented).
5. Begin awareness-raising advertising, e.g. posters.

2–3 months before opening
1. Launch campaign to local and other media with a short lead time, emphasizing the event's contribution to the community, local business, etc. Highlight the contribution of volunteers, sponsors and benefactors.
2. Send out a further progress bulletin together with a brochure to the completed mailing lists and to people who have booked advance tickets already.
3. Provide a site model and publicity displays for the enquiry area or for use in local public places such as libraries and shopping centres.
4. Begin 'behind the scenes' public tours (only if the site is nearly ready).
5. Hold 'hard hat' lunches for invited guests such as media writers.

1–2 months before opening
1. Send out a further progress bulletin, including useful comments from people who have had previews.
2. Undertake a 'mystery guest' enquiry and ticket booking to test the system. Deal with any problems which arise.
3. Establish final plans for the opening ceremony, send out appropriate invitations.
4. Hold the 'soft opening' (an event where you use staff and their families to test the systems, catering, toilets, parking, queuing arrangements, etc.).

The opening month
1. Begin final mailings.
2. Check invited guests attendance at opening.
3. Hold orientation press/media visits.
4. Hold the opening ceremony.
5. Get pictures of opening ceremony to media, same day.

Post event
1. Send out a further progress bulletin, highlighting the success of the opening and especially thanking volunteers, sponsors and beneficiaries.
2. Final media coverage, more photos, success of event, handover ceremony or publish date of next event.
3. Thank you letters.

Figure 9.7   *Outline marketing schedule example for the opening of a garden festival.*

quently, these types of events are based on existing knowledge and techniques, but, as with a book, some changes are made each time, some things perhaps removed, some new things added. Admittedly, the nature of new business often presents a more exciting challenge to event marketers and sales people than might the careful routine of recording, monitoring and caring for an existing target market. Yet it is the attention to the detail of maintaining, and enhancing, an existing business base which is probably the acid test of a good marketing officer. The development of the existing visitor base into repeat business and also as a lead to further new visitors may be very useful indeed.

Careful recording of attendance information about visitors and participants is the first stage in making sure they can be encouraged to return to the next event. It is also important to collect the same information each year, for the sake of consistency and to be able to do accurate comparisons. The basic information which we should be attempting to collect is detailed in the following subsections.

Records of visitor numbers

Total visitor or participant numbers are needed: how many and where from. The where from can be done by sampling surveys or by getting people to fill in some details as part of the booking process – it depends how big your event is, and what resources you can put into recording. With limited resources, such as volunteer staffing, you have no need to collect details from every single visitor. You will know how many tickets you sold, and what types of ticket. If the event is free, volunteers can still be put on the entrances or gates to give a rough count of people coming in. If the event is in an open area estimates can still be made (see also the Deventer Bookmarket case study). More detailed information, such as place of origin or mode of travel, is something that could be put on a simple questionnaire and attached to the ticket to be filled in, if the visitor wants to do it, and placed in a box near the exit(s). Large numbers of questionnaire replies are not necessarily needed to gather this kind of information. If only 100 questionnaires were returned (note the limitations of doing this without control of a representative sample, preferably one which should include some non-attenders to find out why they didn't come), this would still be enough for a modest analysis of the information, and not be too much to collate and write up in a short 'visitor attendance report'. Gathering this information will help you to promote the event in the right places next time.

Case Study 23

Geneva Motor Show

The Geneva International Motor Show attracts a huge number of exhibitors and visitors to the Palexpo halls in Geneva. The show lasts for eleven days in early March of each year and includes some eleven sectors of activity, from car exhibits through equipment and components to events and interactive displays. It is one of a series of motor shows throughout Europe, each country being allowed one international motor show, plus domestic shows and dealer exhibitions. The show in 2000 was of such importance that it was opened by the President of Switzerland, together with the President of the Council of State, other major political figures and celebrities being present at the opening ceremony.

Location

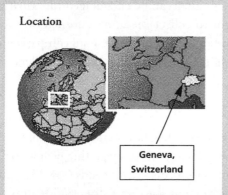

Geneva, Switzerland

Factbox
- Geneva Motor Show.
- Attracted over 714,000 visitors from 87 different countries.
- 4,700 journalists attended.
- There were 275 stands showing 900 models of cars, covering 90,000 square metres of exhibition space.

The eleven-day event takes over two weeks to set up beforehand, inside the exhibition hall – from the initial layout of where the respective stands will be, through the construction of the stand shells, the delivery of exhibitors' stand equipment, the fitting of power and lighting, the arrival of major exhibits (including the cars which are covered with tarpaulins), to the final fitting out of the stands with furniture and promotional materials ready for the opening day. This sequence of construction can be seen in a series of development pictures in the motor show website.

For marketing purposes, the motor show organization, in conjunction with Palexpo, records and publishes admissions information and also breaks the information down into various segments:

Total number of visitors:		714,000	
Total number of Swiss visitors		421,000	59%
Total number of external visitors		293,000	41%
Number of countries of visitor origin:		87	
Main countries of origin with number	France	228,500	32%
of visitors:	Germany	14,250	2%
	Italy	14,250	2%
	All others	37,750	5%
Total number of visitors in age group 18–54		628,000	88%
Total number of visitors in other age groups		86,000	12%
Total number of male visitors		521,000	73%
Total number of female visitors		193,000	27%

Based on this case:

Identify how the breakdown of visitor information can be useful in marketing terms. Examine a local event (or tourist attraction) in your region for which you can obtain visitor information. How can this information be used for marketing purposes? What kind of details would it be especially useful to know about the visitors at the event if you had a further edition of the event to prepare for a coming year?

Related websites for those interested in the Geneva International Motor Show:
www.salon-auto.ch/autos/salon2000/ang/index.html
www.palexpo.ch

Details of spending or use patterns

This examines how much was spent and what on, how many people did what and when. This kind of information helps you to find out what kinds of things were most popular. Your event might have included several different components or activities (the product service mix). In the next edition you might want to add or remove some of these things or make some of them better, or try out new layouts or locations for them. To do this you need information on what components of the event people are using and what is popular. This information can be obtained from spot checks and from sampling of things such as queue lengths at given times. More detailed information can be found from ticket sales and from sales records of catering or other activities. Even where no money changes hands, volunteers can count the number of people using parts of the event, or visitors can be given tokens or ticket strips (carnet strips) to hand in at the various locations, activities or stands as they use them. These can be counted, or just weighed. Gathering this information will help you to decide what parts of your event are most popular, and which should be kept or changed next time.

Marketing effectiveness

What parts of the marketing, publicity and public relations effort were successful? It is quite common for people to be asked on a questionnaire: 'How did you find out about us?' You can ask people how they found out about you by getting them to tick boxes on a questionnaire ('advert in the newspaper; advert on the radio', etc.) but, bearing in mind what we have already noted about how people decide and what influences them, it would be better to do this by having some informal chats to visitors. These can, in fact, be loosely structured by writing down a few short questions and using these as your guide during each chat. Following the chat, write out the responses on a summary sheet (just a list: chat 1, chat 2, etc.). You will be surprised what you learn and, most importantly, this gives people the opportunity to tell you more about what they did and how they found out about you than giving them a list (provided you use open-ended questions – e.g. 'How did you get here?' – rather than 'yes/no' questions: 'Did you come by car?'). Gathering this information will help you to find out what part of your marketing effort was the most useful and how you could improve it.

Expectations and satisfaction

What did your visitors expect, and were they happy with their experience? Did your event fulfil their expectations? As with checking the effectiveness of your marketing, checking expectations and satisfactions is probably best done by talking to people. It helps to explore their expectations by chatting to them, as you probably would not get the full breadth of possible expectations by getting them to fill in a questionnaire. Be careful how you ask things, though. For example, it is very common, when you are in a restaurant, to be asked 'Is everything all right?' Remember what we just noted about asking open-ended questions. The response to 'Is everything alright?' is almost always 'Yes, it's fine.' This is for two reasons: first, the question is framed in a yes/no way; second, it is socially difficult for people to respond to this question by saying 'No, the food is terrible, the service is slow, the carpet is sticky and the toilets smell' (or whatever). Therefore, in exploring whether your visitors are satisfied you need to think carefully about what you will ask them, and what opportunities there are during your event when visitors will be socially comfortable to answer questions. Although we may not necessarily use questionnaires during the event itself, it will probably be a useful exercise to give some out for people to take away, or mail some out a day or two later, in order to obtain opinions after the event or after people have had time to reflect. Clearly, though, the most useful purpose in getting satisfaction information is to help to identify strengths and weaknesses and to help to grow the potential number of people attending by knowing what went well and what didn't.

Summary

Marketing is one of those subjects which is attractive to many people as an interesting and stimulating activity, one which they enjoy doing. However, as with the other component subjects of events management, from logistics to finance, it requires a high level of knowledge and ability to be undertaken properly. Good knowledge of the kind of people who will attend an event, whether as participants, visitors or guests, is essential to promoting the event and ensuring its success. This knowledge helps the event marketer to understand how to raise awareness, advertise, promote, improve an image or maintain the event's impact in the media. Part of the marketing function is also to evaluate how an event is received. Sometimes this is done as an event is progressing, sometimes it is done by feedback at the end. In those cases where there will be a further edition, the knowledge gained from evaluation should enable improvements or changes to be made for the future.

Reference List

Hill, E., O'Sullivan, C. and O'Sullivan, T. (1995) *Creative Arts Marketing*. Oxford: Butterworth Heinemann, pp. 26–34.

Kotler, P., Bowen, J. and Makins, J. (1996) *Marketing for Hospitality and Tourism*. London: Prentice Hall, pp. 217–36.

McDonald, M. (1995) *Marketing Plans*. Oxford: Butterworth Heinemann, pp. 427–35.

Richards, B. (1992) *How to Market Tourist Attractions, Festivals and Special Events*. Harlow: Longman, pp. 21–35.

Russell, V. and Cotton, V. (1999) 'Marketing strategies for European meetings', *The Meeting Professional*, **19** (2): online: (www.mpiweb.org/tmp/1999archive/tmp0299/marketing.htm). (26 September 2000)

Smyth, H. (1994) *Marketing the City: the Role of Flagship Developments in Urban Regeneration.* London: E&F Spon, pp. 127–61.

Swarbrooke, J. (1995) *The Development and Management of Visitor Attractions.* Oxford: Butterworth Heinemann, pp. 58–68.

CHAPTER 10

Managing the Event as a Project

Aims
- To provide a framework for managing event projects.
- To discuss the range of risk management, licensing, health and safety and insurance requirements which are the key to secure operations.
- To provide an overview of the operational activities which take place immediately prior to, and during, an event.

Introduction
The purpose of this chapter is to look at events from the operational viewpoint, how to operate the event as a project and how to address some of the complexities of what might be called the legal side, as these often receive insufficient attention. In addition, the chapter considers how to make the final preparations, those things that need to be done immediately before an event opens. These final preparations should be taken in conjunction with those noted in Chapter 8 about logistics (pp. 142–64) and Chapter 11 about how to run events on the day (pp. 249–54). These sections overlap somewhat, depending on how an event is timed and organized. In some cases they will happen all at once in one day, in others the groundwork and preparations may take several days and have to be ready well before the public arrive.

The Event as a Project
There are considerable similarities between the management of projects and the management of events, so much so that many of the techniques developed in the management of large-scale building, logistical or public projects could be used to bring organizational discipline to many kinds of events. As such, the application of project management techniques to events should provide a vehicle for ensuring the modest success of an event, as opposed to spectacular failure. Why only modest success? Events management, rather

like project management, can be a somewhat thankless task. The world will not see the event coordinator toiling away for weeks on end, coping with late nights, wrestling with tricky problems and recalcitrant suppliers to make the event a success, but the first time that the most minor thing goes wrong ('Oh no, the flowers are red, they should be pink . . .') the event coordinator will get the blame. Reiss (1998), in a usefully chatty book about project management, makes these points very well, and also highlights the opportunities a project manager may have to show how much work is going on behind the scenes. The management of a project (Morris, 1994) covers much the same process as the management of events. Both are unique, time-limited operations (see Figure 10.1).

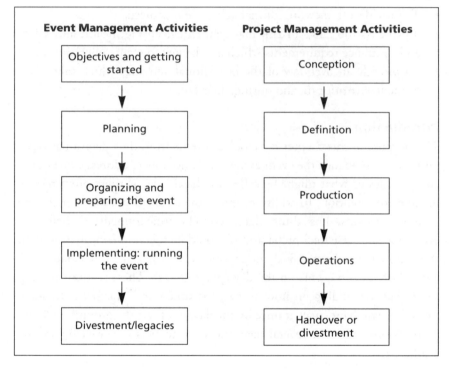

Figure 10.1   *Event and project activities.*

The processes involve very similar approaches, which the event coordinator or organizing committee can seek to use. Objectives for an event can be tested using the SMART approach:

Specific; Measurable; Achievable; Realistic; Timely

If the objectives are framed badly, worded badly or confusing (rather than being specific and precise), then we will have difficulty creating the event from them. The objectives must be measurable, in terms of being able to know whether they are being achieved or whether progress is being made towards them. This highlights the need for progress meetings and schedule deadlines. The objectives must be achievable. It must be genuinely possible to get the event done, especially given the limitations of money, staff, management or volunteer expertise that might be present. Similarly, the objectives must be realistic, bearing in mind what flights of fancy (or fantasy) the clients might want you to achieve. Finally, the objectives must be timely, taking into account what can be done in the time available, what deadlines there are and the natural tendency for time scales to slip. We can plan to put on a party in a tent a week from now, but are we being realistic? Is the timing possible? On the wonderful computer plan we have prepared, it may seem so, but in reality the weather may be bad, the tenters may take frequent coffee breaks, the ground may be wet, the tent may be dirty and need scrubbing, the lorry delivering the poles may get stuck in the mud. Who would be an event coordinator?

When the objectives have been tested, techniques from project management that can be adopted include:

- the use of work breakdown structures;
- project planning, including identification of critical tasks and external dependencies;
- Gantt charting (related to critical path analysis);
- risk assessment.

Naturally, these are only a few of the possible techniques that an event organizer can adopt, or easily obtain suitable software to help deal with, and after all, if the event is going to be huge, then you should hire a project manager and get in all the other fancy computer software and gismos you need.

Work breakdown structures
A work breakdown is just what it says it is: the job broken down into its rough component parts. At this stage detail is not needed or expected. The work breakdown is simply the first stage in looking at what has to be done, identified in its respective component parts by the work that one person or a related team of people can do. It looks rather like an organization chart, in so far as it is hierarchical. Starting at the top, with the event, or major event activity, you work down the chart until you get to the point where the one person or team has been arrived at (see Figure 10.2).

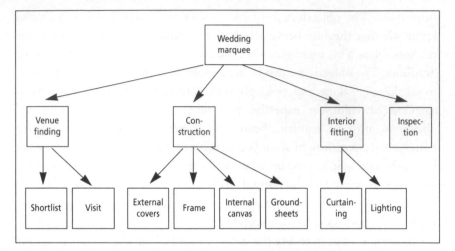

Figure 10.2   *Work breakdown structure for a wedding marquee. Source: adapted from Nickson and Siddons (1997).*

Project planning techniques

There are various project planning techniques that an event coordinator could usefully adopt. These include the identification of critical tasks and external dependencies. Once a work breakdown structure has been drawn up, it should be possible to start to identify those activities that are critical to the event's success. Critical tasks are essentially those things which must be completed first, in any sequence of activities, for the activity to proceed. This not only helps to concentrate attention on the jobs within the event that are central to the task, but also provides the framework for setting deadlines whereby progress on preparing the event can be checked, because the critical tasks must be completed on time for the following activities to be carried out. In the example of the wedding marquee, two critical tasks might be identification of the venue followed by construction of the tent. The key parts of the construction are the setting up of the framework and the fitting of the external covers. Once these things are achieved other activities can take place. For example, once the marquee is weatherproof, the electrician could start installing the lighting at the same time that the tenters were still fitting the internal canvases and the curtaining. These follow-on tasks are called dependencies. External dependencies are those issues which are outside the event coordinator's direct control. Hiring furniture for an event is an external dependency – it relies on the furniture hire company turning up with the correct items at the time and place that we ordered them for. Without the furniture, there will be no event. Arguably, the more external dependencies a project has, and the more unusual they are, the more risk there will be of the project going wrong or failing completely.

It is necessary to turn an initial work breakdown sheet into something which not only is more detailed, but also shows the exact sequence of activities, and how long each will take. This can be done on computer (using software such as Microsoft Project), or, if you had a very small event, could be done by hand using graph paper (for the classically inclined), but doing it by hand has the limitation that any time you need to add something, as you are doing the planning, you have to redraw the chart. You need to identify tasks clearly enough that you know what is going on, but not over-specify them in such detail that you prevent the free thinking and association needed for creativity. 'Decorate venue' (with due regard to safety) may be a perfectly adequate statement of a task. 'Put green balloons one metre above the doors' is over-specification.

Gantt charting

There are a range of ways in which task sequences can be shown visually. These include charts which show resource charting and critical path analysis using PERT charts (which are OK for the experienced; see Morris, 1994), but the easiest and most applicable kind of chart that event organizers can adopt from the project management sphere is the Gantt chart. The Gantt chart simply shows the various tasks that have to be done and puts them in a time-sequence order. This way, it is easy to see what the various tasks are and, most importantly, how long they should take, when they should be completed and what happens if a task, especially a critical task, is delayed.

A project started on 1 May, and the Gantt chart example (see Figure 10.3) gives a snapshot of the work as things are going on 14 June. Various things were ordered and arranged at the beginning of the process, including the venue, the marquee, the furniture and the caterers. Only one thing is shown as having been ordered during the snapshot period; that is, the flowers, which have a shorter lead time than, say, getting a marquee.

There are some limitations to the Gantt chart. It does not show, in our example, the resources available to do the job or if you have given someone too much work to do in the time available; nor is it really suitable for huge projects, as it would be enormous. However, for the modest kind of help it gives to planning events, it can be of very considerable use, not least in that it means that the organizers have to sit down and think through the steps needed to do the work. In some cases, this planning technique might be best applied backwards; that is, start at the deadline (the end) and work back in order to find out how long doing something will really take. Do not come along and say, 'Hey, we've got three days to get the tent up and sorted, just cram it onto the chart . . .'.

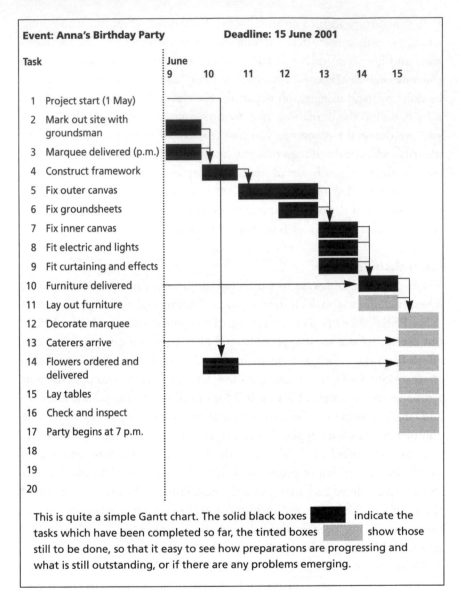

Figure 10.3 *Example of a Gantt chart.*

The other important activity that Gantt charting will compel you to do is to find out how long things genuinely take to do. Without this accurate information, the chart will be useless. For example, will it really take two days to get the outer canvas on the marquee? In our example, yes it does. If you have ordered a marquee, ask the tenters how long it will really take them to put it up.

Risk Management and Emergency Services

For the events coordinator the possibility that something might go wrong at an event has to be acknowledged. Most risk is minor and of little potential impact, but we need to be sure. Risk assessment is a way of attempting to identify potential risks and taking steps to reduce or militate against them. It is also the starting point for being able to produce contingency plans and emergency procedures. Although we will concentrate on risk as a threat to safety, it is important to recognize that the more general approach of risk management is to look at any aspect of the operation of a project or activity to identify its risks. In this more general approach, the risk inherent in putting up a marquee is that, as well as the chance that it might fall down on top of 200 guests, it might not arrive at all. Perhaps the marquee company went bankrupt and forgot to tell you, so what contingency is available in the event of that type of risk? (A contact name and number for another marquee company and event insurance.) Risk categories include:

- Risks to staff and others, owing to confused organization, poor health and safety practice or the presence of chemicals or other potentially dangerous substances and items.
- Risks in marketing an event, perhaps due to (natural) enthusiasm or optimism about what the event will do. There is, therefore the risk of expectations not being fulfilled, but also the risk of the media finding a negative story about an event and making a big performance of it.
- Risks in health and safety, especially for the public, and especially at outdoor events which are large and complicated, or involve some inherently risky activity.
- Risks in catering provision, especially for concessions and food stalls, hygiene and sanitation provision.
- Risks in crowd management, overcrowding, potential crush points, the siting and availability of emergency exits, alcohol provision, noise control and rowdy or violent behaviour.
- Risks in security, particularly at large events or where VIPs are present.
- Risks in transport of items to and from the venue, deliveries and movement at the site of unusual or large items.

It is of considerable importance that we maintain a sense of proportion. It is very easy to get carried away about the potential risks and threats that an event or activity might represent. The first meeting about risks that an event coordinator holds with an organizing committee might raise a long list of potentially horrible consequences of a simple activity (think of the potential dangers of boiling a kettle), but these risks must be put into some kind of context and evaluated, as otherwise nothing will get done for fear of the consequences. The media, particularly television and the lesser quality newspapers, increasingly seem to take an unpleasant delight in making the most innocent activity appear to be something terrible and dangerous. The consequence of this is unnecessary public fear about many activities which are relatively safe. The purpose of risk management is therefore to help us to consider what risks are genuine threats and what risks are not. The risk management approach is one of assessment, evaluation, moderation and recording. Ridley and Cheney (1999) consider risk management in detail.

The first stage in this process is identification of risks. For large or VIP events a professional consultant could be employed. For smaller events, a brainstorming meeting with the organizing team and one or two significant outsiders, such as the fire brigade, ambulance service and police representatives (or specialists, e.g. for outdoor activities), would be a useful starting point. More formally (Nickson and Siddons, 1997, p. 42), interviews can be held with the heads of department to assess risks. It is important that everyone understands the significance of doing this. The outcome of careful risk management might be saving someone's life. From this process a risk management table can be drawn up, identifying and classifying risks, which will then enable plans to be made to moderate or control those risks which are identified as significant (see Figure 10.4). This process should be seen as ongoing. Anyone who feels that he or she has identified a risk, perhaps while some activity is taking place, must be able to flag that risk, and have it dealt with immediately. For this reason, all events must have an appointed safety officer, who has the power to stop an activity on the spot, or order the necessary resources to sort it out, and has contact lists for the events team and for the emergency and back-up services.

In the example of a risk assessment in Figures 10.4 and 10.5 (provided by courtesy of Tendring District Council, some details and names having been amended for publication), the event is a small regional kite flying championship, which happens to be taking place next to a cricket ground, on the same day as a cricket match. This being the case, there are some limited risks attached to things flying through the air. The event does not attract huge numbers of spectators, so overcrowding in the arena area of the championship is not thought a major risk. The catering tent is small, and in bad weather could get quite crowded. Thus, with many people in it, and various

Event: Eastern Regional Kite Flying Championships
Location: Long Road Recreation Ground   Date of event: 10 and 11 June 2000
Date of this assessment: 20 March 2000   Assessed by: A Dangerfield

Risk Ratings

	People at risk			A, Worst case outcome			B, Likelihood			Rating
Hazard	Staff	Contract-ers	Public others	Slight 1	Serious 2	Major 3	Rare 1	Pos. 2	Likely 3	A×B
1 Spectator being hit by cricket ball	✔	✔	✔		✔		✔			2
2 Cricket player being hit by kite		✔			✔		✔			2
3 Spectator being hit by kite	✔	✔	✔		✔				✔	4
4 Over-crowding in event arena	✔	✔	✔	✔			✔			1
5 Over-crowding in catering tent	✔	✔	✔		✔		✔			2
6 Member of the public being hit by fly-away kite in the area		✔			✔		✔			2

Figure 10.4   *Example of a risk assessment form.*

catering equipment, in this particular event it has a somewhat higher risk associated with overcrowding than the main arena. Naturally, each event is different, and the impact must be assessed individually.

The risk management of an event takes place in several linked stages; first, the assessment; second, the evaluation, which results in the preparation of the risk moderation form; third, the control measures, which also stem from the risk moderation form, but which may lead to either special preparations before the event, or special measures during it; finally, a recording activity, which is particularly important where a further edition might take place, and especially so if other risks were identified during the event itself. These need particularly careful recording and review, as they are often surprisingly important and are learned from experience rather than foresight. The implication of this last matter is that we cannot foresee

Event: Eastern Regional Kite Flying Championships
Location: Low Road Recreation Ground — Date of event: 10 and 11 June 2000
Date of first assessment: 20 March 2000 — Assessed by: A Dangerfield
Date of this review: _____ Reviewed by: _____

Risk Control

Hazard found	Existing control measures	Additional control measures required	Priority	Person responsible for measure	Complete by	Action taken	Review date
1	None	Temporary cordon fence installed 20 metres beyond cricket boundary line.	High	A Dangerfield	8/6/00	Fencing instructions sent to T. Sutton and Company	9/6/00
2	None	All kite flying will be sectioned off in areas away from the cricket pitch.		A Dangerfield and stewards	10/6/00		
3	None	All kite flying will be sectioned off from the public within a 100 metre arena.		A Dangerfield and stewards	10/6/00		
4	None	Stewards and police to take appropriate action.		A Dangerfield, stewards and police	10/6/00		
5	Catering manager makes people queue outside	None, action adequate.		Catering manager	10/6/00		
6	None	Stewards to ensure only competent people to fly properly constructed kites.		A Dangerfield and stewards	10/6/00		

Figure 10.5 *Example of a risk control plan.*

everything that might happen at an event. In the end, although we may have gone to every reasonable effort to manage risk, something might still catch us out. Often such things, which lead to a catalogue of disaster, are small, and, in themselves, of little apparent consequence, but cause a terrible and unforeseen cascade effect.

Case Study 24

The moshpit at Roskilde

One of the pleasures of going to rock gigs and festivals is throwing yourself around the moshpit, the area of the crowd nearest the stage, where the most physical activity is going on, with fans dancing and bodysurfing along with the music. In the natural way of things, this area is crowded, and the physicality is part of the attraction of being there. The Roskilde Festival is one of the longest running rock festivals in the European calendar. Taking place some 25 kilometres west of Copenhagen, the festival attracts almost 90,000 people each year.

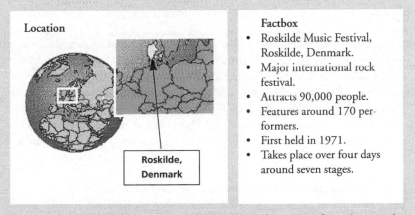

Location

Roskilde,
Denmark

Factbox
- Roskilde Music Festival, Roskilde, Denmark.
- Major international rock festival.
- Attracts 90,000 people.
- Features around 170 performers.
- First held in 1971.
- Takes place over four days around seven stages.

Approaching midnight on Friday 30 June 2000, after a day of steady rain, the moshpit under the orange stage at Roskilde was throbbing with young people enjoying the music of the American rock group Pearl Jam. There were some 70,000 fans at the festival at that point, a large number of them around the orange stage and in particular in the natural crush of the moshpit. As Pearl Jam's set continued it became obvious that the crush was significantly worse than normal and Pearl Jam's singer, Eddie Vedder, asked the crowd to move back. In the sliding mud, in the crush near the stage, nine fans died of suffocation, three from Sweden, one from Holland, one from Germany, one from Australia and three from Denmark itself.

During the days which followed the accident, the television and newspapers, with a typical lack of facts and an excess of speculation, claimed that everything from faulty sound equipment to drug taking, from people being crushed against the stage to scuffles in the crowd, had caused the accident. None of this has been proved to be the case. Tests of the equipment, which found it to be in perfect working order, were barely reported in the media the following week. The Roskilde Festival had a significant reputation for safety, and a measure of this was that first aid staff and police were on the scene immediately. There were few other injuries of any kind beyond those who died. The tragedy also stimulated an excess of pontification about youth culture, with politicians and public officials calling for all kinds of restrictions on what people do at festivals and events, without identifying the real reasons for the accident first.

For the organizers of the Roskilde Festival, the media reaction came as something of a shock, but is an issue to bear in mind in contingency planning for those members of the events organizing team who have media contact and who are involved in the public relations activities surrounding events. The festival was especially criticized for continuing after the accident, but the decision to do so was taken in good faith, and to allow festival goers to retain their original travel plans, rather than have 90,000 people hit the streets in one massed and unplanned departure.

Based on this case:

Is the media reaction to disasters normally measured and reasonable, or is it intended to be hysterical and critical? Why should this be the case, and what effects does the lack of a knowledgeable commentary have on efforts to identify the genuine reasons for accidents? Does this impact on the ability of those involved and those in authority to react to accidents in a way which will make future events more safe not less? Does such media comment result in unexpected outcomes, in cases where the media comment has been based on speculation and hearsay?

Related website for the Roskilde Festival: www.roskilde-festival.dk
For media comment: www.guardianunlimited.co.uk (you will have to search this site and other newspaper website archives)

In assessing the risk at events, our initial judgement of what is involved can be based, in part at least, on existing practice and on an awareness of what constitutes the routine and the predictable and what does not. As a generality, for example, we might consider the level of risk to vary according to the type of event and the activities which will take place in it:

1. *Low-risk events.* These are probably, typically, indoor events, which, while not completely regular or routine, are nearly so, and involve no unusual or specialist activities, where the people involved are well within their own range of experience and where there is considerable existing expertise and experience among management and staff. Examples might be banquets and dinners, either indoor or in marquees.
2. *Medium-risk events.* These might be very large indoor events, in locations the public might not attend regularly, or which are outside their range of experiences (but which a significant number of the attendees,

management and staff have experienced in similar circumstances), where the activities are more complicated than normal. Or these will be outdoor, involving large numbers of people, but with no obvious or perceived dangerous activities. Examples are large-scale sporting competitions, public shows and street festivals.

3. *High-risk events*. These events involve significantly large numbers of people in activities and locations they are unfamiliar with, or have never been to before, where there is little or no existing knowledge or experience of the event or the environment among management, staff or emergency services, or where there are visible, clear and evident dangers of undertaking or participating in the event if the safety features are ignored or inadequate. Examples are high speed racing events, large-scale complicated open air events taking place for the first time (hence public and staff unfamiliarity) and small-scale events, such as corporate outdoor team-building events, where the safety rules and the knowledge of experienced staff are the key to safety, and the activities are risky for those without the experience, expertise or qualifications.

Event managers and coordinators should strive to ensure not only that they provide a safe event and a safe environment for all concerned, but also that the systems and emergency procedures are in place in the event of an accident or other problem arising. In all events, but most especially in high-risk events, the need for adequate and sufficient staff training, especially of volunteers, is absolutely vital.

Case Study 25

Emergency service arrangements at events: Clacton Airshow, England

The small English seaside resort of Clacton-on-Sea hosts a number of annual events intended to attract tourists. These events include an annual carnival, a classic vehicle show, a jazz festival, a real ale festival, a sci-fi convention and its largest annual event, the Clacton Air Show. This range of events helps to stimulate tourism in a resort which relies on its family image, its beaches and its good weather to attract tourists from towns and cities in the east of England and from north London.

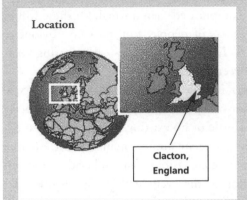

Location

Clacton,
England

Factbox
• The event is run by Tendring
  District Council.
• It consists of two days of air
  displays, including the Red
  Arrows RAF display team,
  parachutists, historic and
  modern aircraft and aerobat-
  ics.
• It attracts 65,000 day trippers.
• Comprehensive risk assess-
  ment and procedures.

The air show is estimated to attract some 65,000 day trippers to the town, in addition to the normal level of tourists. This number is very creditable when compared with some national events, such as the Henley Boating Regatta, which attracts 95,000 people, and the Royal Windsor Horse Show, which attracts some 80,000 people (source English Tourist Board). The economic impact of the air show is quite significant: it is a two-day event making a con-tribution to the local economy of about half a million euros (an average of €14.50 per visitor). Visitors to the air show spend money not only at the show ground but also in local pubs and restaurants, shops and other retail outlets, and at a range of other local facilities and services, including the pier, gift shops and other local attractions.

Many of the events which take place in the resort, like the air show, are orga-nized by the local council's Economic Development Department. The tourism section of this department is responsible for three main areas of activity:

1. The promotion of the resort and the surrounding area.
2. The running of the town's tourist information centre and other informa-
    tion centres in the district.
3. The organization and management of a number of larger special events,
    including the air show.

The air show requires careful organization, especially in terms of risk manage-ment, crowd management, emergency services, transport, access and coordination between various public service departments, including the coast-guard, the fire service, the police, the ambulance service and air traffic control. These are crucial owing to the large number of people attending and the poten-tial dangers associated with air displays, aerobatics, parachuting and similar activities at the show. In addition to full risk analysis, the planning phase includes a series of briefings between the public service departments and tourism officer, and other council departments, including the Department of Emergency Planning, the Department of Highways and the Environmental Department. This is followed up by briefings to staff and volunteers for the event.

For each air show a set of emergency service briefing notes is prepared, which states the allocation of resources and manpower for various kinds of emergencies. These include back-up plans for dealing with emergencies ranging from an air crash to a bomb alert or other types of accident, in order to ensure that the public are as safe as reasonably possible while at the show. This liaison process also includes coordination with the council's own staff who run information points and acts as guides, together with a range of voluntary organizations such as the St John's Ambulance Service, who take part to assist the main emergency services.

Based on this case:

Has your local council got a department or unit which deals with tourism in general and events in particular? If so, how is it organized and what does it do? What other types of events might require a major input from emergency services? Do even small events require a risk analysis and thought for the emergency procedures? What training should take place to ensure the safety of the public at an event?

Related information for those interested in this location: www.essex-sunshine-coast.org.uk

For event safety guidance, the European code is *The Event Safety Guide*, which can be obtained from: www.hsebooks.co.uk

Source: With grateful thanks to Tendring District Council.

Legalities and Insurance

Organizers of events need to bear in mind that there are a large number of legalities and similar issues associated with undertaking an event. These issues include licensing, health, safety and insurance requirements, which are the key to secure operations. Practice about how these are dealt with varies considerably in the various countries within the European Union, making it difficult to generalize. However, permits and licences are generally dealt with at a local level (town, city or district), although a few may be dealt with at regional or provincial level, within a framework of national and European Union legislation. It will be necessary for events organizers to check locally to identify what legal requirements prevail for aspects such as staffing, permits, licences and other regulatory issues (for the UK, see Croner, 2000). Figure 10.6 provides some possibilities, but is by no means definitive.

Permit	Suggested Place of Enquiry (UK only)
Alcohol	Licensing justices/Local council Licensing Committee
Bingo, lottery or gaming	Local council Licensing Department/Licensing justices
Fireworks	Fire Brigade
Food handling	Local council Environmental Health Department
Marches and parades	Police/Local council Highways and Transport Department
Music	Copyright owners/Broadcast Authority
Occupancy (maximum numbers)	Fire Brigade/Local council Licensing Department
Parking	Local council Highways and Transport Department/Police
Parks (use)	Local council Parks Department/Park owners
Public assembly/entertainment	Local council Licensing Department
Sea or beach use	Coastguard/Local authority Tourism Department
Signs and banners	Local council Highways and Transport Department
Street closure	Local council Highways and Transport Department/Police
VAT (sales tax)	Department of Customs and Excise. For 2001, the UK registration threshold is approximately £50,000

Figure 10.6   *Permits, licences and legalities.*

The applications procedures for these vary from country to country, so local documentation should be checked for where to apply for permits, and what kinds of permits are needed (licences for the sale of alcohol are obvious, but even the placing of a waste skip on a public road may need the permission of the local authority). In addition to permits and licences, requirements for insurance need to be investigated with a reputable insurance broker or with insurance companies specializing in the events field. Insurance, however, does have some commonality of approach, and various insurance companies have experience of dealing with cross-European events. Normal events insurance would cover items such as cancellation, venue operator's bankruptcy, non-appearance of stars, failure to vacate the venue, damage to property or premises, legal liabilities, damage to equipment and public liabilities.

Apart from permits and insurance, various kinds of contracts will be needed if the event provides entertainers, musicians, pyrotechnologists (fireworks experts), guest speakers or celebrities, in order to ensure the arrangements are correctly made. Contracting of this kind needs to be undertaken carefully, bearing in mind that bookings for specialists have to be made long in advance, together with some kinds of payments in advance, and arrangements in the event of cancellation of either party to the

Case Study 26

Insuring international events: I-tech Fair, Maastricht, Netherlands

Events activities range from the inherently safe to the rather dangerous. Certainly, in terms of public perceptions you might feel safer at a family dinner party than you would being involved in the Annual International Parascending Competition, even though you might get run over by a bus the moment you left the dinner party, but might not so much as receive a bruise while parascending. But the nature of risk and why an event might run or be cancelled could be more complicated. Suppose you were the organizers of the I-tech International Armaments Fair – what risks might you want your event to be insured against?

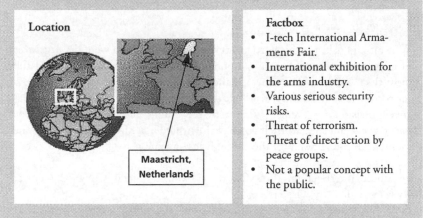

Location

Maastricht, Netherlands

Factbox
- I-tech International Armaments Fair.
- International exhibition for the arms industry.
- Various serious security risks.
- Threat of terrorism.
- Threat of direct action by peace groups.
- Not a popular concept with the public.

The I-tech International Armaments Fair is an annual opportunity for defence buyers and sellers to get together, in just the same way that any other industry might showcase its products at a major international trade show. This trade exhibition originally took place in Düsseldorf, Germany, but became the focus of action by the German peace movement, to the extent that during heated protests at the exhibition shots were fired and the exhibition organizers cancelled the event.

The event was insured against cancellation and as an immediate consequence it was moved to Maastricht in the Netherlands. Maastricht has a major exhibition and congress centre, which was opened in 1988, with a capacity of 17,000 square metres in three interlinked exhibition halls, and 24 conference rooms, the largest of which can accommodate up to 350 people. The centre has extensive facilities, including a 500-seater restaurant, a business centre, a bank, a hairdresser, a pub and two hotels, the Golden Tulip with 180 rooms and the Hotel Tulip Inn with 103 rooms.

The insurance arrangements for the event are:

1. Public liability cover up to €5 million.
2. Employer's liability cover for staff, including casual and volunteer staff .
3. Cover for equipment loss or damage.
4. Cancellation or abandonment cover (including severe adverse weather conditions).

For this particular event the cover included 'financial cause insurance' (e.g. exhibitor going broke) and insurance for damage to the venue. It is also possible to cover for the non-appearance of key speakers or entertainers, and failure to leave the venue at the prescribed time (e.g. snow blocks the venue). Exclusions for event insurance typically include small items damage (up to first €400), damage to ground/grass surface, mechanical fairground rides and bungy jumping.

Based on this case:

Why are the risks for this particular event unusual? If you were the organizer of a less sensitive event, such as a public carnival or festival, what might the most risky activities be, and would these be considered high, medium or low risk? Is this classification of risk linked in any way to the nature of the insurance provision for events? What activities might constitute high risk for participants and spectators? If you have identified a need for insurance of your event, have you allowed for the cost of it in your budgets?

For those interested in the Maastricht Exhibition and Congress Centre: www.mecc.nl
For those requiring more information regarding events insurance: www.expo-sure.com
For some wider legal issues (UK only): www.croner.cch.co.uk

Source: With grateful thanks to Albert Kemp of Insurex Expo-sure.

contract. Where such a contract is likely to be used, some legal advice should be taken, especially if the contract is out of the ordinary or non-standard in some way.

Systems Set-up

When you are setting up an event, it is very easy to become deeply involved in the weight of effort and detail needed to get the event off the ground and, for public events, the effort and the excitement of promoting it. A word of warning is needed here, in this case in the form of a definition of marketing by Gerry Draper (in Lickorish and Jenkins, 1995, p. 136). The marketing activity, according to Draper, is: 'ascertaining customer needs, tailoring the product as closely as possible to meet those needs, persuading the customer to satisfy his [*sic*] needs, and, finally, ensuring the product is easily accessible when the customer wishes to purchase it'. The organizer of special events should take careful note of the last point. A common failing in events organization is found at the beginning of the delivery stage, and that delivery stage starts with enquiries and the issue of tickets. By way of example, here are a few words that you may have heard over your phone: 'If you would like to know about availability, press button one; if you would like to make a booking, press button two; if you know the extension of the person you require please dial it now' (as if you had the faintest chance of knowing the extension of the person you require or knowing which button to press when the automated system hasn't got a button for what you really want). Experienced events coordinators might join us in asking how long it might take for a customer to find out what a ticket actually costs in this type of situation. In short, no amount of money spent on marketing will do us any good if we make it difficult for visitors and participants to make enquiries and get tickets.

For all its modern complexity, the final piece of the events jigsaw, the buying (that is, the purchase of tickets), still depends on one piece – the visitor picking up the phone and wanting a ticket or walking in and getting the money out. 'Picking up the phone' may mean faxing you, e-mailing you, using the Internet or sending granny down with a hand-basket and a wad of cash on the bus, but it is still down to someone showing an interest in the event, and that show of interest has to be dealt with efficiently and effectively.

Setting up a system to deal with enquiries and sell tickets might be as simple as putting your phone number on the posters for the village fête and getting Giorgio the barman to sell them from the village bar. In all probability, though, for those events for which the public can buy tickets, you need to give some careful thought to making it easy for them. Do not exclude part of your potential target market by making it difficult, or impossible, for them to get the tickets or make the booking they want to. Ideally, you should have as many ways of selling tickets and as many outlets (besides the central enquiry and ticket office) as you can imaginatively think of and can reasonably service (Pick and Anderton, 1996). That is, you have to be able to supply outlets with tickets, to monitor what is being sold and to react to increased sales at any one point by being able to increase the allocation, if that is reasonable given the number of people you can admit (or have seats for, within the capacity of the venue). A central computer at your main office, with a software programme such as Ticket Pro, should be able to cope with these demands easily, and within a system set-up, perhaps, to report daily sales.

Let us not beat about the bush: if you make it difficult for people to get tickets, you will have an empty event. The next person who says 'Oh, yes, we'll open the office from 9 a.m. to 5 p.m. during the week and people can come and buy them . . .' will get a large boot in the buttocks. You will do no such thing. Make sure the office is open when people want to buy them, make sure it is easy to pay, make sure you have lots of outlets, make sure you can buy on-line, or by e-mail, or, if necessary, by carrier pigeon, and make sure it is someone's job and responsibility to respond to these enquiries and requests, and answer the e-mail. Get it together!

Case Study 27

Event on-line booking systems: PIMRC, London, England

The process of booking for events varies considerably depending on the type of event and the target market. On-line booking systems are becoming a feature of certain types of events, especially in the organizational category, where large numbers of people in the target market have access to the Internet. The annual PIMRC conference is an international event taking place in a different host country every year. Destinations have included Boston, Yokohama, Helsinki, Toronto and London. The conference deals with electronic communications and the organizing body is the Institute of Electrical and Electronic Engineers.

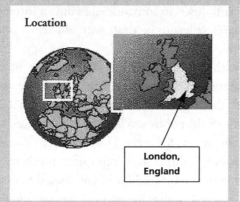

Location

London, England

Factbox
- PIMRC 2000, London.
- International conference dealing with electronic communications.
- Around 600 delegates from up to 40 countries.
- Has a four-day programme, including workshops, seminars, technical sessions, a welcome reception and a conference banquet.

The conference has an international reputation and includes an intensive programme of sessions over the four-day period. Delegates include not only industrialists and professionals in the industry but also academics and students, the event being organized in such a way that delegates can attend the whole four days and as many sessions as they are interested in, or select particular activities. The conference outline, reproduced from the public website, was:

	Monday 18/9/00	Tuesday 19/9/00	Wednesday 20/9/00	Thursday 21/9/00
a.m.	Tutorials and workshop	Opening and keynote address Technical sessions	Technical sessions	Technical sessions
Lunch				
p.m.	Tutorials and workshop	Panel session Technical sessions	Panel session Technical sessions	Panel session Technical sessions
Evening	Welcome reception		Conference banquet	

Potential delegates wishing to participate have to register (book) prior to the event. This is normal for this kind of event, for which registration can be undertaken in a number of ways:

- booking by phone, post or fax to the organizers themselves;
- booking by phone, post or fax to an organizing agency or professional conference organizer;
- booking by e-mail or Internet.

In the case of this particular event, potential delegates are informed that the preferred method of booking is on-line (provided by Inntel), and they are encouraged to use this method in preference to any other. Clearly, as this is a conference, not a public event, there is no booking on the day at the entrance, as final numbers are needed for room layouts, meal ordering, etc. beforehand. Potential delegates are encouraged to book well in advance by having all those who book before 19 August entered in a prize draw to win one of ten free tickets to the conference banquet, held (like the conference itself) at the Hilton London Metropole Hotel.

This approach to booking, where there is one preferred method, has the advantage of administrative efficiency. All bookings go to one central location where they can be coordinated and confirmed on-line, giving the ability to check the status of bookings in real time, on a common system, without, say, having to check through and count individual correspondence. The system has the further advantage of saving staff time, as the potential delegate fills in the requirements on a standard on-line form.

Nevertheless, this approach, while useful for some types of events, is not suitable for all. It could not be used alone for sporting events, as many people will make a short lead time decision on attending and will buy a ticket on the gate. It is similar with many voluntary and charitable events, public open events and so on, where the equipment and systems do not exist to deal with this kind of on-line activity, nor might the potential target market have access to on-line systems or even be computer literate. For these reasons, event organizers must think carefully about the ticketing and booking systems they wish to set up in relation to their target markets and the usual way in which those target markets might buy a ticket or pay an entrance fee for an event.

Based on this case:

Why is on-line booking very suitable for organizational events of this type? Why might such systems not be suitable for, perhaps, a public garden show? What systems must be set up to support the booking process, by way of recording, dealing with enquiries, controlling total numbers, monitoring demand and gathering market research data about attendees?

Related websites for those interested in the PIMRC conference and the IEEE: www.pimrc2000.com and www.ieee.org

   In setting up your advance ticket sales effort, there is no reason why you should not use various methods and channels. If your main method is from your own central ticket office, then think about how the weight of demand can be taken off it if you have other sales channels, such as selling tickets on-line. On the other hand, you might decide you have a big event to prepare and only modest expertise, in which case the activity could be contracted to a ticketing agency, which will earn a small commission from each ticket it sells, but relieve you of the whole activity. Finally, you might have an event where the number of tickets is strictly limited for genuine reasons. In such a case, one central office, with carefully considered limitations, might have to be your solution.

   Taking tickets 'on the door' also requires a little forethought. The most important issue is whether your 'door' will be able to cope with the demand. If only 20 people turn up, there is no problem. But what if 2,000 turn up? That's going to be a bit of a queue, isn't it? So what do we know about selling tickets 'on the door'? What we do know, from research done in cinemas (which obviously have to have quite good 'on the door' systems), is that the average time taken to process a ticket request from a member of the public is about 20 seconds (Slack *et al.*, 1998). So, a little simple maths: 2,000 members of the public waiting at your (narrow) gate for tickets for your evening extravaganza of sound and light (followed by a fish supper at Giorgio's bar). Three a minute, or almost 670 minutes. Oh, a mere eleven hours. By which time the fish supper will be cold. More gates, more ticket sellers, people to deal with odd enquiries that might block up the system; you name it, you need it.

Operational Activities

The big day is almost upon us, we have done as much planning as was needed, we have organized all the various people, parts, organizations, supplies and equipment that we planned for, it's six in the morning and time to throw ourselves out of bed with enthusiasm and get the kettle on. You thought I was joking didn't you? Actually, I'm not. You are going to be awfully busy on the big day, and you might have little or no chance to eat and drink. If that happens you become dehydrated and your blood sugar levels fall, you become poor at decision-making, and you won't notice problems quickly enough. So make the time, have a decent breakfast (or whatever meal before the event) and drink a lot during it. It will help to ensure you are competent. And while you're having your breakfast, check the weather report and local travel news.

Correspondence and schedules check

To help to prioritize your activities, check for any last minute changes, notes left for you, correspondence, phone messages or e-mails. Once you have done this, re-read your planned schedule for the set-up and make any amendments or notes. Carry a notebook around with you. People have a habit of mentioning things as you go round which you may need to deal with. It will be a busy day, and you will forget otherwise. Whenever you sit down to rehydrate (have a drink), check your notebook. As the event coordinator or floor manager you would normally expect the arrival of other staff, volunteers and helpers early on the day, or, in the case of large events, possibly before (particularly if staging, rehearsal or complex setting up is required). A check can then be made of arrangements between coordinator and staff to deal with any final requests or changes to the booked details. Experienced clients can be expected to phone or call in up to a week beforehand or the day before, in order to make general checks. This is to be encouraged, as is a 'pre-con' meeting between the venue, yourself and the other organizers to iron out any last minute problems.

The event office

In order to reduce stress on organizers, helpers, staff and visitors and ensure there is a central point of enquiry for an event. An organizers' office should be provided whenever an event is going to be large, long running or VIP in nature. Where possible offices should be in a convenient location (not a

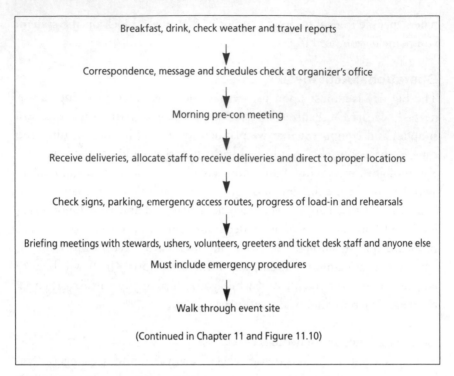

Figure 10.7   *Pre-operations on the day.*

hotel bedroom), and can be anything from a portacabin to a desk in the park-keeper's potting shed. As a minimum, everyone should know where it is and that it should be supplied with a landline phone and, preferably, a fax machine. Without this the venue itself (in the case of a hotel or public hall) will become the clearing house for any activity relating to the event, or people will simply stop and ask the first person they find ('Excuse me, mate, where do you want these boxes of very delicate glasses?' 'Er, no idea, chum, put them inside that yellow dumper truck, while I go and look for somebody that knows'). The arrival of the staging, lighting and PA equipment, suppliers and speakers with queries, the sponsor's chief executive wanting somewhere for a 'quiet meeting' before the event; all will have to be dealt with. Providing a room is not a matter of politeness. Without it, the staff can be inundated with enquiries which they may not be able to deal directly with, or find the organizer in time to deal with them. If you, as an event organizer, are out and about around the venue, get a cell phone or a walkie-talkie radio sorted out, and if it stops ringing, that is because it is broken, not because no one wants you. Make sure you go back to the office at some specified times to check things are going OK and to deal with anything that can't follow you around.

Deliveries of supplies

Various things will be delivered as preparations progress. Make sure these are carefully checked against the purchase orders by the designated person. One of the difficulties events organizers face is that an event is at the end of a supply chain which is very time specific. To highlight this, if you had 300 best porcelain plates delivered to a hotel as new stock, and they were the wrong size, the wrong colour or the wrong design, the hotel could send them back and continue to operate using its older, existing plates. However, because events are unique and one-off, perhaps limited to a few hours of high-pitched activity, and 300 best porcelain plates are delivered which are the wrong size, what do you do? First, you don't send them back, as they might be the only ones you could get in time, and you can't serve 300 chicken dinners on the tablecloth. You accept them, writing on the delivery note that they do not comply with purchase order number whatever, and then phone the suppliers to see if they can get you the right ones in time. Be careful to set up a controlled delivery receival system. The system might have to be a volunteer helper standing next to the main gate with a list, whose job is to check what is coming in, sign for it and point it to the place where it needs to go, but better that than to have to chase around every time a surprise in a lorry turns up.

Transport and parking

With some major events, particularly international ones, there may be a need to make suitable arrangements to transport participants to and around the event, to deal with baggage and materials and equipment in advance and afterwards. For this type of activity there are various companies involved in ground handling; that is, transport, baggage and goods moving. Related to this are activities such as venue–terminal and venue–hotel transfers. In the case of these transfers the nature of transport provision varies, depending on distance and the ease of finding the venue. Participants and visitors may be able to walk, there may be public transport laid on or taxi services may be appropriate and provided formally or informally. There are many events, in all categories, where transport and transfer of people are significant. At the top end of this scale is the provision of chauffeur-driven executive cars to deal with VIPs and dignitaries. Coaches might also be hired. These typically range from 18 to 52 seats and may be luxury vehicles with on board toilets, drinks, video facilities and host/hostess guides. Coach hire of this kind is particularly useful for both executive travel and transfers of large numbers of people to remote venues. On the other hand, for many kinds of events, people will arrive on foot, by public transport or by car.

Adequate and convenient car parking arrangements will need to be made, including arrangements for mobility impaired visitors, for which close liaison with the local authority and the police, who have a role in traffic flow and control, will be necessary in advance. You may also need to provide volunteer or staff car park stewards on the day.

Load-in

The most likely thing to arrive following the organizer at a large event is large staging (some may take several days to construct and this should be foreseen in the scheduling and booking of the venue). A ground plan should be made by the coordinator and a copy left with the venue, to enable work to proceed if the organizer is not yet present or has been held up. A stage set will often be followed by the technical equipment, lighting, sound rig and so on. This part of the set up is sometimes referred to as 'load-in' or 'bump-in'. Doing this properly, with stage and layout plans, and with the area clearly marked out (having been carefully measured for the original plans), should help to ensure that getting a set and its technical equipment up and running is done quickly and efficiently so it can be tested or used for rehearsal.

At this point, once all the equipment is in place, cleaning can be done, message boards and signing put up and other support activities, such as the layout of arrangements for visitors' arrival, organized. It is important that the event is properly signed. Signs are needed for two main purposes: information and emergencies. Information signs deal with things like normal entry and exits, the location of services and activities, where to queue from and how to do things. Emergency signs deal with emergency procedures, emergency exits and escape routes, how to operate emergency equipment and how to call for help.

The design of these two types of sign must be distinctly different. In general, emergency signs of various kinds can be obtained from specialist suppliers, from office or workplace suppliers or from suppliers listed in the phone book. Most indoor venues will already be properly signed for emergencies, as this is a legal requirement. This can be checked during the risk assessment process. For events which are using an unusual venue, or are outside, careful thought needs to be given to emergency signposting. As part of the planning stage, a ground plan of the site should have been drawn up, including the layout of emergency exits, access for emergency vehicles such as ambulances or fire engines and emergency routes. These can then be signposted and roped off, with stewards allocated to keep them clear during the event.

The design of the information signs depends on what sort of event you have. If this is going to be a large-scale professional event, then you can employ a professional sign-making company. If this is a modest volunteer event, then the design of the signs depends on your skill with a computer. You will not even need any fancy software: keep your sign design simple so the signs can be seen from a distance, and if you draft them up on A4 paper using the largest font you can get on it, you can always get them enlarged and laminated at a print shop to A3 so they are easier to see from a distance. Ensure they are all the same design and font. This is not just a matter of how professional your signs will look – visitors should be able to recognize information or emergency signs from the mass of background material they will encounter when visiting your event.

Security and the media
Certain types of event will involve security issues. For VIP or political events a security check may take place at some point prior to the event starting, usually between set-up and public arrival (in these cases the set-up will have to be completed at least a day prior to the event). Police or interior ministry security (in Britain called The Home Office) may want to check the venue site and may well use sniffer dogs and metal detectors to do so. In some cases visitors or the audience may be required to pass through metal detectors of the kind found at airports, with specialist security staff on duty, video surveillance and security checks of staff. At this level it is also likely that staff may be required to hold special passes, though it is common for all staff to be badged in some way, not only for the purpose of courtesy to the delegates, guests and visitors but as a routine security issue. Advice on security can also be sought from the local police for smaller events, and from security companies, some of whom specialize in security at events such as rock festivals. Security is a serious issue, but a note of caution – do not make a big performance out of it. Making security into a major issue can be counterproductive to people's feeling of being secure. If security is too obvious people will wonder why it is there, possibly leading to them feeling more fearful, not less. Second, remember media reactions. If your marketing department organizes a press call, or gets a TV crew to your event, the media will almost naturally look for the bad news. You will watch the TV later to see what great pictures of your event are shown across the national network, to find that the TV presenter stood in front of the largest security guard (usually holding the most enormous dog on a leash) on the entire site, said one positive thing about your event and then talked on national TV for five minutes about the heavy security.

This tendency to latch on to the tiniest whisper of bad news can give your marketing and public relations team nightmares. Reporter: 'Did the ceremony go well?' Your press officer: 'Yes, we had an excellent day, with 30,000 people attending, although there was a bit of an argument between two blokes in the catering tent over a cream bun; ho, ho, ho . . .' Later, you read the paper, which has the headline: 'Public brawl ruins opening ceremony'. In case you think this can't happen in real life, here is the headline from the opening ceremony of the Welsh Highland Railway on 7 August 2000: 'Tractor protest mars Welsh Highland opening' (Johnson, 2000). During the culmination of a ten-year, €5 million effort by volunteers, a farmer left his tractor across the track and 'the police were called'. This is rural Wales. Some fool leaves a tractor on your railway and you have to give the police a ring, the nearest 'copper' is probably 30 km away on serious police business but the impression given in the media is of a major incident. Nevertheless, due care should be taken of the media, and adequate and proper facilities provided for them. This might include their own media centre, tent, etc., equipped with its own power (for broadcasts) and its own phone lines, fax lines and computer workstation(s), as well as adequate and sufficient refreshment (but not alcoholic, in case they write about how extravagant the hospitality was on public finances!).

Rehearsal and briefings
A rehearsal may take place of the technical facilities, particularly of sound and presentation systems for many kinds of events. While this rehearsal may be a purely technical activity for certain types of high-profile organizational events, product launches or public relations events, it is possible that the rehearsal may be of the 'full dress' kind, including practice by actors, musicians, entertainers or other artists, timing arrangements, acoustics and so on. Ushers, if required, can be briefed at this point, together with any meeters/greeters the organizer may have arranged.

Briefings for casual and specialist staff should include elementary issues such as what the event is for, who is coming and the opening and closing times; details such as the location of toilets, cloakrooms, organizer's office, refreshment areas, check-in areas; what to do with the VIPs (such as direct them to a VIP hospitality room); how to assist mobility impaired visitors into the event; and what action is required in an emergency, including the nature of the alarm system, emergency exits, assembly points, the location of the medical centre if there is one or how to get a first aider quickly if there is not (Maitland, 1996). All staff at the event must be given a copy of the site map, information sheet, emergency contact list and emergency procedures. The site map and information page should be one sheet of A4, the emergency contact list and procedures should be on another sheet of A4. Any more than this and staff will not read it. Clarity is essential. The pre-event briefing can be summarized as:

1. The purpose of the event, type of visitors, likely numbers.
2. Opening and closing times, the programme, facilities and services.
3. Parking and access, facilities for the mobility impaired.
4. Who you report to and arrangements for staff refreshment.
5. Emergency contacts, systems and procedures. Keeping access clear.
6. Who to direct the media to.
7. Questions and answers.

Visitor welcome

The entrance areas or visitor reception area should be ready for use prior to the start time, even if this, in the case of a small informal event, amounts to no more than a table with programmes for people to pick up as they arrive. At large events, for convenience of organization, the layout of the arrival area might be arranged with several entrances. It may also be necessary to provide greeters or an information desk, or both, as minor queries by incoming arrivals can slow down the entry process. Queries can be dealt with by the greeters going along the queues. The greeters have the additional function of helping to direct visitors. While signage is necessary and important, people arriving in unfamiliar locations will look first for someone official to ask, and only secondly for (inanimate) directions. Toilets should also be located near the entrance areas: the first thing that will be needed, especially if your event attracts the public, and particularly families, will be the toilets.

Where this would help, packs, site maps, entry badges and tickets (such as refreshment tickets) and programmes should be laid out in boxes (e.g. alphabetically) to ensure the arrival process goes quickly. It is preferable that this lay-out process should actually take the form of all items (programme, site map, badges, tickets and pack) being put into large envelopes or 'goody bags' and stacked (for those events where the visitor is going to receive a pack). Not only does this increase the speed of entry, it also saves a great deal of stretching over a vast array of material spread on a table. Any urgent messages can be displayed on a board at the arrival point or even highlighted on stage screens during refreshment breaks. It would also be preferable to have your most experienced staff available at the entrances, as first impressions count, and an impression of confusion, given by inexperienced staff at the doors, will reflect badly on the event as a whole. In the planning of the arrival areas, thought should also be given to providing power and phone points for tills (for both enquiries and if automated transactions are to take place), and to the way in which the tills will be supervised, supplied with cash and change, then emptied, with income recorded and banked.

If the event is a conference or VIP invitation-only event, a list of delegates or guests expected, plus badges (for conferences) or some suitable small gift (for invited events, such as corsages), should have been made up prior to the event. (Where security is an issue, guests must be politely required to wear their badges, though normally most guests are happy to wear badges; at informal events or where there is no security issue, not everyone may wish to wear a badge and should not be compelled to if they do not want to.) But it is important that guests are checked against the guest list as this will provide accurate final numbers of the people attending and can be passed to catering staff for any last minute amendments to be made to seating or refreshment arrangements. This also acts as a key security check.

It is also common at conference-type check-ins to issue information packs, including agendas, working papers, delegate lists and a little information about the venue for delegates to take away with them. The last of these should be provided by the venue's marketing department to the client. If as organizer you are making up their own packs, ensure that a selling opportunity for the venue is not missed. For this kind of event, coordinators would be supported by check-in staff, normally one per fifty delegates, provided either by the organization itself or by the venue, to ensure delegates find the right conference and do not get mixed up with any other activities taking place (Seekings, 1996). Normally the coordinator will be on hand at least half an hour prior to the published start time to deal with supervising the arrival area.

Summary

We have attempted to provide an overview, in this chapter, of some of the more serious issues regarding managing events as projects, including the risk management and key aspects of insurance, legal, health, safety and licensing requirements. At the least, we have indicated where to look for further information about these things. The HSE book *The Event Safety Guide* is especially recommended with regard to health and safety issues for events. We have also sought to provide an overview of the operational activities which take place immediately prior to, and during, an event, noting that efficient preparation and due thought to operational issues will reduce the risk of something going wrong. The set-up process should not be seen as separate from the activities of running the event on the day, as this is often a continuous proces. The reader should also look at the following chapter, under 'Running the Event on the Day' in particular, for more information.

Reference List

Croner (2000) *Croner's Hospitality Management.* Kingston upon Thames: Croner CCH Group.

Health and Safety Executive (1999) *The Event Safety Guide.* Sudbury: HSE, pp. 3–20.

Johnson, P. (2000) 'Tractor protest mars Welsh Highland opening', *Steam Railway*, 18 August, p. 16.

Lickorish, L. and Jenkins, K. (1995) *An Introduction to Tourism.* Oxford: Butterworth Heinemann, p. 136.

McDonnell, I., Allen, J. and O'Toole, W. (1999) *Festivals and Special Events Management.* Milton, Queensland: Jacaranda Wiley, pp. 198–9.

Maitland, I. (1996) *How to Organise a Conference.* Aldershot: Gower, pp. 195–202.

Morris, W. G. (1994) *The Management of Projects.* London: Thomas Telford, p. 245.

Nickson, D. and Siddons, S. (1997) *Managing Projects.* Oxford: Butterworth Heinemann, pp. 17–18.

Pick, J. and Anderton, M. (1996) *Arts Administration.* London: E&F Spon, pp. 103–6.

Reiss, G. (1998) *Project Management Demystified*, 2nd edn. London: E&F Spon, pp. 1–4.

Ridley, J. and Chency, J. (1999) *Risk Management.* Oxford: Butterworth Heinemann.

Seekings, D. (1996) *How to Organise Effective Conferences and Meetings*, 6th edn. London: Kogan Page, pp. 320–41.

Slack, N., Chambers, S., Harland, C., Harrison, A. and Johnston, R. (1998) *Operations Management*, 2nd edn. London: Pitman, pp. 383–6.

CHAPTER 11

The Organization Manager and the Team, During the Event

Aims
- To identify the kinds of organizations found at events.
- To explore organizational effectiveness.
- To discuss recruitment issues for paid, voluntary and permanent staff.
- To consider issues about event management 'on the day'.

Introduction

The organization and staffing of special events varies considerably. Personal events, for example, often involve friends, family and volunteers. Organizational events may employ event management companies or professional events organizers. Both paid and volunteer helpers are common at a large number of events, notably those involving community activities, sports and so on. Professional organization is common, but expensive for some kinds of event. As a typical example, weddings could be undertaken entirely by volunteer help or entirely by professional help, or a mixture of both – it may simply depend on the budget. The event organizer must be aware, though, that this is not the only criterion – the issue is partly one of knowing what volunteer help can accomplish or when to bring in professionals for reasons of size, safety, standards or whatever else.

As with many other labour-intensive service industries, the events business has a considerable need for staff. This need is satisfied by both on-the-job training and the recruitment of staff from outside, whether direct from the labour pool or by recruiting from colleges and universities. Unlike other service industries, however, there are very few events-specific courses in the current academic world. This means that the events business has to rely very heavily on adapting its staff from other sources, such as from the hospitality or tourism industries, and from courses in these fields as well as marketing, business and leisure programmes.

For all the considerable effort that goes into planning an event, running it on the day can still prove a challenge. The coordination of a wide range of disparate and even unusual activities, facilities and services can be overwhelming. Events management has to be effective, and events managers must be good communicators and good delegators in situations that may be constantly changing. The importance of planning in this situation is that it reduces the variability and uncertainty of what is taking place during the event, and allows the event coordinator to concentrate on those matters which require immediate or constant attention.

Organization

One of the themes which has emerged in the preceding chapters is the diversity of events, anything from celebrity weddings to tennis tournaments. The organizational issues mirror this diversity. It is extremely unlikely that any two events would have exactly the same organization structure or staffing. This said, there are some similarities and we would expect core services to be organized in broadly similar ways. There is some probability, therefore, that event organizational structures will include five main functions: visitor services operations, support services operations, marketing, administration and finance. These five functions can be further subdivided depending on the nature and size of the event, but were we to survey the organization charts of a number of events, all five functions would probably be present in some form (see Figure 11.1).

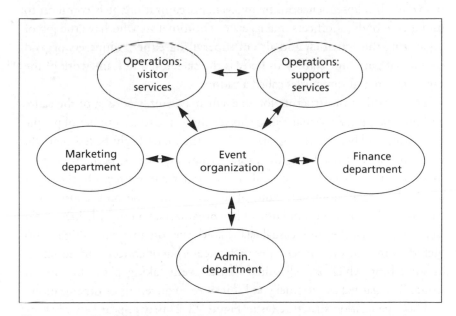

Figure 11.1   *Simplified events organization structure.*

The organizational structure for an event forms the framework around which the various activities and services are provided. It has been previously noted that events provide a mix of products and services; for example, ceremony and celebrations, food and drink services, presentation and technical services, support and ancillary services. These activities will probably come under an operations department, which might itself be subdivided into visitor services and support operations (as in Figure 11.1, the former for parts of the event which have public contact, the latter for those that do not). In addition to this, which will be specific to any given public event, the organizational structure will typically have a marketing department whose role may be to cover sales activities, and also enquiries and ticketing, depending on the type of operation. There is also likely to be an accounts and control function, to deal with both outgoing and incoming invoices and financial business, which may also include a purchasing role, particularly in larger events. Underpinning the support activities will be an administration department covering not only general administration but also personnel issues, recruitment and induction, payment of wages, etc.

In this kind of organizational structure, the key members of staff, or key managers, might be the only paid staff in the event; the actual staff doing the work might all be volunteers. Similarly, if the event is being run by a club or society, the key members of staff might simply be the members of that organization's normal committee. Committees are extremely common in events. In consequence, in many events organizations it is common to find a core body of officers, managers or coordinators who have the job of organizing the activities, and also of supervising either volunteers or paid casual and part-time staff. This body is the skeleton and framework of the organization and sometimes called a cadre.

The organization structure for an event may simply consist of the cadre and their helpers. At a small village flower show, the total number of people organizing and helping to organize and run the event might be less than 20, with only six of these being the cadre, or key organizers, perhaps because they form the village horticultural club's regular committee. On the other hand, the organization structure of an event may become enormously complex. There may be a mixture of key organizers, volunteer helpers, paid full-time, part-time and casual staff, and the organization might also include some outsourced activities such as catering or concessions, resulting in something which is well suited to the event taking place, but which would be regarded as extremely odd if it were a conventional organization.

The organization structure (as in Figure 11.2) may appear very conventional, because there is a need, in an organization where unfamiliar people

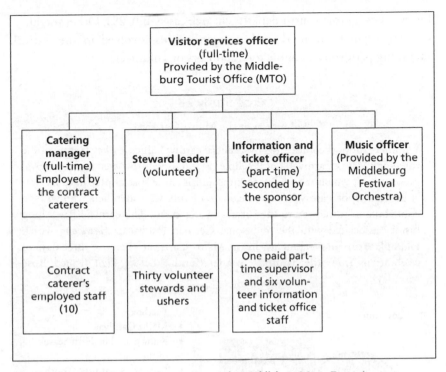

Figure 11.2 *Visitor services department at the Middleburg Music Festival.*

are working together, to know exactly who is in charge. There must be no ambiguity for reasons of the safety of the public and the efficiency of the organization, which may, having been created to run an event, be a relatively short-lived entity.

The lines of communication, in events organizations, not only pass up and down the hierarchy, but also run from side to side. This is essential to ensure that information gets passed around the organization quickly and does not get bogged down by having to be transferred up to line managers and then back down again. For example, if there is a change in the music programme, the music officer needs to tell the visitor services officer, but also needs to be able to speak directly to the information and ticket office, without waiting for other managers or officers to turn up, who might be part-time or only around the venue at certain times. The one person who is slightly detached in this example system is the catering manager, whose own organization is rather self-contained.

In this type of organization, we can also see a mix between paid and volunteer staff, with staff perhaps originating from a number of sources. Suppose a festival is being organized by a city tourist department, rather than by a voluntary committee – in this case the core cadre may be provided by members of that tourist department (see case study 29). Other members of staff might be from the other organizations involved in the festival, including performers, contractors, sponsors or volunteers.

Case Study 28

Volunteers at the Mainz Carnival

Volunteer support coordinated by a central carnival office is a key feature of the three-day Mainz Carnival. Local people are intensively involved in the carnival preparations, which take many months and include special preparations by a large number of 'carnival clubs', made up of volunteer members who wish to contribute in some way to the success of the event. The carnival has a long history associated with the traditional German festival of *Fastnacht*, which takes place on Shrove Tuesday. In the Mainz Carnival, there are three days of celebrations from the Saturday to the Monday before Lent (called Rose Monday).

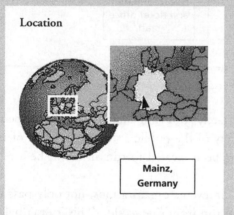

Location

Mainz,
Germany

Factbox
- Mainz Carnival.
- Known as 'The Fifth Season of the Year'.
- Comprises Saturday Youth Carnival, Sunday Carnival Guards Parade, Rose Monday Carnival Procession and three days of costume balls.
- Admission ticket, with grandstand seats, a costume ball and a carnival show: €70.

The Mainz Carnival is organized by a carnival office (secretariat), the Mainzer Carnivals Verein. It coordinates the efforts of official bodies, professional organizations and the many volunteer carnival clubs. The carnival office has a small permanent staff, which increases for the carnival itself, by the use of volunteers and additional casual staff, who have many years' experience of running the event. Carnival organization officially begins in the previous October, to give enough time for the complex work of providing an intensive three-day celebration in March. In practice, however, preparations and planning are more or less continuous for such a large-scale activity throughout the year.

The carnival organization is a combination of efforts by public, voluntary and private sector bodies. Local government involvement helps to provide tourist promotion and logistics support. The private sector, in the form of local businesses, helps with funding, sponsorship, displays and other support for the voluntary organizations involved. The voluntary element makes up a very significant part of the carnival effort, with the carnival clubs, together with many other local clubs, societies and recreational organizations involved. These range from sporting clubs to theatrical clubs, from music clubs to historical re-enactment societies, provide marchers in the procession, floats, displays and tableaux, and ensure the carnival is loud and colourful. A very wide range of activities takes place besides the major carnival processions, including carnival shows with stands and displays, and costumed and masked balls, where participants, guests and visitors can dress up to get wined and dined, and enjoy dancing and other social activities.

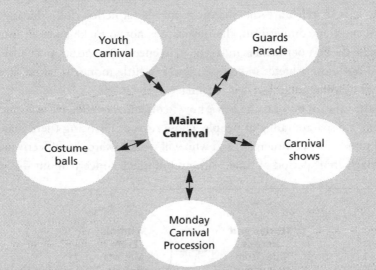

Based on this case:

What role do the various voluntary organizations play in making the carnival a success? What is the function of the carnival secretariat? How does the existence of carnival clubs improve the standard of the carnival and the range of activities being put on? Compare this organization with your own local carnival or annual festival: how do they differ?

Related website for those interested in visiting the Mainz Carnival: www.mainz.de

Source: Information kindly provided by Touristik Centrale Mainz.

Organizational Effectiveness

The culture of an organization has an impact on its efficiency and ability to do its job. However, most research into culture has centred on permanent organizations. The modest research undertaken on short-lived organizations, such as that quoted by Mullins *et al.* (1993), suggest that culture may be of only secondary importance to identifying, transmitting and delivering 'the main objective', which Mullins *et al.* (wrongly) suppose is the 'generation of profit for stakeholders'. In the events business, there may be some types of events whose purpose is indeed to make a profit, but we should be careful not to generalize about profit. Perhaps we could more legitimately say that events are about creating wealth – wealth of experiences, wealth in socialization, wealth in community spirit – but profit is too limited a concept. In our analysis of events so far, we have repeatedly made the point that it is the purpose of only certain types of events to make a profit. For the family and friends organizing a wedding the objective is not to making a profit, it is to celebrate the wedding; for the athletics club running its annual sporting competition, the objective is not to make a profit, but to showcase the best performers in its sport, to encourage and support athletes and to test those athletes in competition. If a little money is taken on the gate, all well and good, but it is secondary to the sport.

So the issue for event managers is how to organize an effective event, with possibly a disparate range of people whose reasons for being there may be social rather than commercial, and who will work towards an objective over a relatively short period of time, without too much concern about the style

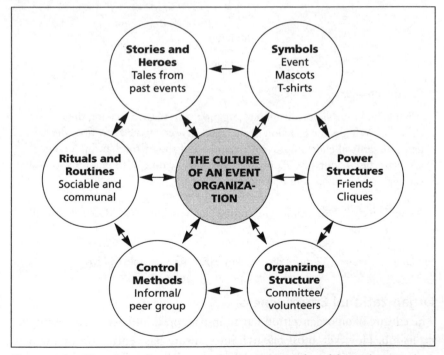

Figure 11.3   *The culture of an event organization. Source: adapted from Johnson and Scholes (1999).*

of the organization they are working with. Additionally, although an event may be undertaken by a professional organization, the nature of many events is still largely informal and social. Events are significant social activities, and they are often communal and good natured, which is reflected in their culture (see Figure 11.3).

The typology of events in Chapter 1 noted the difference in the scale of organizational complexity and levels of uncertainty. In organizational development terms, the simpler an event, the fewer contributing organizations and individuals will be involved; consequently, the development of the organization's culture may be faster, and this culture may also impact more quickly on its effectiveness. It is rather easy to assume that simply because events organization might be made up of happy, jolly volunteers who want to contribute their skills and enthusiasm, an event will be a runaway success. We should exercise a little caution in believing this. Richards (1992) makes the eloquent point that while volunteers 'can be the backbone' of an organization, they may also have their limitations, an initial rush of enthusiasm may fade away, they may have volunteered for reasons completely unrelated to the needs of the event (hence the requirement for a selection procedure even for volunteers) or they may be diverted from their task by other enthusiasms. For this reason, careful thought needs to be given to how to make the best use of volunteers, but also how to reward those whose efforts are genuine and add considerably to the event.

The volunteers are people who choose to contribute their time, skills, effort and experience without pay to benefit a cause, or the community in which they live. As such, their motives for volunteering are personal and probably social. By volunteering they may be involved in hobbies they enjoy, or be undertaking a role which enables them to meet new people or spend time with friends or which might provide satisfaction or self-esteem. It might also enable them to exercise their skills or remain active if they are retired. These motives must be taken into account when volunteer labour is being used. In the creation of an effective volunteer organization or team, it will naturally help to know what their reasons are for being there, and what they hope to get out of it.

The creation and development of teams in short-lived organizations and their effectiveness in situations which may be unusual or new to them can vary. The classical approach to team building is that teams go through a number of processes before they become effective; for example, the 'forming, norming, storming and performing' scenario, bearing in mind that not all teams reach the performing stage. However, this approach presupposes that there is sufficient time to organize teams and for them to socialize through the process. In the case of special events this method and approach to team building may not be appropriate or suitable. There may simply not be sufficient time to team build, in which case a participative style of management will be needed by the team leader. Additionally, as many events are reliant on volunteer staff, the time scale for organizing them and socializing them into the culture of the event organization may be very short indeed. In this case, the effectiveness of the organization may not rely on group development at all, but on a wide range of factors, some of which may ultimately be beyond the control of the organizing group.

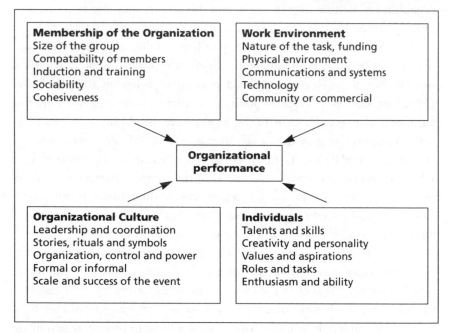

Membership of the Organization
Size of the group
Compatability of members
Induction and training
Sociability
Cohesiveness

Work Environment
Nature of the task, funding
Physical environment
Communications and systems
Technology
Community or commercial

Organizational performance

Organizational Culture
Leadership and coordination
Stories, rituals and symbols
Organization, control and power
Formal or informal
Scale and success of the event

Individuals
Talents and skills
Creativity and personality
Values and aspirations
Roles and tasks
Enthusiasm and ability

Figure 11.4   *Framework for an event organization's performance. Source: adapted from Mullins (1992).*

The event we have worked so hard to organize may not be a success. It may be a failure for any number of reasons, internal or external. Success is sometimes elusive, and for all our market research, for all the effort put in to producing something which we hope will be excellent, in the end the public might not actually buy tickets, and the reasons for this might possibly be beyond the control of the event organizers.

However, let us assume that everything is going wonderfully well. We have a packed programme, enthusiastic and knowledgeable volunteers, advanced sales of tickets are going like a French TGV and what we need to do is keep up the momentum. With volunteer staff, how effective we are depends on good leadership, clear objectives, thorough communication and the volunteers being adequately supported by the event organization. Volunteers should be given proper encouragement and praise for their efforts, be carefully listened to for their ideas and comments (and that these are acted on), be given flexibility in how they can perform a task, be in relatively small teams so they can socialize and enjoy themselves, and be given suitable rewards. The emphasis with volunteer staff is that they have volunteered because they are committed and interested, but they are unpaid. This lack of pay should be offset by careful thought about the support and rewards they get for doing the task. Support may be anything from providing proper meals for volunteers, and their own dedicated facilities, to proper induction and basic training. Rewards can be anything from special uniforms, badges, custom made sweatshirts or small leaving gifts, to holding social events and parties, or giving celebrations and prizes for the volunteers at significant points in the event, rather than just a farewell party at the end, in order to recognize their efforts. It is also important that volunteers are mentioned in the internal and external marketing of the event, in newsletters and press releases, and that following the closedown of the event careful efforts are made to thank volunteers by writing to them. It may also be necessary to provide some financial support in the form of the payment of travel or other subsistence expenses, or the provision of a travel pass where an event is so large that it has its own transport arrangements.

Staffing

If you were the client for an event, perhaps a company wanting a product launch or a celebrity wishing to hold a charity benefit, then there is a reasonable degree of certainty that you would wish to employ a professional organization to provide it. The events industry has not only management companies, but also production companies, as well as individual professional organizers and consultants. To put your event on, you simply employ one of these and pay them a given fee to get on with it, having set up a project brief. In fact, some companies employ or retain an events management operator, perhaps on a contractual basis. In this type of relationship, events operators may be invited to tender for the business, based on a brief of what is required, in much the same way that marketing agencies can tender for promotional programmes for client companies. Event management companies (EMCs) and organizers can be found in the phone book, and may be standalone operations or have grown out of a related service provider, such as a caterer, some being divisions of catering companies, out of production companies or as part of a hotel or venue booking agency. EMCs tend to be involved where the organizers have a requirement for major or high profile events, specialist dinners, celebrity parties, high-profile charity fund-raising events or where an event demands specialist design, innovation or a major media impact.

Looking at an event, the organizing body, client or buyer may simply say, 'Our event requires a professional paid organization, let's get some quotations in and watch some presentations, then we will choose an organizer and pay them to get on with it.' However, the diversity of events is such that this is only one way of doing it. The alternative is that the organizers, clients or buyers do it themselves. This is also extremely common and takes two forms. The first is where the organizing body employs a full-time person or even a department to undertake events organization. This is especially the case for trade activities, such as conference organization and fund-raising activity among companies, associations and charities. It is also the type of structure found in public sector organizations such as town and city council tourism, leisure or economic development departments. These departments often have the task of providing events to support council aims, such as to increase tourism, community inclusion, economic expansion, etc. Second, where the activity is directly run, but not part of a separate department within the client's organization, it might be that whoever wants an event in an organization just gets on and does it singly or in a group. This is often the case for conferences, staff parties, birthdays and so on.

CREATIVITY

Events Coordinator

We are a leading provider of corporate hospitality and event management services, working for a range of high profile companies in Europe. Our activities include sport, the arts, corporate incentives and conferences. We are seeking an experienced event coordinator with the following qualities:

- At least two years' event management experience.
- The ability to create imaginative programmes to meet specific briefs and budgets.
- Must be confident, self-reliant and mature. Own vehicle essential, knowledge of French or a second language useful.

Salary €30,000 plus attractive benefits package.

For further information contact Trudi van Heater, Creativity Ltd, 150 Festival Park Road, Middleburg, SG1 3PP or phone us on 00 44 (0) 1786 123456. Closing date 1 March 2001.

Figure 11.5 *Example job advertisement for an events coordinator. Source: adapted from an advertisement in the* Guardian.

Probably by far the most common type of events organization is none of these, it is the committee of volunteers. This committee might be in the position where it normally runs special events as part of its role. This is very common. Alternatively, a special committee might be set up just to deal with a given event. (We could even interpret the organization of a wedding by the respective families as a kind of volunteer committee.) But what if you have to start completely from scratch? Here you are with a brief to organize an event on your own. Most people at this point will pick up the phone and ring their friends ('Hello Anna, I've got to organize a party for Giorgio. It's going to need a few of us to do, any chance you could lend a hand?'). Well, you might not exactly ring your friends, you might talk to them in the pub or whatever, but instinctively, you probably do two things:

1. Think about who you know has the ability to help.
2. Think about who you know might like to help.

In setting up something slightly more formal than a few friends knocking together a dinner party, much the same approach can be considered, if in a rather more formalized way. You need to know some basic details about the event you are planning, but essentially you need to consider what talents or skills you will need and who might have them. Some people are good organizers, some people are good communicators, some people are good with their hands, some people are good with figures, with computers, with design. But it is not as simple as this. You will be putting together a team of volunteers, which means you will not necessarily get exactly the skills and talents you think you need. You are most likely to have a disparate group of people who want to be involved and who are enthusiastic (otherwise they probably wouldn't have volunteered), but who might need to take up tasks they have never done before (although this can be one of the enjoyments of volunteering for something). In short, you may simply attach the most suitable people to the various tasks you have identified by intuition.

On the other hand, you might look around your team and think 'Now what?' First, this is a special event, you have a tight time scale, it might have to be enough that you have some helpers and you will probably just be thankful they have turned up. For short-lived organizations there is little time for group development (though this will come up later in relation to operating cadres), and because of this you may wish to get this group of individuals to choose their own roles. This is to ensure they are doing something they like, or know a little about, and will put their best efforts into it. There are a couple of things to bear in mind. Individuals are just that, what is one person's best effort will be completely different from the next person's, and taken together with their abilities and experience you may get two completely different results from two people doing the same job. Bearing in mind the limitations or opportunities of the skills and talents they have, in order to guide the group and get the event going, in addition to letting them identify the jobs they might most like to do (someone will always say, 'I'll do anything really'), you can divide up ancillary tasks among them to cover those things that there might be no direct expertise in the group to cover. In this way you should be able to deal with gaps in your group's knowledge and talents, against your original list of what needs to be done. After all, lots of people will probably be able to say 'I can help out in the catering tent' but you may not get anyone who says 'Hey! I'm an expert in health and safety.'

A voluntary committee (or any committee) can vary considerably in the number of people involved in it, what they do, what their titles are and so on, but it will probably form the basic organization structure for many types of events (see Figure 11.6). It is important that the leader of the committee is the best person who can be found for the job. That person would need to have enough time to undertake the role, should have some previous experience of committee work and have some knowledge of organizing events previously. The implication of this is that the person who may have to set up the committee to run an event might not necessarily be the one who becomes the chair of it.

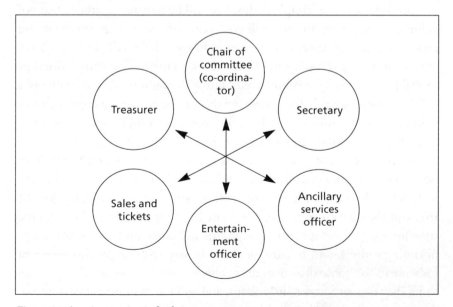

Figure 11.6   *A committee of volunteers.*

Factors Influencing the Number and Type of Staff

With the framework of the event organization up and running, the next stage is for the respective officers or heads of department to identify how many staff they need and what type. This process is often based on experience, either of previous events or of members of the committee. Alternatively, a list of tasks can be drawn up (or the work breakdown structure used) and the number of staff then estimated. This will result in the basic outline of a staff plan, which can then be developed and costed into a staffing budget. A number of factors will affect the number of staff each department will need to run the event:

- The size of the event, numbers attending, likely demand.
- The types of staff: paid, full-time, part-time, casual, volunteer.
- The layout and components of the event.
- The method by which the services are provided.
- What functions are carried out 'in-house' or contracted out.
- The demand for and scheduling of staff, number of staff per activity.
- The expertise required for the event

The size of the event

This is a simple enough place to start. How big is this event going to be? Can you put it on with a few friends and relatives, or will it need thousands (the 2000 Olympic Games is said to have required over 40,000 staff, a very large proportion being volunteers)? Do you know what the likely demand will be? Have you done any market research, or is your event simply limited by the capacity of your venue? If the site capacity is 300 people, or only has licensing for 300, then that is the maximum number of people you need to staff for. (See also Chapter 8 on logistics, especially for catering staff numbers.)

The balance between staffing types

There are variations between what your staff can achieve, given their expertise, ability, knowledge and experience. Full-time paid staff may have all these things in abundance, and it may be that one member of full-time staff can achieve what normally takes two volunteers to do. (But this does not allow for enthusiasm. A volunteer is working at your event because he or she wants to be there and to help. Volunteers may well work harder than full-time members of staff who don't want to be there – this is a variable.) Perhaps you may have a choice about how the event will be staffed. Within the limits of your budget you might decide you can afford three members of full-time staff to cover a particular task, say covering the information office. But that might mean, allowing for days off, that you will only be able to cover the information office with one person on a shift most of the time. Say it is open from 9 a.m. to 9 p.m. and you know it will get really busy in the afternoons. You have a range of choices:

- You can run it with the full-time staff, knowing the one on duty in the afternoons will be swamped.
- You could use one member of full-time staff as supervisor and trainer and have six volunteers to do the work, and use the money you save for another task.
- You could have three full-time equivalents (this perhaps means six half-time staff), which might give you more flexibility to cover the tasks.
- You might not be able to get any full-time staff, and you might finish up using a range of part-time, casual or volunteer staff in various roles to get the job done.

These alternatives depend largely on the circumstances you find yourself in. Full-time staff are not terribly common at the operational level of events, because running one event over a couple of days can hardly be described as full-time. Where there are full-time staff these are in festival cadres, or in those companies, such as contract caterers, that have large numbers of events to put on, with staff, especially at a management or coordinator level, travelling from one to another setting them up, running them and closing them down, then going on to the next one. In some companies, casual staff are taken on for a season, and can then be moved from event to event within a given geographical area. This saves time and money on training, and requires less overall effort on local recruitment (Cole, 1997).

The layout and concentrating staff at key points
The layout of the activities at an event can have a number of impacts on staffing. The wider the area that has to be covered, the more staff may be needed and the more difficult communications with them may become. Ideally, for their own safety and peace of mind, staff should not be on their own in locations isolated from the main centre of activity, without the means to communicate with it. The range of things going on at an event is a major factor in staffing. In general, the more that is going on, and the wider the range of services, facilities or components of an event, the larger is the number of staff needed.

In terms of physical layout, some events can be designed with ease of staffing in mind. It might be possible to concentrate all the services and activities on one central location, where the various staff, being multi-skilled, could do whatever needs doing. These 'service cores' tend to be centralized so that fewer staff can operate and supervise a larger number of activities, concentration of design also reduces transit times for staff going from one part of the venue to another and has the benefit of concentrating utility and store provision in one location.

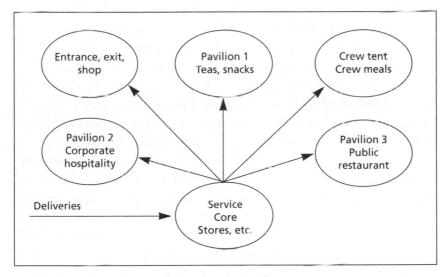

Figure 11.7   *Centralization of core services and staff.*

The method by which the events facilities and services are provided

This is chiefly an issue of the provision of services such as catering or retail where there are opportunities to provide the service 'in-house' (i.e. with your own staff or volunteers), as against contracting the activity to a specialist company. There are advantages and disadvantages of doing either, but in staffing terms, getting a contractor in will have the effect of relieving the organizers of having to bother about covering that particular task with their own staff. Related to this is the issue of quality. The contractor may have highly trained and expert staff and be able to provide something better than you could, within your limited resources.

The demand for and scheduling of staff

Demand is a baseline determinant of staffing. But at any event there will be a fixed level of staff beyond which it is not possible to fall (for example, one administrator may be required to be on duty at any time between 8.30 a.m.

and 6 p.m. five days a week to deal with even a low level of business: visitors, general paperwork, enquiries by phone, fax, e-mail or whatever). The one administrator may be able to deal with greater demand only up to a certain level. Quite simply, as demand increases so will staffing. The issue is about how to schedule the staff to deal with peaks and dips in demand. For this it will be essential to be aware of when the event is going to be busy and when it is not, and, for those peak demand periods, which parts of the event will be most busy and need most staffing. Suppose the peak arrival time at our village fête is between 10 a.m. and 11 a.m. Clearly we would need extra staff at the entrance, selling tickets. The peak period in the catering tent might be between 1 p.m. and 2 p.m., so the spare staff could be transferred from the entrance to the catering tent. The peak period in the arena might be between 3 p.m. and 4 p.m., with visitors buying things at stalls and playing games, so spare staff could be transferred there. This is a simple example, but illustrates the point that we need to give some thought to what parts of an event are busy when, and how we can deploy our staff to cope.

The control of the cost of staffing is also a major concern. Rosters are produced by management to schedule staff, yet cost control is as much dependent on effective forecasts of demand and careful rostering as it is on the sheer number of staff. A comparison of two managers compiling a roster for the same event, the same demand forecast and the same staff could still produce a significant variance in cost due to the ability of each to complete an appropriate roster effectively. More efficient rostering could, perhaps, reduce the number of staff needed and is thus also a factor in staffing, though possibly not a major one (Medlik, 1995).

Paid staff might not be a concern. Even a relatively large-scale event can be accomplished by capable volunteers, provided it is relatively simple in format and requires no major technical expertise. If we consider a play as an example, almost all the aspects of putting on a play, from preparing the stage sets to designing the costumes, could be done by experienced volunteers, but elements such as lighting or electrical systems would need expert volunteers. (The concept of an expert volunteer might seem a little odd, but is perfectly common. The person volunteering to deal with the lighting of the play might be a lighting engineer in real life, or a retired one, or do it as a committed hobby.)

The expertise required
This brings us to probably the most important issue for an events organizer: what kind of expertise is available for the planned event.

The various tasks identified should be developed into a series of job descriptions to help the matching process (an example job description form is given in Figure 11.8). The pool of labour must be considered carefully at this stage. What staff are available, what are they capable of, what is their expertise, what things might need to be done for which either training is needed, or professional help would have to be paid for? Even seemingly simple choices can have serious staffing complications in terms of staffing numbers and knowledge. This implication is often highlighted by catering issues, where organizers might choose a dish they particularly like, only to find it not only completely unsuitable for a wedding reception in a marquee, but also almost unproducable for the numbers involved. Organizers have been known, for example, to put crêpe suzette on a function menu because they saw it once in a restaurant and liked it – only to find, on the day of the reception for 400 people, that only one member of the catering staff had ever prepared it before and had no chance whatsoever of producing more than 20 an hour. This is one reason why many function caterers will test dishes in advance for a customer who requests something unusual. Food is only one example of the problem of expertise. An events organizer is best advised to list the expert knowledge of regular staff, or to ask his or her team of volunteers what they can do, what they have experience of, what the normal job is and what their hobbies are. Such a list will help to identify both where the staffing expertise lies and where it does not.

Staffing is, therefore, as much an issue of identifying what expertise exists as having large numbers of people to do things, unless, of course, the event actually requires large numbers of people to do very simple tasks; but these still have to be organized somehow.

Finding Staff

Recruiting paid staff

The recruitment of paid staff can be done in a relatively conventional way, through advertising in newspapers or events trade magazines. Marketing, tourism, leisure and hospitality magazines are also common sources of staff for events. Paid staff can be found through employment agencies, some of which specialize in various types of personnel. Sources of potential paid staff include colleges and universities, where students are not only looking for a job on graduation, but may also be looking for a part-time job while they are studying to help with their income. Paid staff can be sought through the Internet (newspapers often duplicate job adverts on their websites) and via industry contacts. Many companies that operate in the events business,

Job Title_____

Department_____ Department Leader_____

Base location or area _____ Event Coordinator_____

Needed from_____ To_____

Hours of work _____ Work pattern_____

Duties and responsibilities

_____

_____

_____

_____

Essential skills, talents or qualifications required

_____

_____

Desirable skills, talents or qualifications required

_____

_____

_____

_____

Induction and training to be given:

    Event background and tour ❑   Date:_____   Given: ❑

    Health, safety and fire   ❑   Date:_____   Given: ❑

    Food hygiene   ❑   Date:_____   Given: ❑

    Hosting skills   ❑   Date:_____   Given: ❑

    Manual handling and lifting ❑   Date:_____   Given: ❑

    Specific task training (state): _____

    Date:_____   Given: ❑

Rewards and benefits (pay/expenses/transport/parking permit/meals/
uniform/items in kind)

_____

_____

Any other comments

_____

_____

Copies: one to personnel file; one to department leader's file; one to the
member of staff

Figure 11.8   *Job description form.*

especially those in hospitality and catering, retain staff records for events and activities put on in a particular location. This enables them to use people who they have previously employed for repeat events, especially casual and part-time staff, as lists are kept of these by geographical area, so that if a particular venue is used frequently for different events, there is an existing pool of staff who can be called in.

Getting staff may not always be easy for events companies. There are areas (towns and cities) where the local labour market is stretched; that is, most people have jobs, there is low unemployment and getting part-time staff or casual staff can be extremely difficult. In cases such as these, staff may have to be transported to the event from some distance away, adding to the labour cost of the event.

Recruiting volunteers

This can be done informally, by asking around friends, colleagues, acquaintances and relatives. This might easily yield a range of helpers. However, it will be useful to explore what skills or talents they might have, so whereas a conventional application form for a job might explore a person's background or job roles, an application form for volunteers should contain a 'talent and skills' section, which will be very significant in identifying what a volunteer can bring to our organization and event. We are obviously looking for the kind of expertise that might be useful in an event environment, and can explore: previous experiences of events; hobbies and pastimes; experience of groups, formal or informal, as a member or as part of a committee; whether they have even had experience of visiting similar events, so they know what one could be like (even if not how to run one); what the main elements of their normal work or daily role are; what they did before they retired (if appropriate); and, most important of all, what they would be most interested in doing for the event, as a volunteer.

This means that as event organizers we have to analyse the event to identify the range of jobs and tasks that need to be done and seek to match our available volunteers to them. This matching is part of the selection process. Not all those who apply (even volunteers) are necessarily needed or suitable, and some may have to be refused.

There are various sources of volunteer staff. First are volunteers immediately associated with an event or an event organization as part of their job or hobby. This type of volunteer may be a member of a society or friend, relative or acquaintance of someone involved in that club or society. For example, an annual town flower show may be run by the horticultural club. In order to put on the event members of the club will participate, members

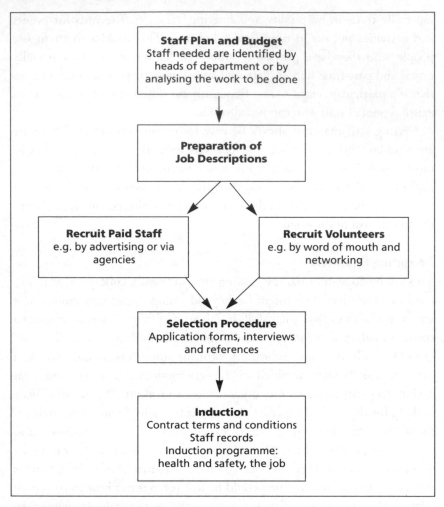

Figure 11.9 *Staff provision for an event.*

of the club's committee will organize friends and relatives of members to be volunteers to help produce the flower show. Second, there are those events which require large numbers of volunteers and for which this type of informal personal networking approach to getting them may not be sufficient. In this case a member of the organizing committee will have to be responsible for getting volunteer labour, or the task may even have to be given to a recruitment agency. In either case we would have to seek to attract volunteers by advertising in the local media, by making presentations to other interested voluntary bodies, by networking (word of mouth) or by organizing recruitment drives (i.e. preparing a comprehensive plan about how many people you need, how you will attract them, what sort of network you might need to do so, etc.).

Finally, we have assumed up to this point that volunteers are individuals, but a large-scale event may involve not only the key organizing body, but also a range of voluntary bodies that wish to participate. This is the case with carnivals and festivals. A central co-ordinating body may well be the focus for the activities of a wide range of participants, from commercial organizations, to voluntary bodies, to charitable organizations and so on, the success of the event depending on the cooperation between them.

Recruiting permanent staff

In order to achieve sufficiently high standards of service and management of event operations it is necessary to employ people with adequate skills and to provide additional training. Even if individual events are short-lived, events management companies, production companies and caterers require permanent staff, as they are dealing with an entire business composed of events of all kinds, in venues and sites within their geographical area. Historically, the acquisition of suitable staff for events management has been achieved by two main methods:

1. The employment of staff with a good basic education to be trained by the organization and developed as skilled member of staff and/or as managers.
2. The employment of staff with an appropriate vocational and educational background in the field or a related field.

The first method, effectively on-the-job training, is the most prevalent for operational staff. Staff and managers have been developed in-house by experience or by the company providing some form of basic training. Relatively unskilled jobs, such as steward leaders or stage crew, have tended to be based on recruiting a person with satisfactory potential and good handling skills, who could learn the job by experience through working with other existing staff. This method is sometimes backed up by additional short-course training in addition to fundamental activities such as induction and fire training. On this basis, it is still possible for members of staff to work their way up through an organization to supervisory or management level by experience over time.

The second method, based on vocational education, provides not only operational staff but also supervisors and managers. Larger organizations recruit from colleges or universities which run appropriate courses and then tend to add their own programme or training course to develop managers with a specific knowledge of their company. Yet it must be noted that there are almost no event industry specific further or higher education courses around Europe, though this position is beginning to change. In order to recruit, say, a junior event coordinator, the most likely educational source would be vocational courses in the hospitality and catering field, or leisure and recreation, or some business studies courses where the programme contains events management as a subject or module. These range from operations-level courses to undergraduate courses at degree level. Only at degree level do some colleges and universities include event management modules or, in a very few cases, events management pathways to their degrees. Other potential sources of vocationally educated people are the travel and tourism fields, sales and marketing and business administration. Typically people employed from these fields, particularly the hospitality field, will have a good background knowledge of business generally and some awareness of events as an activity, but will still need specific training, for two reasons:

1. Every organization is different.
2. Every job is different.

Even using graduates from those colleges and universities where the degree programme contains a specific events element, an events company will need to tailor the graduates employed to the particular organization and role. Nevertheless, there is a good level of cooperation between educational establishments and events companies and bodies. These links range from industry cooperation with assignment work and field visits, up to providing year-length paid placements for undergraduate students. By this method the events industry not only influences the curriculum content of courses, but also effectively provides 'seed corn' for future employment among those students with an interest. A number of the companies providing year placements may well go on to employ some of the placement students once they have completed their course. This system is particularly well established between events venues and the greater hotel schools, and is mutually beneficial and often seen as a model of good practice for other industries.

In addition to the above methods, the ebb and flow of employment in general accounts for a large number of staff and managers within the events business: people moving jobs from one location to another; people moving into events management from related fields (e.g. hotels, tourism, retail, catering, business travel); people newly employed in their first job; and staff being transferred around the larger, more diverse organizations, which may include several divisions besides events. All these methods account for the supply of potential staff. Some are better trained than others, but in all cases there is a good business argument for organizations to have a well trained, well motivated and well managed staff (Swarbrooke, 1995). This also is the reason for many organizations having a definite staff development policy, progression routes and comprehensive staff training programmes, some of which are targeted at quality issues, such as 'Investors in People' programmes, which are intended to achieve not only high levels of staff training and good service for visitors, but also public recognition in general.

Running the Event on the Day

For all the considerable effort that goes into planning an event, running it on the day can still prove a challenge. The coordination of a wide range of disparate and even unusual activities, facilities and services can be overwhelming. Events management has to be effective, and events managers must be good communicators and good delegators in situations that may be constantly changing. The importance of having done the planning for this situation is that it reduces the variability and uncertainty of what is taking place, and allows the event coordinator to concentrate on those things which require immediate or constant attention. Some things are essential, on the day of the event, for the event coordinator: drink enough so you don't dehydrate; eat enough to keep your blood sugar levels up, as otherwise your decision-making and problem-solving abilities will decline; wear the most comfortable pair of shoes you have and keep a change of clothes somewhere convenient, because you never know when some fool is going to spill a load of Chateau Tour de Langoiran '99 all over you.

The nature of the event business is such that each occasion is unique and a production line approach can rarely be adopted. The activities undertaken to provide one event effectively may not necessarily accomplish the next so effectively, though there are clearly common features. Thus the recurrence of routine tends to be in the framework – the approach, the organization and the management – rather than in the implementation or the operation. On a simple level, the same ordering system can be used almost universally for all events; but the number of people, the timing, the amount of supplies and requirements will be unique for each event. It is this uniqueness which systems and staff must be sufficiently flexible to cope with. Systems and staff are intended to work hand in hand. In general, to reduce costs, especially labour costs, if an operation can be systematized or automated, it should be, but this supposes a more or less standard product. Nevertheless, many event-related activities, such as food production, can be systematized – whether this is cookery according to standard recipes or the buying in of a standard dish from a supplier.

Case Study 29

Organization at the Deventer Bookmarket

The fine old eastern Dutch city of Deventer, in the province of Overijssel, famous for its history as a member of the Hanseatic League (an association of medieval trading cities in Northern Europe), holds a number of events each year. These include the annual Bookmarket, the Christmas Dickens Festival, Deventer on Stilts and Op Den Berghe, a popular and colourful medieval festival. The Bookmarket, held each year on the first Sunday in August, attracts not only the general public, but also booksellers and antiquarians from throughout the Netherlands and other parts of Europe.

Location

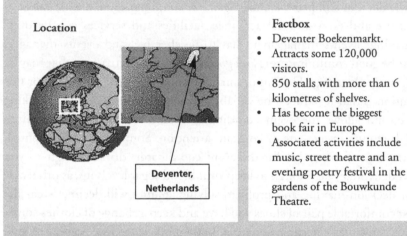

Deventer,
Netherlands

Factbox
- Deventer Boekenmarkt.
- Attracts some 120,000 visitors.
- 850 stalls with more than 6 kilometres of shelves.
- Has become the biggest book fair in Europe.
- Associated activities include music, street theatre and an evening poetry festival in the gardens of the Bouwkunde Theatre.

The Deventer Bookmarket is organized by the Events Bureau of the Deventer Tourism Department (Vereniging voor Vreemdelingenverkeer: VVV). The department has the equivalent of some twelve and a half staff (some being full-time and some part-time) who cover five departments. The operation and running of events is funded from a range of sources including Deventer City Council, local business members of the organization, such as catering, retail and market trade businesses, sponsoring organizations, and through admission charges and related income, such as the sale of programmes and city maps.

For the running of the event, an operating group of five or six key people, including the Director of the Bureau and his assistant, plus, at most, a further ten helpers, will be on the ground during the Bookmarket to coordinate activities. This is deliberately not a large number in order to prevent confusion. It also ensures that the Director can maintain informal contacts with participants, visitors, local businesses and officials to ensure the smooth running of the event. This process is, in effect, management by wandering around. Contact is maintained by mobile phones and the Director is seen to be there.

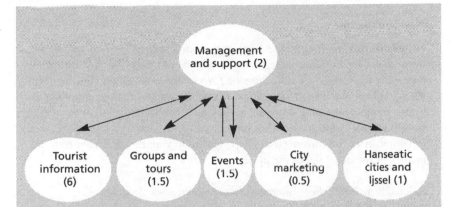

The Bookmarket attracts between 90,000 and 120,000 people each year. This varies because of the weather and other incidental factors (e.g. alternative events). The measurement of attendance is done by comparison of data from sales outlets (e.g. comparing the event days' sales of ice cream against a normal day's sales) and from information supplied by the railway company (Nederlandse Spoorwegen, which is able to report the difference in ticket sales to Deventer for the Sunday of the Bookmarket as against a normal summer Sunday). Knowing the number of people who travel to the market by rail, as a proportion of the total number, allows the total number to be estimated. However, the number of visitors is not always promoted in press releases, as, clearly, the attendance varies as does the amount visitors spend. In one year you might have more visitors who spend less, and the next, fewer visitors who spend more – there is considerable variation, even though averages can be given, such as the average spend for day trippers being of the order of €25 a day. (This helps prevent negative press coverage.)

The Bookmarket and the other major festivals, Dickens, Deventer on Stilts, Op Den Berghe and a smaller comedy festival, are key to the strategy which the Events Bureau operates. This strategy has a number of central objectives:

- to stimulate cultural tourism in Deventer and its nearby region of Overijssel;
- to generate added value for tourists to Deventer;
- to improve the marketing and the image of the city;
- to generate positive publicity in order to attract tourists;
- to highlight the strengths of historic Deventer and stimulate return visits;
- to make the city livelier;
- to improve the living and working environment;
- to encourage residents to be involved in the art and culture of the city;
- to encourage people to use the city for recreation and culture.

Based on this case:

How is the organization of the Bookmarket undertaken? In what way do the festivals in Deventer satisfy the strategic objectives of the VVV? What reasons, excluding the weather, might there be for variations in visitor numbers and average spend at an event? How might the media react to changes in published visitor numbers in headlining their stories, and would the view that the media gives make the strategic objectives difficult to fulfil? Identify a festival or event in your district and consider how that event fits in with the style, environment, history or surroundings of the place.

Related website for those interested in Deventer: www.deventer.nl

Source: Kindly provided by Mr Hein te Riele, Director, Deventer VVV.

The maintenance of standards in non-routine service activities is a significant concern of management in a business such as events. The non-routine and non-systematized nature of anything from site layout to variances in individual audience requirements needs to be accommodated by allowing flexibility of operations, while maintaining adequate supervision and control (Lovelock, 1994). Simple managerial control may be exercised by detailed supervision and the use of checklists, by techniques such as 'management by exception' or by improving the quality of staff and staff training to the level at which quality control can largely be placed in the hands of the staff themselves. This can be difficult in short-lived organizations at events, because there is limited time to train staff and limited time to get to know what abilities they have.

Perhaps the most common management technique used by events coordinators is management by wandering around. Draw up a checklist of things you need to keep an eye on and give yourself a route to go round, preferably covering your main department leaders and those places you regard as 'pinch points'. Pinch points are where things are likeliest to go wrong, or be busiest, or need support at crucial times. A regular events coordinator will know this from previous experience, but for the beginner, the best advice is to follow through what your potential visitors will do, including driving into the visitors' car park when you arrive and entering the site or venue through the same entrance as they will. In this way you will find out in time if things are signposted badly, if the area is not clean enough and so on. Do a walk through of all the things a visitor will do, including the toilets. Test the things a visitor will ask for. For example, go and have a coffee in the catering tent. Don't just get a coffee and walk out, take it and sit where the visitors will sit. By doing so you will find unexpected things which can make or break people's experience of your event.

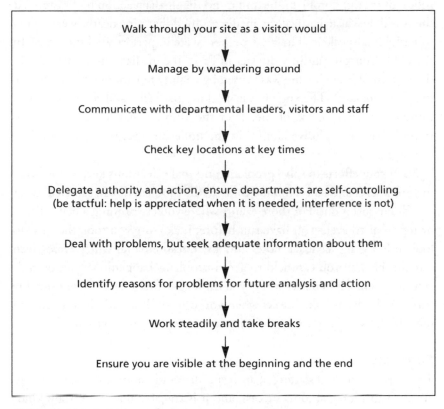

Walk through your site as a visitor would

↓

Manage by wandering around

↓

Communicate with departmental leaders, visitors and staff

↓

Check key locations at key times

↓

Delegate authority and action, ensure departments are self-controlling
(be tactful: help is appreciated when it is needed, interference is not)

↓

Deal with problems, but seek adequate information about them

↓

Identify reasons for problems for future analysis and action

↓

Work steadily and take breaks

↓

Ensure you are visible at the beginning and the end

Figure 11.10   *Activities on the day.*

Above all, communicate actively and frequently as you do your rounds. It is important you delegate wherever you can, so that your regular staff learn to handle and solve problems for themselves. Step in if you have to, but remember, you are the last resort, you should not be trying to sort out minor problems when your staff could do so on their own. In fact, as a manager, if you have to do things which your people should be capable of, then you have failed: you have failed to educate them in their abilities and remits, you have failed to give them the resources and confidence to do the job they need to do.

When you are making decisions and solving problems it is vital to be aware of the factors which have led to the problem and to be able to take the correct action. It may be that you have to take action first and ask questions later, but it is essential to ask the questions, as otherwise you might fail again. If you fail to identify the source and origin of a problem correctly, it will occur again, and you may not be able to get yourself and the event out of it the next time. Therefore a good decision is dependent upon the recognition of the right problem. Bear in mind the media reaction to disasters. At the Roskilde Music Festival the media claimed that nine deaths were owing to faulty loudspeakers. The loudspeakers were in perfect working order. In the 2000 Concorde airliner disaster in Paris, the media at first claimed that the catastrophic engine fire was caused by a faulty repair done hastily before the plane took off. The engine was working perfectly, and the disaster was caused by a small piece of metal on the runway that led to a series of improbable but explosive failures in the undercarriage, the wing and then the engine.

So in your efforts to solve problems and make decisions keep a notebook in your pocket and take a minute to write the problem down, as well as what you did to sort it out. For those events where you are running a new edition or repeat of an event you have run before, make sure you took the time to look at last year's feedback notes and any questionnaires which were given out. In this way you can help to avoid problems happening again or concentrate resources in places where you think they might recur. Work steadily through the event, take breaks when you can, sit down when you can and take drinks when you can. It is important that you pace yourself.

Summary

The organization and staffing of an event, its coordination and management, are all factors integral to its success, and it is arguable that, for certain kinds of events, as much can be achieved with talented amateurs and enthusiastic volunteers as can be achieved with professional paid staff. However, there is a place for both professional and volunteer staff in the events business. Events are varied and diverse, and their organization and staffing reflect this.

Reference List

Cole, G. A. (1997) *Personnel Management.* London: Letts, pp. 110–21.

Johnson, G. and Scholes, K. (1999) *Exploring Corporate Strategy.* London: Prentice Hall, pp. 74–5.

Lovelock, C. H. (1994) *Product Plus.* New York: McGraw-Hill, pp. 160–90.

Medlik, S. (1995) *The Business of Hotels.* Oxford: Butterworth Heinemann, pp. 71–93.

Mullins, L. J. (1995) *Hospitality Management: a Human Resources Approach.* London: Pitman, pp. 52–85.

Mullins, L. J., Meudell, K. and Scott, H. (1993) 'Developing culture in short-life organisations', *International Journal of Contemporary Hospitality Management,* 5 (4), 15–19.

Richards, B. (1992) *How to Market Tourist Attractions, Festivals and Special Events.*
Harlow: Longman, p. 106.
Swarbrooke, J. (1995) *The Development and Management of Visitor Attractions.*
Oxford: Butterworth Heinemann, pp. 226–42.

CHAPTER 12

Closedown and Legacies

Aims
- To discuss the issues involved in closing down an event.
- To consider the activities relating to the evaluation of an event.
- To consider post-event use of sites, divestment and legacies.

Introduction
It is three o'clock in the morning, your guests have just gone, having eaten you out of house and home, told assorted improbable stories and drunk all your best port. You are both happy that the dinner party went well and exhausted. It is best to shut the door on the dining room, and leave the washing up until tomorrow. Of course, if it is three in the morning and you are the coordinator at an event venue where the guests have just gone, you might have a whole night's work ahead of you. The closedown of an event should be approached in much the same way as it is set up, and remember the lesson often quoted in the mountain climbing world: most accidents don't happen on the way up, they happen on the way down. At the end of a long event, you and your staff will be tired, and many will want to get cleared up and get out, but it is important to be able to handle the closedown and clear up properly, and carefully.

Once the whole thing is closed down and handed back, there is still some administration to be done. This will be anything from the filing to sorting out the accounts, from paying the bills to collecting questionnaires. The final administrative details need to be completed, and the event, especially if it is to happen again in the future, should be properly evaluated to see what can be learned from it and what could be done better next time round, not only from the visitors' point of view, but also from your own organizational point of view. It is valuable to look back and assess the outcome.

For some events there will be no next time. The purpose of the event may have been strictly limited to a one-time-only activity, in some of these cases, especially where the objective might have been economic or social in there will be various legacies, some intended, some perhaps unint. The significance of such legacies may have been carefully planned; this is particularly the case for regeneration events. Often, however, it is the physical regeneration that is planned and social regeneration comes as a surprise.

Closedown

There are several elements to closing down an event, besides just clearing the venue out and closing the doors. There will be a range of administrative tasks to tie up too. These include the completion of the accounts, payment of final bills to contractors and other, final marketing activities, such as closure press releases and providing information about plans for the future. There will need to be various personnel completions, in particular the final payments to staff of various kinds and the bringing up to date of staff records for future reference, together with the need to do some evaluation of the event (considered in more detail below).

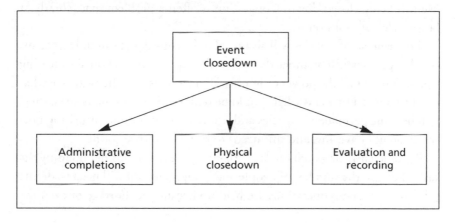

Figure 12.1   *Final phase of event activities.*

The most obvious closedown activities are the physical ones, the big clear-up once the doors have closed and the last visitors have gone. This should be approached in much the same way as the set-up. A work breakdown schedule can be created, based in part on the activities leading up to the opening, but in reverse. Understanding that there is a sequence of closedown is important, as otherwise you will have people making ridiculous attempts to get their gear out before it is safe to do so. In the same way that it is important for everyone to know how to set up, it is also essential for them to know how to break down. This information can be given in a summary sheet to staff during the event, with a closedown briefing given over a meal immediately following the public's departure. Otherwise you will be overrun with tired and frustrated people wanting to throw stuff in a truck, without knowing that the truck doesn't arrive for another hour.

As a general rule, the clear-up operation goes from small items to large ones. You cannot get the stage down until you have cleared the equipment and the furniture. You cannot clear these items until you have cleared at least some of the litter and collected and stored small valuable items. Staff should be properly briefed on this process, with control maintained to the very end, for reasons of safety and of security of goods and equipment. Some tasks can be done in parallel (at the same time), providing there are enough staff to do them, and the various department leaders should continue to supervise these activities. Items of stock to be reused, such as catering stock, linen or consumables, should be returned to a central storage place prior to collection and return to the supplier or to the contractor's central depot. Exit routes for goods, equipment and materials should ideally be separate from the public exit routes, which might still be busy while the event is being closed down. Congestion is often a problem, particularly at large-scale outdoor events.

The removal of utilities will also need to be considered carefully in terms of what goes last. Remember that you will still have people on site clearing up, so don't cut all the power or remove all the toilets straight away; see what can be removed first and what should be removed last. On many sites, there will be some permanent supplies and utilities, but it is often surprising how many do not have any, and this needs to be taken into account.

Be sufficiently prepared for the clear-up operation. Consider not only the tasks, but also the number of people and equipment you will need to do the job. Many clear-up operations are held up because of shortage of even the

---

Case Study 30

Clearing up: the World Golf Championship, Valderrama

Clearing an events site can be a major task. It can involve anything from having to remove large amounts of litter, debris and other general waste, to having to restore lawns, gardens and other natural features. Many events are run in locations which are sensitive to being used by large numbers of people, and care has to be taken that crowds do not damage the area and its surroundings. This is particularly the case for open air events.

Location

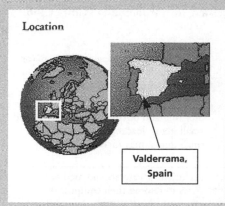

Valderrama, Spain

Factbox
- World Golf Championship, Valderrama.
- Three-day event involving 62 international players.
- Large crowd to watch the golf.
- Top prize of about €1 million.
- Won in 1999 by Tiger Woods.
- Event sponsored by American Express.

The arrangements for major golf tournaments require particular care. Crowds of up to 100,000 people are possible, putting huge strain on the resources at golf courses. For major tournaments, stands have to be built and facilities provided for the media, including locations for broadcasts as well as media centres for journalists and other reporters. Additional facilities have to be provided, including catering and refreshments, first aid, toilets, retailing and power. Thoughtful crowd control is absolutely essential, in order to prevent accidental damage by large numbers of people to the course itself, to the fairways and the greens. As a consequence, most facilities, including parking, tend to be kept away from the main course, and walking routes for the crowd to watch the golf are carefully set up, roped off and controlled by stewards. The international course at Valderrama is extremely well kept and is known for its ecological approach. This being the case, there are areas of the course which are kept isolated from the public, due to the presence of wildlife and rare plants.

The process of clearing up after the championship is quite intensive (see chart on p. 260).

Although the clear-up period is relatively short, the site being more or less clear of its extra structures and equipment within a week, the repair to the areas used by large numbers of visitors, especially where there is damage to the ground due to heavy public use, takes the greenkeepers and groundsmen a great deal of time. Where the green areas have to be resown, the new grass may take up to six months to regrow properly.

Based on this case:

What are the effects on a site of having a large number of the public present? Site damage is mainly caused accidentally or because of the large number of people. How could you attempt to mitigate the effects of large crowds on open air sites (think also of Glastonbury)? How can you plan the closedown of a site, and in what order should things be removed?

Related website for those interested in Valderrama Golf Club: www.valderrama.com

Event finishes Public leaves Cash up	Cleaning begins	Litter picking, bagging, washing up (or removal), dealing with laundry and linen, moving items to a central collection point
	Clear down small items	Stocking and boxing of consumables and small items, loading of transport for small items (may include removal of rubbish)
	Bump out equipment and furniture	Technicians, caterers and media crews to remove their equipment, etc.
	Cleaning and waste disposal	Collection of solid waste Recycling collection Emptying of tanks
	Removal of utilities	Stripping out of telecoms, electricity, gas (not at the same time), removal of temporary water supplies, temporary sewage, generators, etc.
	Removal of structures	Removal of large items, tents, portacabins, mobile cold stores, etc. Removal of rope-work and crowd barriers
	Handover and site restoration	Removal of final waste skips, wash downs, check course for damage, greenkeepers begin work on areas damaged by heavy use and wear and tear from public trampling

most basic equipment, such as brushes, mops and buckets, cleaning materials and refuse sacks. Have these kinds of things stored and ready for collection by department leaders so you can get the work done speedily.

Much of the equipment, materials and resources you may have used for your event will be recoverable for reuse. Ensure that you have an efficient and careful storekeeper to collect this material, and to record what has been returned, take stock and calculate any losses. Careful storekeeping and the ability to redeploy equipment, resources and other materials may save a great deal of money and possibly effort next time, especially for those things which are often overlooked at the planning stage, such as electrical extension leads, special signs and small administrative equipment. Experienced administrators will prepare 'ready boxes' of basic office needs (such as tape, scissors, staplers, glue, blue tack, Velcro fixings, pens) from the returned materials so that a box can be taken out of stores and used easily, at the next event, without wasting time chasing round for a box of staples or a washable marker pen. Many of the contracting organizations also take the same approach. Contract caterers will collect, wash, stock-take and then recount items, such as crockery or cutlery (for example, into batches of 10) ready for their next use.

Allen (2000) makes the point that it is essential to thank all those involved, and in particular key staff, in writing, 'as you never know who you might need again'. It is, in any case, both good manners and a courtesy. In particular, thanks to volunteers and members of the community for their efforts are important, as this is also a matter of good relationship marketing for future events. On the subject of relationship marketing, if you are going to repeat this event, did you put the next date and phone number on the tickets or in the programmes? You want people to return so start by helping the process along. Again, various people may be interested in your event organization or the venue and while they would not normally step out of their way to obtain information, can be asked for their business card or address as they leave, with information being despatched to them. A sales opportunity is a sales opportunity, personal contact being far more effective than advertising.

If there is an element of organization that is neglected by venues and organizers it is the closedown. Some effort should be made to ensure all went well. Coordinators should be around to speak to visitors and VIPs on departure to obtain verbal feedback and pick up comments. Comments need noting as part of a quality control cycle, and can be recorded as part of the 'event history' to be referred to next time round. Even relatively simple issues such as the speakers preferring lapel microphones, or the need to have some spare umbrellas in the central office, while not being perceived as disastrous, are significant issues for that event and one less worry next time.

The final administrative issues about event closedown are those regarding contract acquittal, dealing with outstanding bills and completing the accounts. In contract acquittal, we are in the business not only of making final payments to contractors, but also of deciding, for the future, whether contractors have done a good job. Key to our own success as event organizers is the ability to have the materials and supplies that are required delivered in the way in which they were ordered, on time and correctly. A good relationship with suppliers and contractors is therefore vital, and one of the functions of contract acquittal is to identify those companies which will be retained as suppliers for the future, and those which may have to be changed.

The preparation of the final accounts will be a matter for the treasurer, financial officer or our accountants for the event. The final accounts will tell us how the event ran financially and, where an event has run in the public domain (i.e. it is not commercially private), the accounts can be published as part of a final report to the client body, which might be government, local councils or other funding or sponsoring bodies. In any case, a copy of the accounts should be included in our event history file for future reference and as an aid to planning any new edition.

Evaluation

A short period after the closedown of the event, certainly within a month, there should be a meeting of the various interested parties (organizers, clients, sponsors, etc.) to evaluate the event. The evaluation should use all the various sources of information available to it and should consider not only the visitors' perception of the event, but also that of the organizers, for lessons may need to be learned from all points of view. The potential sources of information are quite extensive, if they are used and are appropriate to the event. However, it should be noted that many events, especially smaller ones, record and keep very little information indeed, sometimes only the number of people who bought tickets and what the various departments took or sold. This limitation is partly due to a lack of expertise at recording, partly due to the effort needed to collect useful information and partly due, for events management and similar companies, to the need to get going with the next event – consequently there is little time to either collect or review what information has been collected. However, care in evaluation is an aid to future planning and should not be overlooked.

Quantitative Information	Qualitative Information
Visitor and participant data, sales	Visitor perceptions
Target market, visitor profiles	Questionnaires returned, exit surveys
Attendance statistics, market target information	Recorded (structured) chats or interviews
Financial reports and accounts	Staff and volunteer feedback
Financial balance sheet	Management notes and commentary
Economic impact analysis	Social impact analysis
General statistical information	Social benefits balance sheet

Figure 12.2   *Types of information for evaluation of events. Source: Richards (1992).*

One of the limitations of evaluation is the inability to make use of the process. Most events organizations will have a meeting to review major events, but the process may end there. 'We had the meeting, and we'll look at the minutes of it next year when we start planning the next edition.' The purpose of evaluation is for managers to learn how an event went and to be able to improve on it for the future. This 'improvement' can be looked at in several ways. First, there might be activities that went well that could be strengthened further. Second, there are those activities that went well in such a way that they are best left untouched (if it's not broken, don't fix it). Third, there are those activities that went badly, that need sorting out. These things have to be evaluated, and even where only a modest amount of information is collected, say by formal means (e.g. questionnaires), there might actually be lots of underused information sources (see Figure 12.3).

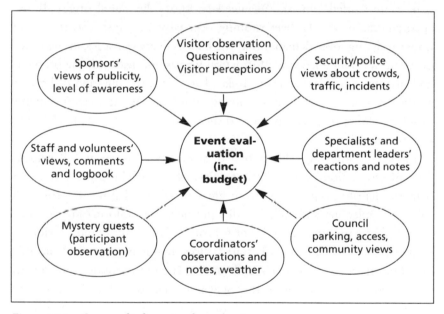

Figure 12.3   *Sources of information for evaluation.*

There are quite a large number of sources of information even for a small event where no formal research has been done. However, where the information is unstructured, we must be careful about its use, as otherwise the analysis of the information could be based on little except someone's opinion, which may be more or less worthless, without support. There are probably two key evaluation issues:

1. Did the event meet its objectives?
2. What can be improved for the next edition, if there is to be one?

A review of the event objectives, in the light of the information available, needs to be carried out, not only for the satisfaction of the event coordinator, but also to ensure that the stakeholders can be reassured of the effectiveness of the event, and that if stakeholders such as councils, sponsors, clients and so on put money into the event, the money was well spent. This is the reason for the publication of final reports and accounts, particularly for big public events.

The usefulness of some formal or structured research and observation at events becomes most obvious when we look at what might need to be done for future editions. The identification and solving of problems can only be done properly if there is enough information genuinely to find out what the causal origin of a problem was. It is no good saying, 'We had a brawl in the beer tent when the beer ran out and the vicar got hit over the head with a two metre stuffed banana.' We need to know the causal origin. If the apparent cause was the beer running out, why was this? Was the cause under-ordering, over-demand, that the beer delivery got stuck in the mud, or what? Without adequate information we cannot deal with the problem and prevent it happening again. Related to this is the question of how to allocate resources and time to solving problems. What were the major problems? Were they serious and did they constitute critical failures in the eyes of our visitors?

In general, knowing what is best or worst about an event will help to increase satisfaction levels and reduce dissatisfaction. This process may also help to identify persistent problem areas which need time and effort to solve: by collecting and collating the 'problem area' information you can then rank the problems in order of priority or seriousness ('most serious – least serious' or 'most frequently stated – least frequently stated'). With this list of priorities, you can attack and sort out the most serious problems, so that in the next event edition they will not occur or at least be less of an inconvenience or difficulty for your visitors, and you will have improved the visitors' experience of your event. It is best to give the task of solving a particular problem to one person who has the authority and the means to solve it, or a small subgroup of the organizing committee, once the problem has been identified, rather than having the problem discussed endlessly in big committees and not get solved.

In any list of problems, the ones which cause the most difficulty should be dealt with first. To do this we need to be able to measure the impact of a problem. Where we are looking fairly informally at our list of problems, it might simply be down to 'gut feeling' about which would be the best to solve, because, given limited management time and expertise, not every problem on a list can be solved (though perhaps some of the lesser problems could be given to junior staff or volunteer helpers to solve; these might even provide more creative solutions than professionals might provide). On the other hand, we might be running a major event again next year, and the effort put into evaluative problem-solving might be well worth the effort (O'Neill *et al.*, 1999). Hence the need for some kind of measurement.

This type of approach is used in various industries. For example, some UK railway companies use a system known as 'golden asset identification'. What happens is that delays to trains are analysed by cause, and the total delay to trains caused by physical assets is measured in minutes. This is then costed, so that the total cost of an asset failure or specific problem is known. Problems are then ranked by severity and the cost of solving them is compared with the cost of delays. By this method it has been found that very large delays (and costs) can sometimes be solved at very small cost indeed. Suppose that a set of points (track turnouts) near a major railway station has been identified as the cause of regular delays. Perhaps 20,000 minutes of delays to trains up and down the line are caused by this set of points, at a cost of €10 a minute (this is less than the real cost but a convenient figure to use). The total cost of the problem is €200,000 a year. The track engineers say that the wrong grease is being used to keep the points moving. This was because someone decided to buy cheap grease at €20 a can less than the proper grease. In this case the cost of solving a €200,000 problem is €20 a year, as one can lasts a year. For those who think this is a fictitious problem, the set of points is just south of Purley in South London.

How can event managers use this approach? It might be felt that an event is more of an unusual service than a railway, and events may be less dependent on physical assets, but it is a useful place to start. Figure 12.4 is a sample visitor satisfaction report from our good friends, the Middleburg Music Festival.

In this example there is a problem with parking. It might be a problem for a range of reasons: not enough space, not enough access, everyone leaves at once creating a queue and so on. In short, the problem may be quite complicated to solve and need several approaches. In order to solve it, we need more information, from other sources, not just the visitor survey. In the case of the car park, we find there are two other sources of information. The first comes in the form of 'mystery guest' reports (see Figure 12.5). The festival organizers employed six people from the local university (three lecturers and three senior students) to visit the festival as customers and prepare a structured report each about their experiences.

Visitor Satisfaction Analysis

Problems identified from structured chats and post event questionnaires returned.

Total attendance this year: 6,400 visitors

Most frequently stated problems (sample of 138 responses):

Parking (exit congestion)	48%
Parking (general congestion)	27%
Catering	26%
Seating too far away from the stage	10%
Printed programme poor quality	7%
Not enough for kids to do	4%
Etc., etc.	

Figure 12.4   *Visitor satisfaction at the Middleburg Music Festival.*

Mystery Guest Report

Question 2.

Were access and parking arrangements adequate?

No, I found a great deal of difficulty getting out of the car park. First there was a huge queue and the car park was not properly marked out, so cars were not flowing in the right direction, but crossing over each other before they could get to the exit. The exit was bad to see out of because of overgrown bushes on the roadside, and it was amazing there were no accidents because of the speed of people coming down the main road and then being surprised by festival visitors trying to pull out of the car park.

Figure 12.5   *Mystery guest report (extract).*

In this example, the mystery guest report was corroborated by Jock Barnett, the Car Park Head Steward: 'Aye, the car park was a mess to get out of, you took your life in your hands when you pulled out onto the main road. We set up signs saying "concealed entrance; slow down" but they didn't look official enough so many drivers on the main road ignored them.'

The problem is an obvious one, and has a safety aspect, so action is essential, without the need for measurement. But the reader may wish to give some thought to how this kind of problem could be measured. The solution in this example clearly includes better liaison with the road authority and the police to have a temporary speed restriction applied to the main road, official signs put up and the bushes cut back. Internally, we need to look at the car park layout, and to re-sign and re-line the car park, to make the traffic flow simpler. It may also help us to take some of the weight of cars away from the car park by providing a 'park and ride' bus to another car park, or a bus to the city centre or rail station. It might mean better sign-posting of the exits, it might mean staggering the finishing of different parts of the event to reduce the rush for the gates. The solutions which get the most management attention should first be the ones that will have the most impact on the problem, then moving down the list of solutions to those which have respectively less, but still positive effect. In the case of this example, we have supposed it has only been identified at the end, but monitoring should be going on during events, and where an event takes place over more than one day, some urgent changes could be made once the event closes for the day, or overnight, or even during the event.

The costs of some problems and service failures may be hidden, perhaps because they deal with visitor satisfaction and enjoyment, or they are not terribly obvious in some way. These costs might involve a hidden loss of revenue, the distraction of event managers from key activities while solving problems, time taken in dealing with complaints because the service was inadequate and so on. Consequently, the related issue to identifying problems is being able to identify satisfaction with events. In simple terms, people might have enjoyed the events, despite the problems they encountered, or alternatively these things might have spoilt their experience altogether. We can make an event look pretty, have fancy marketing, have standardized management systems, provide smart uniforms or whatever, but if the event itself is no good, and our guests have not enjoyed themselves, all these mechanisms will have not added to the impression of the event or to guests' experience of it. You can go to see a play in a clean and well kept theatre, with polite and efficient box office staff, prompt service at the bar during the interval and in the company of good friends, but the play might still have been awful. This is also true of events. So what affects people's impressions?

There is a view that visitors' impressions of an event are influenced by two sets of judgements about it. This view (quoted from Love and Crompton in O'Neill *et al.*, 1999) argues that visitors make their judgement based on things about an event that satisfy them, and things about an event that dissatisfy them. Things that work as satisfiers are the ambience, excitement, social involvement, relaxation and other positive emotional states and some service elements; things that work as dissatisfiers tend to be physical and basic service features, such as the parking, the toilets, availability of information and queues. In the analysis of satisfaction levels using this approach, a formal method of research is needed, using both questionnaires about service quality features of an event and trained observers. This kind of research could be done by a market research agency, but should result in the analysis of visitors' perceptions of the event and identification of those factors which were satisfiers, and thus critical to its success, and those factors which were dissatisfiers, and thus critical failure points. These types of results could also be put into graphical form to illustrate the levels of satisfaction which visitors experienced (see Figure 12.6).

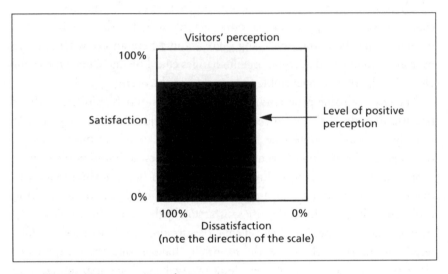

Figure 12.6   *Visitor experience chart.*

It is important to recognize the limitations of what can be achieved in evaluating events. We are never going to achieve complete and total satisfaction. There will be, in the nature of events, many factors which impinge on people's perception, even though we might go to considerable lengths to identify and deal with the critical incidents.

Divestment and Legacies

Many events are repeat editions, some are not. Some events are designed for a single 'one-time-only' purpose (such as garden festivals, whose purpose was regeneration); some events do not recur in the same place twice (such as the Olympic Games), even though they may leave substantial legacies in terms of buildings and facilities; some events leave only social legacies.

If the event has been a one-off, with regeneration or reuse in mind as objectives for the site, the divestment needs to be planned into the process at the beginning. There will be a target date for the handover to the site's new owners or managers, and the site must be given over in the condition that the original objectives intended, or that the plans specified (unless this is done properly, financial or other penalties may be incurred in order to put things right). It will be essential to hand over not just the site, but also the knowledge that goes with it, about its nature, utilities, environment, problems and limitations. Consequently, a handover may not simply be a case of saying 'here are the keys' and leaping into your Lamborghini.

There should be a period of overlap between the event organization closing down and departing, and the redevelopment organization, agency or new owners starting work. In some cases this may even mean the continuance of certain jobs or roles between the two organizations, perhaps for posts such as site manager or marketing officer. This will improve the transfer of important information between the organizations concerned. Copies of important documentation will also be handed over, including copies of the final reports and the events history file (in case parts of the event occur again or certain suppliers need to be contacted). In some cases a formal handover ceremony may take place, with the media being present, to stress the change in the site's circumstances.

The type of post-event use of an event site, where regeneration or reuse has been planned, may vary, as may the kind of organization taking over the site. In the case of the series of garden festivals held in the UK in the 1980s and 1990s, most sites were handed over to local development agencies (public sector bodies), whose task was to re-use the sites to create employment and other positive development outcomes, and to retain some of the site as public open space parkland or nature reserves. For more recent development of event sites, such as the Millennium Dome site and parts of the Hannover 2000 site, development companies have purchased these with various projects in mind. In the case of the Dome, for economic regeneration, in the case of parts of the Hannover site to create residential housing (an aspect which was planned for the parts of the Hannover site at the beginning and as a method of re-use of exhibitors' accommodation).

Re-use varies, according to what facilities were provided for the event. In the case of the World Student Games, in Sheffield, the re-use has been primarily in sporting and leisure facilities. In the case of the Hannover site, the objective was not primarily re-use, as the Hannover objectives stressed ecological sustainability. Thus the Expo was intended to make use of existing exhibition facilities rather than create new ones, and consequently the re-use objectives at Hannover were considerably more modest than those for any previous Expo, such as that in Seville in 1992. For smaller-scale events, re-use may not actually imply any new use or transfer of ownership. Where events recur year after year in new editions, the site may simply have to be restored to its normal condition as parkland, or as a public venue of some kind. The effort in these cases is mainly directed towards restoration and maintenance rather than any form of rebuilding

Case Study 31

Events legacies: the World Student Games, Sheffield

The legacies which events leave, range from the negligible and intangible (perhaps only a memory or a few photographs of a day out) to the significant and tangible (such as area regeneration and major buildings). Legacies can be social in nature, such as having made friends by participating in an event; they can be economic, with the creation of jobs afterwards, such as with the legacies of some of the garden festivals; they can be political and developmental, as with the Millennium Dome. The World Student Games, held in Sheffield, England, in 1991, left an interesting mix of legacies, some positive, some less so, and a sufficient time has passed to be able to reflect, dispassionately, on these.

Location

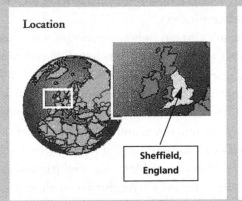

Sheffield, England

Factbox
- World Student Games, Sheffield.
- Investment of €225 million in various sports facilities, including the Sheffield Arena, the Don Valley Stadium and the Ponds Forge Pool.
- Enhanced and improved Sheffield's image.
- Left the city with a large debt.

The purposes of staging the games for Sheffield were:

- to play an integral role in the economic regeneration of the area;
- to encourage local participation in sport and collaboration in the games;
- to improve Sheffield's image, nationally and internationally;
- to leave the city a legacy of world-class sporting facilities.

There is no mistaking the controversy which surrounded the games and Sheffield's efforts to re-create itself as a modern sporting city. The pages of the *Yorkshire Post* (the major regional newspaper) long resounded with the arguments. However, there is no misunderstanding that Sheffield's role as a steel-making and manufacturing city was in steep decline by the late 1980s, and in no way could these activities be kept alive in the face of international competition. The city had to address its decline and had to take action. The games provided the vehicle and impetus for this action.

With the exception of Ponds Forge, which is in the city centre, most of the new facilities were constructed in the Don Valley, an area that had become a grim industrial wasteland, desperately in need of restoration. The city threw itself at the task of regeneration: 'Make no little plans. They have no magic to stir men's blood. Make big plans: aim high in hope and work' (D. H. Burnham). Sheffield made big plans. The fruition of these plans and their triumph can be seen today. The Don Valley has its great sporting facilities, it has the tremendous regional shopping centre of Meadowhall, it has a cross-city tram system, one of the first to be built in England for almost seventy years, and it has new residential areas and public entertainment facilities, including a multiplex cinema.

The games were popular, were short-lived and made a huge loss. They caused controversy, argument and the resignation of city councillors. But they provided the mechanism by which Sheffield could propel itself into the modern world. Sheffield could not be said to have been a pretty city, not the kind that appear on chocolate boxes, but it looked forward and took the risk, something many cannot say they have done.

Based on this case:

What was more important, the games or the legacy? What other mechanisms could Sheffield have used to stimulate regeneration? Are legacies something that every event can provide? Or would this be too much to expect? The games were a one-off event. Do repeat editions leave legacies, and if so, of what kind?

Related website for those interested in Sheffield:
www.shef.ac.uk/staff/links/sheffield.html

Source: Adapted from Watt (1998).

The legacies of many kinds of events may not be conceived in physical terms. Although much regeneration activity is regarded as physical and economic, making a derelict or previously damaged area into something usable and better, many events do not have these impacts. The impacts of an event whose aims are not targeted at re-use are probably much more limited and social. They may be intended to improve the image of an area, they may be intended to sustain tourism by increasing awareness of a destination (Hall, 1992) or they may simply aim to enhance social integration and improve the confidence of a community in itself. These social aims may be more than worthwhile, and have more positive outcomes for a community than the physical legacies. It depends on what the event objectives were.

Summary

Event closedown is one of those aspects of management which receives insufficient attention. The temptation is to let everyone in to get cleared up and finished as soon as possible. But this can be a recipe for disaster, or at least accidents. The large number of people milling round, moving heavy items or trying to get out of the venue in a hurry has to be overseen, with modest control achieved. Once closedown is over, and the event team has had time to sit back a moment and reflect, the opportunity should be taken to evaluate and to learn for the future. For repeat events this process is necessary and important to running a better event, or one at least as good, again. For one-off events, there are still lessons which the team can learn for its own benefit. Perhaps the evaluation process might have to feed into some closing report, so information should be collected and analysed to help to wrap up the loose ends. Finally, events leave a legacy. This may be in personal memories or in friendly social contacts made at the event, or it may be in some item handed over; anything from a park bench, bought from the modest surplus of the village fête, to a donation to an honourable cause, to the grand arena built to regenerate a city. It may be transient or long-lasting. Either way, some thought should have been given, in the setting of objectives at the beginning, to the legacy.

Reference List

Allen, J. (2000) *Event Planning*. Etobicoke, Ont.: Wiley, pp. 235–8.

Hall, C. M. (1992) *Hallmark Tourist Events*. London: Belhaven, pp. 164–75.

Kotas, R. and Jayawardena, C. (1994) *Profitable Food and Beverage Management*. Sevenoaks: Hodder and Stoughton, pp. 215–20.

Nickson, D. and Siddons, S. (1997) *Managing Projects*. Oxford: Butterworth Heinemann, pp. 120–2.

O'Neill, M., Getz, D. and Carlsen, J. (1999) 'Evaluation of service quality of events', *Managing Service Quality*, 9 (3), 158–6.

Richards, B. (1992) *How to Market Tourist Attractions, Festivals and Special Events*. Harlow: Longman, pp. 61–2.

Smyth, H. (1994) *Marketing the City: the Role of Flagship Developments in Urban Regeneration*. London: E&F Spon, pp. 237–58.

Watt, D. C. (1998) *Event Management in Leisure and Tourism*. Harlow: Longman, pp. 13–21, 75–9.

Glossary

---

assembly a large group of people gathered, convention style, for deliberation, legislation, worship, lobbying or some political activity.

attendees a group of people attending an event, for a range of purposes, from watching the event take place to actively participating in some or all of the event's activities.

audience the group of people engaged in watching an event or (usually) passively participating in some aspect of the event activities.

blag to attempt to get into an event by gatecrashing, or to get tickets under false pretences.

bowser a tanker designed to stand by at events to provide fresh water (or other liquids).

bump-in (also **load-in**) the arrival of equipment, stage crew, staging, materials, sound and lighting rigs and other various items of event set-up.

bump-out (also **load-out**) as bump-in, but leaving.

breakdown that part of the close-down activities of an event after load-out, when the final jobs of site clearance and infrastructure dismantling are taking place.

break-even the point at which an event's costs equal the revenue received for it.

break-out session where small groups formed from the delegates of a larger event work together, usually in separate areas or rooms, breaking out from the main event.

brief a document or specification prepared by a client to state the requirements for an event, which is used as the basis for an EMC or PEO to tender, or as a basis for the design of the event itself, or both

capacity the maximum number of people who can be accommodated at a venue (due to physical, legal, quality or other limits).

cash bar a bar set up during a function where the guests or delegates, rather than the host, pay for drinks individually.

cherry picker a vehicle with an extendable arm and platform on the end, used for reaching high places.

client the person or organization purchasing or specifying an event.

chill out room a place set aside for attendees (usually at events such as gigs) to cool off and relax in quieter surroundings than the main arena or stage area of an event.

concurrent sessions when sessions of a meeting are held at the same time in different rooms, usually allowing delegates to choose which to attend.

conference   a meeting whose purpose is the interchange of ideas.

contingency   an alternative plan of action if problems occur in a given situation.

convention   a conference gathering of greater importance, size and formality; perhaps with over 300 people in attendance.

corporate hospitality   corporate hospitality (or 'corporate entertaining') involves inviting groups of people, usually clients of a company or high profile organization, to public events for a meal or entertainment.

critical success factors   those issues which are key to the success of an event, as laid down by its objectives, and which are criteria by which its success can be judged or measured.

critical path   the key time-limited route through a number of time-critical activities in the planning of an event.

critical tasks   those tasks or jobs which must be completed in a sequence, before any other, or all others, can be done.

cut-off date   the designated date when an organizer must release reserved, but unconfirmed, space or confirm a booking by payment.

day delegate rate   the price quoted by conference venues for providing one delegate with meeting facilities and refreshments, such as morning coffee, lunch and afternoon tea, normally for one 9 a.m. to 5 p.m. session.

delegates   the main term used to describe people who attend confer-ences, seminars, workshops and similar events.

delegate day   a measure of the number of people attending a conference each day. Thus, ten people attending a conference for one day equals ten delegate days.

dumper truck   a truck used at building sites for moving heavy stuff around, such as sand or gravel, usually painted yellow.

EMC   event management company.

event coordinator (see also **PEO**) that individual who manages an event on behalf of a client.

event organizer   the individual, or organization, that promotes and manages an event.

external dependency   a task performed by a person or organization outside the direct control of the event organizer, perhaps a contractor's or suppliers' task

'external' events   an event arranged by an organization, particularly in the corporate market, to disseminate information to external audiences (e.g. to wholesalers, distributors, dealers, consumers, the press).

final exit   the termination of an escape route from an event site in the case of an emergency, giving exit to a place of safety or dispersal to an open space (for example, in case of fire).

Gantt chart   a project planning chart like a horizontal bar diagram.

gig   a concert of rock, pop, house or another popular musical style.

guaranteed number   the minimum number of guests at an event, for which the host has paid or will pay, irrespective of the actual number attending.

guest   a person attending an event, perhaps by free invitation, or by paying for the pleasure of attending.

gully emptier   a tanker lorry designed to suck drainage out of gullies or drains or clear septic tanks.

head count   the actual number of people attending a function or event.

incentive   an event designed to be a perk or reward for staff in an organization. Although some incentives have a serious element, the principal purpose is to motivate, encourage or reward. Incentives are often for salespeople (and may sometimes include their partners).

'internal' events   events where attendance is confined to personnel inside the organization, such as the sales force, departments and groups and people attending internal – as opposed to external – training courses (thus 'in-house' or 'in-company').

jam session   a practice or friendly session before or after a set.

letter of agreement   a document that confirms all the requirements, services and costs as agreed between the organizer and the venue. In effect a contract.

load-in (also **bump-in**)   the arrival of equipment, stage crew, staging, materials, sound and lighting rigs and other various items of event set-up.

load-out   (also **bump-out**) as load-in, but leaving.

logistics   the discipline of planning and organizing the flow of goods, equipment and people to their point of use.

means of escape   a structural way of providing a safe route for people to travel from any point in a building or site to a place of safety, without assistance (such as a marked corridor or pathway enclosed by rope).

moshpit   the place at the front of a gig audience where the most energetic activity takes place.

occupant capacity   the maximum number of people who can safely be accommodated at a venue.

PEO (see also **events coordinator**) professional event organizer.

PERT   programme evaluation and review technique. A project management planning technique for plotting work to be done in a given time scale, generally using a computer program.

participant   a person attending an event who is actively taking part in it or in some activity related to it.

pit   the place immediately in front of a stage providing a gap between the audience and the performers.

pre-con   a meeting between the organizers, the coordinator or floor manager and other key team leaders to confirm details just prior to the event.

production schedule   the scheme of work to be done, in time order, to ensure an event is set up properly

product launch   a 'show' to introduce an audience such as the media to a new product or service. It may also be aimed at an organization's internal management and staff, sales force or external dealers and customers.

programme   the schedule of events.

public event   an event attended by members of the general public.

road show   where the same event is staged in several different geographical locations.

seminar   a small gathering similar to the break-out session, where a group, not the whole plenary, discusses an issue.

set   the performance given by one individual or group at a concert or gig.

set-up time   the time needed to arrange, or rearrange after a previous function, the necessary facilities for the next event.

show   a full sequence of sets or, more simply, the event itself (in terms of musical, artistic or similar activities).

skip   a large waste or rubbish container which is moved by lorry.

special event   that phenomenon arising from those non-routine occasions which have leisure, cultural, personal or organizational objectives set apart from the normal activity of daily life, whose purpose is to enlighten, celebrate, entertain or challenge the experience of a group of people.

syndicate   *see* break-out session

trade show   a gathering for a trade or competitive exhibition, often with accompanying social events, a conference or workshops and entertainment, which is probably not open to the general public

visitor   an individual attending a special event, usually for the purpose of watching the event or of engaging in audience activities

VIP   very important person

work breakdown structure   a schedule of the various jobs which have to be done to complete an entire event

workshop   a small gathering of people to discuss a specific topic, to exchange ideas or to solve a particular problem

Organizations in the Events Industry

Europe

Association for Conferences and Events International
   Riverside House, High Street
   Huntingdon
   Cambridgeshire
   PE18 6SG
   England
   Tel 00 44 1480 457595
   Fax 00 44 1480 412863
   www.martex.co.uk/ace

Association of Event Managers
   PO Box 935
   Finchingfield
   Braintree
   Essex CM7 4LN
   England
   Tel 00 44 1371 810999
   Fax 00 44 1371 810520
   www.world-of-events.co.uk

Association of Festival Organizers
   PO Box 296
   Aylesbury
   Buckinghamshire
   HP19 9TL
   England
   Tel 00 44 1296 394411
   Fax 00 44 1296 392300
www.mrscasey.co.uk

Association of National Tourist Offices
   4 Conduit Street
   London
   W1R 0DJ
   England
   Tel 00 44 2074 994694
   Fax 00 44 2074 994694
   www.tourist-offices.org.uk

Corporate Hospitality and Event Association
   Firdene House
   Windsor Walk
   Weybridge
   Surrey
   KT13 9AP
   England
   Tel 00 44 1932 831 441
   Fax 00 44 1932 831 442
   www.eventmanager.co.uk/cha

European Arenas Association
   Palau Sant Jordi
   Passeig Olimpic 5–7
   08038 Barcelona
   Spain
   Tel 00 34 93 325 6565
   Fax 00 34 93 325 5162
   www.eaaoffice.org

European Association of Exhibition
Organizers
   XM Europe Group
   PO Box 23293
   1100 DT Amsterdam
   The Netherlands
   Tel 00 31 30 662 1838
   Fax 00 31 30 666 3336
   www.xmeurope.com

European Association of Event Centres
   Elisabeth Pietrek
   EVVC Geschaftsstelle Berlin
   Messedamm 22
   14055 Berlin
   Germany
   Tel 00 30 3038 5800
   Fax 00 30 3038 5802
   www.evvc.org

European Federation of Conference
Towns
   BP 182, B 1040 Brussels
   Belgium
   Tel 00 32 2 732 6954
   Fax 00 32 2 735 4840
   www.efct.com

European Festivals Association
   120B, rue de Lausanne
   CH – 1202 Geneva
   Switzerland
   Tel 00 41 22 738 6873
   Fax 00 41 22 738 4012
   www.euro-festival.net

European Sponsorship Consultants
Association
   ESCA Secretariat
   Marash House
   2 Brook Street
   Tring
   Hertfordshire

   HP23 5ED
   England
   Tel 00 44 1442 826 826
   Fax 00 44 1442 826 826
   www.sponsorship.org

European Stadium Managers Association
   24 Rue de Commandant Guilbaud
   92514 Boulogne
   France
   Tel 00 33 14215 2552
   Fax 00 33 14215 1039
   www.venue.org/ESMA.htm

Incentive Travel and Meetings Associa-
tion
   PO Box 195
   Twickenham
   TW1 2PE
   England
   Tel 00 44 20 8892 0256
   Fax 00 44 20 8891 3855

International Association of Confer-
ence Interpreters
   10 avenue de Secheron
   CH – 1202 Geneva
   Switzerland
   Tel 00 41 22 908 1540
   Fax 00 41 22 732 4151
   www.aiic.net

International Association of Congress
Centres
   AIPC Secretariat Office
   55 Rue de l'Amazone
   1060 Brussels
   Belgium
   Tel 00 32 2 534 5953
   Fax 00 32 2 534 6338
   www.aipc.org

International Festival and Events Association – Europe
c/o Netherlands Board of Tourism
PO Box 458
2260 MG Leidschendam
The Netherlands
Tel 00 31 70 370 5296
Fax 00 31 70 320 1654
www.ifeaeurope.com

International Visual Communications
Association Limited
Bolsover House
5/6 Clipstone Street
London
W1P 8LD
England
Tel 00 44 020 7580 0962

Meeting Professionals International
Avenue des Gaulois, 7
B 1040 Brussels
Belgium
Tel 00 32 2 743 1544
Fax 00 32 2 743 1550
www.mpiweb.org

Production Services Association
Unit 3a Endeavour House
2 Cambridge Road
Kingston upon Thames
Surrey
KT1 3JU
England
Tel 00 44 20 8392 0180
Fax 00 44 20 8541 0247
www.psa.org.uk

Union des Foires Internationales
35bis, rue Jouffroy d'Abbans
F-75017 Paris
France
Tel 00 33 14267 9912

Fax 00 33 14227 1929
www.ufinet.org

North America

Association of Destination Management Executives
3333 Quebec Street, Suite 4050
Denver
CO 80207
USA
Tel 00 1303 394 3905
Fax 00 1303 394 3450
www.adme.org

Canadian Association of Exposition
Management
6900 Airport Road, Suite 239A,
Box 82
Mississauga,
Ontario, L4V 1E8
Tel 00 1905 678 9377
Fax 00 1905 678 9578
www.caem.ca

International Association of Assembly
Managers
635 Fritz Drive
Coppell
TX 75019
USA
Tel 00 1972 255 8020
Fax 00 1972 255 9582
www.iaam.org

International Association of Convention and Visitor Bureaus
2025 M Street, Suite 500
Washington
DC 20036
USA
Tel 00 1202 296 7888

Fax 00 1202 296 7889
www.iacvb.org

International Association of Fairs and
Expositions
  PO Box 985
  Springfield
  MO 65801
  USA
  Tel 00 1800 516 0313
  Fax 00 1417 862 0156
  www.iafenet.org

International Festival and Events Association
  PO Box 2950
  115 E Railroad Ave, Suite 302
  Port Angeles
  WA 98362
  Tel 00 1360 457 3141
  Fax 00 1360 452 4695
  www.ifea.com

International Special Events Society
  9202 N Meridian St, Suite 200
  Indianapolis
  IN 46260-1810
  USA
  Tel 00 1317 571 5601
  Fax 00 1317571 5603
  www.ises.com

Stadium Managers Association
  President: Bill Lester
  HHH Metrodome
  900 S 50th Street
  Minneapolis
  MN 55415
  USA
  Tel 00 1612 335 3316
  Fax 00 1612 332 8334
  www.venue.org/SMA.htm

Asia-Pacific

Asian Association of Convention and
Visitor Bureaus
  AACVB Secretariat
  c/o Macau Government Tourist
  Office
  2/F Tourist Activities and Conference Centre
  Rua Luis Gonzaga Gomes
  Macau
  Tel 00 853 7984 156
  Fax 00 853 703 213
  www.aacvb.org

Asia Pacific Exhibition and Convention Council
  Secretary General: Jong-Hoon Kim
  c/o CoEx, World Trade Centre
  Kangnam-gu
  Seoul 135-731
  Korea
  Tel 00 822 6000 1130
  Fax 00 822 6000 0117
  www.venue.org/APECC.htm

International Special Events Society
Australia
  PO Box 1375
  Maroubra 2035
  Australia
  Tel 00 6102 9344 4755
  Fax 00 6102 9344 4755
  www.ises.org.au

South Pacific Tourism Organization
  Level 3, FNPF Place 343–359
  Victoria Parade PO Box 13-199
  Suva
  Fiji Islands
  Tel 00 679 304 177
  Fax 00 679 301 995
  www.tcsp.com

Index